双语阅读世界经典童话

（英汉对照）

王尔德童话

The Fairy Tales of Oscar Wilde

【英】奥斯卡·王尔德 著
【英】查尔斯·罗宾逊 杰西·金 绘
丁立福 译

北京师范大学出版集团
安徽大学出版社

图书在版编目（CIP）数据

王尔德童话：英汉对照/（英）奥斯卡·王尔德著；丁立福译. —合肥：安徽大学出版社，2023.3
（双语阅读世界经典童话）
ISBN 978-7-5664-2558-4

Ⅰ.①王… Ⅱ.①奥… ②丁… Ⅲ.①英语—汉语—对照读物 ②童话—作品集—英国—近代 Ⅳ.① H319.4：I

中国版本图书馆 CIP 数据核字(2022) 第 258276 号

王尔德童话（英汉对照）

[英]奥斯卡·王尔德　著
丁立福　译

出版发行：	北京师范大学出版集团 安 徽 大 学 出 版 社 （安徽省合肥市肥西路 3 号　邮编 230039） http://www.bnupg.com http://www.ahupress.com.cn
印　　刷：	安徽利民印务有限公司
经　　销：	全国新华书店
开　　本：	787 mm × 1092 mm　1/16
印　　张：	17
字　　数：	476 千字
版　　次：	2023 年 3 月第 1 版
印　　次：	2023 年 3 月第 1 次印刷
定　　价：	58.00 元

ISBN 978-7-5664-2558-4

策划编辑：李　梅　葛灵知	装帧设计：李　军
责任编辑：葛灵知	美术编辑：李　军
责任校对：高婷婷	责任印制：赵明炎

版权所有　侵权必究
反盗版、侵权举报电话：0551-65106311
外埠邮购电话：0551-65107716
本书如有印装质量问题，请与印制管理部联系调换。
印制管理部电话：0551-65106311

译者序

童话在人间，人间非童话
——王尔德和他的童话

所谓王尔德童话，顾名思义，是王尔德创作的童话。王尔德，即被后世称颂为英国唯美主义经典作家的奥斯卡·王尔德（Oscar Wilde, 1854–1900），早年家境殷实且才华横溢，于1888年开始广泛地涉猎小说、戏剧、诗歌、散文、随笔及童话等领域的创作，但真正为其赢得盛誉的正是童话集《快乐王子和其他故事》(The Happy Prince and Other Tales)，抑或说直到"《快乐王子和其他故事》问世之后，人们才真正将他视为有影响力的作家"[①]。《快乐王子和其他故事》是王尔德于1888年出版的第一部童话集，包括《快乐王子》《夜莺与玫瑰》《小气鬼巨人》《忠诚的朋友》《了不起的火箭炮》等5篇童话；3年后即1891年，王尔德出版了第二部童话集《石榴之家》(A House of Pomegranates)，包括《少年国王》《公主的生日》《渔夫和他的灵魂》《星孩儿》等4篇童话。一般所言王尔德童话，就是这两部童话集所包括的9篇童话故事。这9篇童话故事全部为本书所囊括，因此本书亦算是王尔德童话的全译本了。

笔者在翻译王尔德童话的过程中，除了坚守翻译的基本原则即严复所言的"信、达、雅"，还要注意以下几点：

（一）坚守童话翻译的初衷，利于儿童心智的发展。这既是童话创作

---

① 徐海华：《中西方文学语境下的王尔德童话》，硕士学位论文，上海外国语大学英语学院，2004年，第8页。

和翻译的初衷，也是出版社与笔者共同的理想目标。本书译文精练又不失严谨，既能为儿童读懂，又有利于儿童认知水平尤其是标准语言使用能力的发展。

（二）灵活运用童话翻译的方法。谈及翻译策略或方法，笔者主张兼采异化和归化，或兼顾直译和意译，以使童话翻译的效果最大化，更好地服务读者。首先，异化和归化，抑或直译和意译，都是就具体译文相对而言的，在整篇童话乃至整部童话集中，肯定是存在适用不同策略或方法的文本。其次，王尔德童话在国内译介已经有百余年，其中的《快乐王子》《夜莺与玫瑰》等童话早已通过诸多渠道为中国青少年所感知乃至熟悉，这使得一定程度的异化或直译有了坚实的基础。另外，青少年相对较低的认知水平以及基础教育阶段相对规范的语言使用都是客观存在的，这使得面向青少年翻译的童话需要适度采用归化或意译。

（三）尽可能保留童话翻译的底本风格。王尔德童话的原文风格，从语言的形式铺陈到结构的巧妙构思、从角色的至善追求到主题的现实批判等都有其独特之处，这在译文中皆有体现。

此处所言童话翻译的底本风格之保留，主要指保留王尔德童话的非童话性——既是忠于原文的完整性和风格，也是展示王尔德的批判光芒。王尔德开始发表童话时儿子才3岁，他坦诚创作童话的初衷"既是写给孩子们，也是写给那些仍具孩子般好奇心的快乐人们，以及那些能够在简单中体会出特别滋味的人们"[②]。这样一来，其童话中非童话的另面世界——成人世界就得以一定程度地展现。当然，言及王尔德童话中的非童话性，主要是就主题内容而言的。从深层次背景来说，王尔德生活于

[②] 唐蓓：《论奥斯卡·王尔德童话中的"成人世界"》，硕士学位论文，暨南大学英语语言文学系，2012年，第14页。

维多利亚时代的中后期,一面是盛世相伴的纸醉金迷,一面是日益扩大的贫富差距,这使得当时社会以及生活其中之人充满了多变性,因此一言难尽。个人的美与丑、社会的善与恶,在那个时代并非非此即彼的对立,而是由此及彼的对照。在时代和社会面前,大多数人犹如尘埃,几经飘浮挣扎终究要归落于地。进而言之,王尔德9篇童话的主题内容的非童话性主要表现在两个方面:一是人与社会之复杂,二是生活与命运之无奈。例如《快乐王子》,快乐王子生前不知忧愁为何物,死后被雕塑成像却心怀悲悯,在燕子的帮助下向穷人散尽身上珠宝,其形象逐渐高大起来,故事似可收尾了——但王尔德接着补充,王子的雕像因不再珠光宝气而被世人推倒,并与冻死的燕子一同被弃于灰堆之上,寥寥数笔写出世间生死、冷暖、悲欢、善恶等,不禁让读者唏嘘不已。

总而言之,童话即童言童语,只有人间方能听得到;现实生活中,童话已升格为文学体裁的范畴,专指"通过丰富的想象、幻想和夸张来编写的适合于儿童欣赏的故事"③,当然也只有人间才能创作得出。言及童话创作,主要是通过丰富的想象及夸张来塑造形象与创设离奇情节,以期对儿童进行思想教育。从创作主体观之,童话创作可以分为两类,即民间创作和作家创作,前者如广为流传的白雪公主和灰姑娘等,后者如世界知名的安徒生童话和王尔德童话等。无论是民间创作还是作家创作的童话,其最大的共同点就是面向儿童——这与童话创作的初衷即"对儿童进行思想教育"是相吻合的。进而言之,童话创作是为了对儿童进行思想教育,同时又必须兼顾儿童的方方面面,不可随心所欲。也就是说,童话作为一种特定文学体裁,有着一些固有的特征,如语言浅显生动、情节富有童趣、角色人格化,再如结局往往是正义战胜邪恶——既是对

---

③ 中国社会科学院语言研究所词典编辑室编《现代汉语词典(第7版)》,商务印书馆,2016年,第1315页。

儿童进行潜移默化教育的初衷，也是对美好生活向往与追求的直接流露。一般来说童话原文所具有的这些特点，在翻译时亦应尽可能地体现出来，但是具体到不同童话，理应有所区别。王尔德童话的独特魅力在于直面现实，其对世人及社会的批判较好地展现了人世间冷落与残酷的一面，真可谓人间非"童话"，尽管童话在人间。

2022 年 11 月 6 日
于淮南王故里梅园小区寓所

目录 CONTENTS

上篇　快乐王子和其他故事
THE HAPPY PRINCE AND OTHER TALES

快乐王子 / 2

THE HAPPY PRINCE / 12

夜莺与玫瑰 / 22

THE NIGHTINGALE AND THE ROSE / 29

小气鬼巨人 / 36

THE SELFISH GIANT / 41

忠诚的朋友 / 46

THE DEVOTED FRIEND / 58

了不起的火箭炮 / 70

THE REMARKABLE ROCKET / 83

下篇　石榴之屋
A HOUSE OF POMEGRANATES

少年国王 / 96

THE YOUNG KING / 110

公主的生日 / 125

THE BIRTHDAY OF THE INFANTA / 143
渔夫和他的灵魂 / 162
THE FISHERMAN AND HIS SOUL / 196
星孩儿 / 231
THE STAR-CHILD / 247

上 篇
快乐王子和其他故事
THE HAPPY PRINCE AND OTHER TALES

［英］查尔斯·罗宾逊 / 图
Charles Robinson / Illustrator

快乐王子

高高的圆柱上矗立着快乐王子的雕像，直入城市上空。王子浑身贴满薄薄的纯金叶片，双眼由两颗明亮的蓝宝石做成，一颗硕大的红宝石镶嵌在他的剑柄上，闪闪发光。

王子的确让人非常羡慕。"他美如风信鸡。"一位想表现自己有艺术品位的市参议员如此评论。"只是没有风信鸡那么实用。"他又补充道，唯恐有人认为自己不务实。

"为什么你不能像快乐王子那样呢？"一位通情达理的母亲对正在哭着要月亮的孩子说，"快乐王子连做梦都不会想到哭着要东西呢。"

"我很高兴世上竟有人这么快乐。"一个灰心失落的男人凝视着这座妙不可言的雕像喃喃自语。

"他看上去就像位天使。"慈善院的学童们赞叹着。他们正从大教堂走出来，披着大红色的斗篷，穿着干净的白色围裙。

"你们怎么知道的？"数学老师问道，"你们从未见过天使呀。"

"啊！但是我们见过，在梦里见过。"孩子们答道。数学老师皱起眉头，表情严肃，毕竟他不赞成小孩们做梦。

一天晚上，城市上空飞来一只小燕子。他的伙伴们都在六个星期前就飞往埃及了，只有他落在后面，因为他爱上了那株天下最美的芦苇。小燕子早在初春时节就遇见了芦苇姑娘，其时他正追着一只大黄蛾顺着河流一路飞过来，一下子迷上了腰身纤细的芦苇姑娘，于是停下来跟她搭讪。

"我可以爱你吗？"燕子张口就说，他素来喜欢直言直语，而芦苇则向他深深地弯下了腰。于是燕子围着她飞了一圈又一圈,用双翅轻抚水面,泛起层层银色的涟漪。他这是在求爱,就这样一直持续了一整个夏天。

"爱得荒唐!"其他燕子叽叽喳喳地说,"这姑娘没有钱,亲戚又多得离谱。"确实呢,河边长满了芦苇。随后,秋天来临,他们都飞走了。

伙伴们都飞走后,燕子感到孤单,并且对心上人也开始生厌。"她总是不说话,"他说,"还有啊,我怕她是个卖弄风情的女子,你看她老是跟风眉来眼去的。"这倒是真的,风一吹起来芦苇就会行屈膝礼,无比优雅动人。"我承认她惯于居家,"燕子继续说道,"可是我喜欢外出旅行。作为我的妻子,她也应该喜欢旅行才对。"

"你愿意跟我走吗?"燕子最后问她。然而芦苇摇了摇头,她是那么地恋家,舍不得离开。

"你一直在拿我寻开心哪!"燕子大喊道,"我要去金字塔了。再见吧!"说完他就飞走了。

燕子飞了整整一天,入夜时他飞入这座城市。"我应该在哪儿过夜呢?"他说,"希望城里人已经为我准备好住处了。"

随后,燕子看到了高柱上的那座雕像。

"我就到那儿过夜吧,"燕子叫道,"这可真是个好住处,新鲜空气有的是。"于是,他飞落下来,恰好停在快乐王子两脚之间。

"我找到一间纯金卧室啦!"燕子环顾四周,轻声自语。然而就在他把头插入翅膀下面准备入睡时,一滴大大的水珠掉落在他身上。"真是奇怪!"他喊道,"天空中连朵云都没有,星星又明又亮,竟然下起雨来了?北欧的天气,真是糟糕透顶。芦苇姑娘以前喜欢下雨,但那不过是她的私心罢了。"

接着又有一滴掉落下来。

"如果都不能用来挡雨,这座雕像还有什么用呢?"燕子说道,"我得找一个好住的烟囱管帽去。"他决定离开这里。

可是还没等燕子张开双翅，第三滴水珠又落了下来。他仰头一看，只见——啊！他看见了什么？

快乐王子双眼噙满泪水，泪水正顺着他的金色脸颊往下流。他的脸庞在月光的衬托下显得如此动人，让小燕子顿生怜悯。

"你是谁呀？"燕子问。

"我是快乐王子。"

"那你为什么要哭呢？"燕子问道，"你都把我浇透了。"

"从前我活着，还拥有人心时，"雕像答道，"我并不知道眼泪是什么，因为我住在无忧宫，忧愁和悲伤一律不许入内。白天我跟伙伴们在花园里玩耍，晚上我领着大家在大殿里跳舞。花园周围砌有高墙，但我从未关心过墙外的世界，我的一切都那么美好。臣子侍奉我，都称我为快乐王子。如果开心就是快乐的话，我确实是快乐的。我就这样活着，也就这样死去。现在我死了，他们把我供在这儿，立得这么高，让我可以看到城中的所有丑陋和一切苦难。虽然我的心是用铅做成的，但我还是忍不住哭了。"

"怎么，王子不是纯金的？"燕子自言自语道。他非常有礼貌，从不大声评头论足。

"远处，"王子雕像继续说，声音低沉而悦耳，"远处的一条小街上，有一间破屋。透过开着的窗户我看到一个妇人坐在桌旁。她的脸庞消瘦、憔悴，双手粗糙、发红，扎满了针眼，原来她是一个裁缝。她正在一件缎袍上绣西番莲花，这是给皇后最宠信的侍女参加下一次宫廷舞会准备的。在角落里，她的小儿子正生病躺在床上。孩子发烧了，嚷着要橘子吃。然而，母亲除了河水，什么也给不了他，所以孩子一直在哭。燕子，燕子，小燕子，你愿意把我剑柄上的红宝石拿去送给她吗？我双脚固定在这个底座上，动弹不了。"

"有人正在埃及那边等着我呢，"燕子说，"我的伙伴们在尼罗河上飞来飞去，正和大朵大朵的莲花说着话哩。一会儿，他们就要到伟大国王的坟墓里睡觉。国王自己也在，就睡在彩绘的棺材里，浑身裹着黄色亚麻布，涂满了香料，脖子上围着一条淡绿色的翡翠项链，双手就像枯叶似的。"

"燕子，燕子，小燕子，"王子说，"你就不愿意陪我一个晚上，做我的信使吗？瞧那孩子多渴，妈妈有多伤心啊！"

"我不喜欢男孩子。"燕子答道，"去年夏天，我待在河边时，有两个野小子，就是磨坊主的儿子，他们总是拐石子打我。当然，他们从来没有打中过；我们燕子飞得可厉害了，根本打不中，何况我出身的家族更是以身手敏捷而著称；可不管怎么说，那么做都是不礼貌的行为。"

然而，快乐王子看上去是那么地悲伤，让小燕子难过起来。"这儿很冷，"他说，"不过我愿意陪你一晚，做你的信使。"

"谢谢你，小燕子。"王子说。

于是，燕子从王子的剑柄上啄出那颗硕大的红宝石，衔在嘴尖，挨着城中高高低低的屋顶向远处飞了过去。

他飞过大教堂的塔顶，看见了顶上雕着的白玉天使像；他飞过皇宫，听见宫内传来阵阵歌舞声。一个美丽的少女和她的恋人一起迈步来到阳台。"星星有多么美，"恋人对她说，"爱情的魅力就有多么妙！"

"希望我的礼服及时做好，能赶上国宴舞会，"她答道，"我已经吩咐要绣上西番莲花，可是做针线活的妇人太懒了。"

他飞过河面,看见一盏盏灯笼悬挂在船桅上。他飞过贫民区,看见犹太老人相互讨价还价,把钱放在铜天平上过秤。最后,小燕子来到破屋前,朝里看去:男孩发着烧,在床上翻来覆去;妈妈已入睡,因为她太累了。他跳了进去,把那颗硕大的红宝石放在桌上,紧挨着那妇人的顶针。然后他轻轻地绕着床飞,用翅膀给男孩的额头扇风。"真凉快啊!"男孩说,"我肯定快好啦。"说着,他就沉入了甜美的梦乡。

然后,燕子飞回到快乐王子的身边,把自个儿刚做的那些事儿告诉了他。"真是奇怪,"燕子说,"我现在觉得挺暖和的,虽然天冷得很。"

"那是因为你做了件善事。"王子说。小燕子开始思索王子的话,跟着就睡着了。动脑筋的事儿,总是令他昏昏欲睡。

天刚亮起来,燕子就飞到河边洗了个澡。"多么异常的一个现象啊,"正在过桥的鸟类学教授感叹道,"冬天还有燕子!"于是他就围绕这个给地方报纸写了一封长信。信被大家传得沸沸扬扬,其中含有那么多他们不能理解的词句。

"今晚我就去埃及。"燕子说,一想到要走他就欢欣鼓舞。他参观了所有的公共纪念碑,并在教堂的塔顶上坐了好一会儿。无论他到哪里,麻雀都会叽叽喳喳地叫个不停,并互相说道:"真是一位尊贵的稀客啊!"所以他游览得十分尽兴。

月亮升起时分,他飞回快乐王子的身边。"你有什么事需要我在埃及效劳吗?"他喊道,"我要出发了。"

"燕子,燕子,小燕子,"王子说,"你难道不愿意再陪我一个晚上吗?"

"有人正在埃及那边等着我呢,"燕子说,"我的伙伴们将飞往上游的第二大瀑布。那里有河马藏在菖蒲里,巨大的花岗岩宝座上端坐着门农神。他整夜看着星星,启明星亮起时他就快乐地大喊一声,随之归于沉默。中午时分黄狮来到河边喝水。他们有绿宝石一样的眼睛,吼起来比瀑布的声音还要响亮。"

"燕子,燕子,小燕子,"王子说,"远处,在城市的那边,我看见一个小伙子住在阁楼上。他正俯身于一张铺满稿纸的桌上,旁边的大玻璃瓶里插着一束枯萎了的紫罗兰。他有一头棕色短发,嘴唇红如石榴,双眼大而好看。他正在赶工给剧院导演写一个剧本,但是他太冷了,冷得写不下去。而且炉子里没有火,他也饿得头昏眼花。"

"我再陪你一个晚上吧,"好心的燕子说道,"需要我再拿一颗红宝石给他吗?"

"唉!我现在没有红宝石了,"王子说,"只剩下一双眼了。做成这双眼睛的是两颗珍贵的蓝宝石,是千年前从印度买来的。挖出其中一颗,给他送去。他会把这颗宝石卖给珠宝商,然后买点儿食物和柴火,好把他的剧本写完。"

"亲爱的王子呀!"燕子说,"我下不了狠心哪。"说着他开始哭起来。

"燕子,燕子,小燕子,"王子说,"照我的吩咐去做吧。"

于是燕子啄出王子的一只眼睛,飞往小伙子所住的阁楼。进阁楼很容易,因为屋顶上破了一个洞。通过这个洞他飞了进去,进入房间。小伙子双手抱头,所以没有听到燕子翅膀扑棱的声音。他抬起头时,看到了那颗美丽的蓝宝石正卧在枯萎的紫罗兰上面。

"开始有人赏识我啦!"小伙子大叫道,"不知是哪位崇拜者慷慨相助。现在我能写完剧本了。"他露出非常快乐的样子。

第二天燕子飞下来,到了港口。他落在一艘大船的桅杆上,看着水手们用长绳把大箱子从船舱里拉上来。"起——嗨!"他们每拉上来一个箱子,都大声地叫一声号子。"我要去埃及了!"燕子高声喊叫,可是没有人在意。月亮升了上来,他便飞回到快乐王子的身边。

"我是回来跟你告别的，"燕子喊道。

"燕子，燕子，小燕子，"王子说道，"你就不愿意再多陪我一个晚上吗？"

"冬天了，"燕子答道，"寒风大雪马上就要来了。埃及那边，太阳正暖暖地照在绿油油的棕榈树上，鳄鱼躺在泥里懒洋洋地打量着周围。我的同伴们正在巴尔贝克城的太阳神庙里筑巢呢，粉红的和雪白的鸽子一边看着他们，一边咕咕地叫着。亲爱的王子，我非走不可了，但我永远也不会忘记你。来年春天，我会给你带回两颗美丽的宝石，以弥补你慷慨送人的那两颗。我带回的红宝石会比红玫瑰还红，蓝宝石会像大海一样蓝。"

"在下面的广场上，"快乐王子说道，"在那儿站着一个卖火柴的小女孩，她的火柴掉进了水沟，全废了。如果她不带点钱回家，她爸爸就会打她，她正哭着呢。她没有鞋、没有袜，也没有戴帽子。挖出我的另一只眼睛，给她送去，她爸爸就不会打她了。"

"我再多陪你一个晚上。"燕子说，"可是我不能挖掉你的另一只眼睛。那样你就全瞎了。"

"燕子，燕子，小燕子，"王子说，"照我的吩咐去做吧。"

于是燕子挖出王子的另一只眼睛，衔起来飞走了。他俯冲着掠过那卖火柴的小女孩，让宝石轻轻地落进她的手心。"多好的一块玻璃啊！"小女孩高喊道，一路笑着往家跑去。

然后燕子又飞回王子的身边。"现在你双眼都瞎了，"他继续说，"所以我要陪着你，永不离开。"

"不，小燕子，"可怜的王子说道，"你应该离开去埃及。"

"我愿意陪着你，永不离开。"燕子说着，就在王子的脚边睡下了。

第二天，他从早到晚都一直坐在王子的肩头，给他讲自己在异国他乡的诸多见闻。他给王子讲红朱鹭，这些鸟儿一长排一长排地站在尼罗河岸边，用嘴捕捉金鱼；讲到斯芬克斯，这种狮身人面怪物和世界一样古老,家住沙漠,无所不知;讲到那些商人,他们与骆驼为伴慢慢地前行,手里捏着琥珀念珠;讲到月亮山的国王,他的皮肤黑得像乌木,还崇拜一块大水晶;讲到那条大青蛇,睡在棕榈树上,竟有二十个僧侣喂它吃蜜糕;还讲到那些小矮人,乘着又大又扁的叶子航行于大河大湖,还老是跟蝴蝶开仗。

"亲爱的小燕子,"王子说道,"你给我讲的都是一些不可思议的奇闻怪事,但最不可思议的怪事莫过于天下大众的苦难。大众的苦难才是天下最怪的事。到我的城市上空飞一飞,小燕子,再把你看到的告诉我。"

于是,燕子飞到这座大城的上空,看到富人在他们的豪宅内寻欢作乐,而乞丐们却坐在门外受冻挨饿。他飞进黑暗的小巷,看到饥饿的孩子们脸色苍白,无精打采地望着黑蒙蒙的巷道。在一座桥的拱门下面躺着两个小男孩,相互搂抱在一起,只想暖和一点点。"真饿啊!"他们说。"你们不许躺在这里。"巡夜人吼叫起来,他们只得茫然地走入雨中。

然后燕子飞回来,把自己看到的告诉了王子。

"我浑身镀有纯金,"王子说,"你得摘下来,一片一片地摘,再给穷人们送去。在世的人啊,总是觉得金子能使他们幸福起来。"

一片又一片的纯金,燕子逐片啄下,直到快乐王子看上去暗无光泽,灰不溜丢的。一片又一片的金子,他逐一送给穷人们,孩子们脸上红润起来,笑呵呵地在街上玩起了游戏。"我们有面包啦!"他们大声叫着。

接着下起雪来，雪后又是结霜。一条条街道看上去像是用白银堆砌而成的，闪闪发亮。长长的冰凌像一把把水晶利刃从家家户户的屋檐悬挂下来，人人外出时都穿上皮衣，小孩们则戴着鲜红的帽子，在冰面上滑行起来。

可怜的小燕子感到越来越冷，可是他不愿意离开，着实是太爱王子了。在面包师傅没留意的时候，他就在门外捡点儿面包碎屑，还使劲地扇动翅膀，尽量地让自己暖和一点儿。

但是到最后，燕子知道自个儿快要死了。他用尽最后一点力气，再一次飞到王子的肩头。"别了，亲爱的王子！"他喃喃地说，"你愿让我亲一下手吗？"

"我很高兴，你终于要去埃及了，小燕子，"王子说，"你在这儿逗留得太久了，不过要亲就亲我的嘴唇，因为我爱你。"

"其实我不是要去埃及，"燕子说，"我要去的是死亡之家。死亡是睡眠的兄弟，不是吗？"

然后，他亲过快乐王子的嘴唇，就掉落在他的脚边，死去了。

就在这时，雕像里面传出奇怪的破裂声，好像有什么东西裂开了。原来是，快乐王子的铅铸之心一下子碎裂成两半了。

第二天清早，市长和议员们一起在雕像下面的广场上散步。他们路过那根柱子时，市长抬头看了看雕像，惊叹道："天哪，瞧这快乐王子有多么寒酸！"

"确实是够寒酸的！"议员们嚷道。这些人，往日里总是附和市长的意见，此时听到市长的话后便都走上前去看个究竟。

"红宝石从剑上掉了，双眼没了，身上也不再金光闪闪了，"市长说道，"说真的，他比乞丐好不了多少！"

"比乞丐好不了多少。"议员们回应道。

"而且在他的脚下竟然有一只死鸟！"市长继续说，"我们应该颁布一项公告，禁止鸟儿死在这个地方。"市长秘书赶忙记录下这条建议。

于是他们把快乐王子的雕像推倒了。"他不美了，也就不再有什么用了。"大学的美术教授说。

然后他们把雕像扔进火炉中熔化。市长还召开一次工作会议来决定如何处置这些金属。"当然，我们必须再建一座雕像，"他说道，"这座雕像理应雕我的像。"

"雕我的像，"每个议员都争着说，于是他们大吵起来。我最近听说，他们仍在吵呢。

"真是怪事！"铸造厂的监工说道，"瞧这颗铅心，碎都碎了，却在炉中烧不化。我们应该把它扔掉。"于是他们把它扔到一个灰堆上，那儿还躺着那只死去的燕子。

"去把那座城里最为珍贵的两件宝贝给我取来。"上帝吩咐自己的一位天使说。天使就把铅心和死去的燕子拿给了上帝。

"你选得真对。"上帝说道，"因为在我的天堂花园里这只小鸟会永远放声唱歌，在我的黄金城内快乐王子会赞美我。"

THE HAPPY PRINCE

High above the city, on a tall column, stood the statue of the Happy Prince. He was gilded all over with thin leaves of fine gold, for eyes he had two bright sapphires, and a large red ruby glowed on his sword hilt.

He was very much admired indeed. "He is as beautiful as a weathercock," remarked one of the Town Councillors who wished to gain a reputation for having artistic tastes; "only not quite so useful," he added, fearing lest people should think him unpractical, which he really was not.

"Why can't you be like the Happy Prince?" asked a sensible mother of her little boy who was crying for the moon. "The Happy Prince never dreams of crying for anything."

"I am glad there is some one in the world who is quite happy," muttered a disappointed man as he gazed at the wonderful statue.

"He looks just like an angel," said the charity children as they came out of the cathedral in their bright scarlet cloaks and their clean white pinafores.

"How do you know?" said the mathematical master. "You have never seen one."

"Ah! But we have, in our dreams," answered the children. And the mathematical master frowned and looked very severe, for he did not approve of children dreaming.

One night there flew over the city a little swallow. His friends had gone away to Egypt six weeks before, but he had stayed behind, for he was in love with the most beautiful reed. He had met her early in the spring as he was flying down the river after a big yellow moth, and had been so attracted by her slender waist that he had stopped to talk to her.

"Shall I love you?" said the swallow, who liked to come to the point at once, and the reed made him a low bow. So he flew round and round her, touching the water with his wings, and making silver ripples. This was his courtship, and it lasted all through the summer.

"It is a ridiculous attachment," twittered the other swallows. "She has no money, and far too many relations." And indeed the river was quite full of reeds. Then, when the autumn came they all flew away.

After they had gone he felt lonely, and began to tire of his lady love. "She has no conversation," he said, "and I am afraid that she is a coquette, for she is always flirting with the wind." And certainly, whenever the wind blew, the reed made the most graceful curtseys. "I admit that she is domestic," he continued, "but I love travelling, and my wife, consequently, should love travelling also."

"Will you come away with me?" he said finally to her. But the reed shook her head; she was so attached to her home.

"You have been trifling with me," he cried. "I am off to the Pyramids. Good-bye!" And he flew away.

All day long he flew, and at night-time he arrived at the city. "Where shall I put up?" he said. "I hope the town has made preparations."

Then he saw the statue on the tall column.

"I will put up there," he cried. "It is a fine position, with plenty of fresh air." So he alighted just between the feet of the Happy Prince.

"I have a golden bedroom," he said softly to himself as he looked round, and he prepared to go to sleep. But just as he was putting his head under his wing a large drop of water fell on him. "What a curious thing!" he cried. "There is not a single cloud in the sky, the stars are quite clear and bright, and yet it is raining. The climate in the north of Europe is really dreadful. The reed used to like the rain, but that was merely her selfishness."

Then another drop fell.

"What is the use of a statue if it cannot keep the rain off?" he said. "I must look for a good chimney pot." And he determined to fly away.

But before he had opened his wings, a third drop fell, and he looked up, and saw— Ah! What did he see?

The eyes of the Happy Prince were filled with tears, and tears were running down his golden cheeks. His face was so beautiful in the moonlight that the little swallow was filled with pity.

"Who are you?" he said.

"I am the Happy Prince."

"Why are you weeping then?" asked the swallow. "You have quite drenched me."

"When I was alive and had a human heart," answered the statue, "I did not know what tears were, for I lived in the Palace of Sans-Souci, where sorrow is not allowed to enter. In the daytime I played with my companions in the garden, and in the evening I led the dance in the Great Hall. Round the garden ran a very lofty wall, but I never cared to ask what lay beyond it, everything about me was so beautiful. My courtiers called me the Happy Prince, and happy indeed I was, if pleasure be happiness. So I lived, and so I died. And now that I am dead they have set me up here so high that I can see all the ugliness and all the misery of my city, and though my heart is made of lead yet I cannot choose but weep."

"What! Is he not solid gold?" said the swallow to himself. He was too polite to make any personal remarks out loud.

"Far away," continued the statue in a low musical voice, "far away in a little street there is a poor house. One of the windows is open, and through it I can see a woman seated at a table. Her face is thin and worn, and she has coarse, red hands, all pricked by the needle, for she is a seamstress. She is embroidering passion flowers on a satin gown for the loveliest of the Queen's maids-of-honour to wear at the next court ball. In a bed in the corner of the room her little boy is lying ill. He has a fever, and is asking for oranges. His mother has nothing to give him but river water, so he is crying. Swallow, swallow, little swallow, will you not bring her the ruby out of my sword hilt? My feet are fastened to this pedestal and I cannot move."

"I am waited for in Egypt," said the swallow. "My friends are flying up and down the Nile, and talking to the large lotus flowers. Soon they will go to sleep in the tomb of the great King. The King is there himself in his painted coffin. He is wrapped in yellow linen, and embalmed with spices. Round his neck is a chain of pale green jade, and his hands are like withered leaves."

"Swallow, swallow, little swallow," said the Prince. "Will you not stay with me for one night, and be my messenger? The boy is so thirsty, and the mother is so sad."

"I don't think I like boys," answered the swallow. "Last summer, when I was staying on the river, there were two rude boys, the miller's sons, who were always throwing stones at me. They never hit me, of course; we swallows fly far too well for that, and besides, I come of a family famous for its agility; but still, it was a mark of disrespect."

But the Happy Prince looked so sad that the little swallow was sorry. "It is very cold here," he said. "But I will stay with you for one night, and be your messenger."

"Thank you, little swallow," said the Prince.

So the swallow picked out the great ruby from the Prince's sword, and flew away with it in his beak over the roofs of the town.

He passed by the cathedral tower, where the white marble angels were sculptured. He passed by the palace and heard the sound of dancing. A beautiful girl came out on the balcony with her lover. "How wonderful the stars are," he said to her, "and how wonderful is the power of love!"

"I hope my dress will be ready in time for the state ball," she answered. "I have ordered passion flowers to be embroidered on it; but the seamstresses are so lazy."

He passed over the river, and saw the lanterns hanging to the masts of the ships. He passed over the Ghetto, and saw the old Jews bargaining with each other, and weighing out money in copper scales. At last he came to the poor house and looked in. The boy was tossing feverishly on his bed, and the mother had fallen asleep, she was so tired. In he hopped, and laid the great ruby on the table beside the woman's thimble. Then he flew gently round the bed, fanning the boy's forehead with his wings. "How cool I feel!" said the boy. "I must be getting better." And he sank into a delicious slumber.

Then the swallow flew back to the Happy Prince, and told him what he had done. "It is curious," he remarked. "But I feel quite warm now, although it is so cold."

"That is because you have done a good action," said the Prince. And the little swallow began to think, and then he fell asleep. Thinking always made him sleepy.

When day broke he flew down to the river and had a bath. "What a remarkable phenomenon," said the professor of ornithology as he was passing over the bridge. "A swallow in winter!" And he wrote a long letter about it to the local newspaper. Every one quoted it; it was full of so many words that they could not understand.

"Tonight I go to Egypt," said the swallow, and he was in high spirits at the prospect. He visited all the public monuments, and sat a long time on top of the church steeple. Wherever he went the sparrows chirruped, and said to each other, "What a distinguished stranger!" So he enjoyed himself very much.

When the moon rose he flew back to the Happy Prince. "Have you any commissions for Egypt?" he cried. "I am just starting."

"Swallow, swallow, little swallow," said the Prince. "Will you not stay with me one night longer?"

"I am waited for in Egypt," answered the swallow. "Tomorrow my friends will fly up to the Second Cataract. The river horse couches there among the bulrushes, and on a great granite throne sits the God Memnon. All night long he watches the stars, and when the morning star shines he utters one cry of joy, and then he is silent. At noon the yellow lions come down to the water's edge to drink. They have eyes like green beryls, and their roar is louder than the roar of the cataract."

"Swallow, swallow, little swallow," said the Prince. "Far away across the city I see a young man in a garret. He is leaning over a desk covered with papers, and in a tumbler by his side there is a bunch of withered violets. His hair is brown and crisp, and his lips are red as a pomegranate, and he has large and dreamy eyes. He is trying to finish a play for the director of the theatre, but he is too cold to write any more. There is no fire in the grate, and hunger has made him faint."

"I will wait with you one night longer," said the swallow, who really had a good heart. "Shall I take him another ruby?"

"Alas! I have no ruby now," said the Prince. "My eyes are all that I have left. They are made of rare sapphires, which were brought out of India a thousand years ago. Pluck out one of them and take it to him. He will sell it to the jeweller, and buy food and firewood, and finish his play."

"Dear Prince," said the swallow. "I cannot do that." And he began to weep.

"Swallow, swallow, little swallow," said the Prince. "Do as I command you."

So the swallow plucked out the Prince's eye, and flew away to the student's garret. It was easy enough to get in, as there was a hole in the roof. Through this he darted, and came into the room. The young man had his head buried in his hands, so he did not hear the flutter of the bird's wings, and when he looked up he found the beautiful sapphire lying on the withered violets.

"I am beginning to be appreciated," he cried. "This is from some great admirer. Now I can finish my play." And he looked quite happy.

The next day the swallow flew down to the harbour. He sat on the mast of a large vessel and watched the sailors hauling big chests out of the hold with ropes. "Heave a-hoy!" they shouted as each chest came up. "I am going to Egypt!" cried the swallow. But nobody minded, and when the moon rose he flew back to the Happy Prince.

"I am come to bid you good-bye," he cried.

"Swallow, swallow, little swallow," said the Prince. "Will you not stay with me one night longer?"

"It is winter," answered the swallow. "And the chill snow will soon be here. In Egypt the sun is warm on the green palm trees, and the crocodiles lie in the mud and look lazily about them. My companions are building a nest in the Temple of Baalbec, and the pink and white doves are watching them, and cooing to each other. Dear Prince, I must leave you, but I will never forget you, and next spring I will bring you back two beautiful jewels in place of those you have given away. The ruby shall be redder than a red rose, and the sapphire shall be as blue as the great sea."

"In the square below," said the Happy Prince, "there stands a little match-girl. She has let her matches fall in the gutter, and they are all spoiled. Her father will beat her if she does not bring home some money, and she is crying. She has no shoes or stockings, and her little head is bare. Pluck out my other eye and give it to her, and her father will not beat her."

"I will stay with you one night longer," said the swallow. "But I cannot pluck out your eye. You would be quite blind then."

"Swallow, swallow, little swallow," said the Prince. "Do as I command you."

So he plucked out the Prince's other eye, and darted down with it. He swooped past the match-girl, and slipped the jewel into the palm of her hand. "What a lovely bit of glass!" cried the little girl. And she ran home, laughing.

Then the swallow came back to the Prince. "You are blind now," he said. "So I will stay with you always."

"No, little swallow," said the poor Prince. "You must go away to Egypt."

"I will stay with you always," said the swallow, and he slept at the Prince's feet. All the next day he sat on the Prince's shoulder, and told him stories of what he had seen in strange lands. He told him of the red ibises, who stand in long rows on the banks of the Nile, and catch gold fish in their beaks; of the Sphinx, who is as old as the world itself, and lives in the desert, and knows everything; of the merchants, who walk slowly by the side of their camels and carry amber beads in their hands; of the King of the mountains of the moon, who is as black as ebony, and worships a large crystal; of the great green snake that sleeps in a palm tree, and has twenty priests to feed it with honey cakes; and of the pygmies who sail over a big lake on large flat leaves, and are always at war with the butterflies.

"Dear little swallow," said the Prince. "You tell me of marvellous things, but more marvellous than anything is the suffering of men and of women. There is no mystery so great as misery. Fly over my city, little swallow, and tell me what you see there."

So the swallow flew over the great city, and saw the rich making merry in their beautiful houses, while the beggars were sitting at the gates. He flew into dark lanes, and saw the white faces of starving children looking out listlessly at the black streets. Under the archway of a bridge two little boys were lying in one another's arms to try and keep themselves warm. "How hungry we are!" they said. "You must not lie here," shouted the watchman, and they wandered out into the rain.

Then he flew back and told the Prince what he had seen.

"I am covered with fine gold," said the Prince. "You must take it off, leaf by leaf, and give it to my poor; the living always think that gold can make them happy."

Leaf after leaf of the fine gold the swallow picked off, till the Happy Prince looked quite dull and grey. Leaf after leaf of the fine gold he brought to the poor, and the children's faces grew rosier, and they laughed and played games in the street. "We have bread now!" they cried.

Then the snow came, and after the snow came the frost. The streets looked as if they were made of silver, they were so bright and glistening; long icicles like crystal daggers hung down from the eaves of the houses, everybody went about in furs, and the little boys wore scarlet caps and skated on the ice.

The poor little swallow grew colder and colder, but he would not leave the Prince, he loved him too well. He picked up crumbs outside the baker's door when the baker was not looking, and tried to keep himself warm by flapping his wings.

But at last he knew that he was going to die. He had just strength to fly up to the Prince's shoulder once more. "Good-bye, dear Prince!" he murmured. "Will you let me kiss your hand?"

"I am glad that you are going to Egypt at last, little swallow," said the Prince. "You have stayed too long here; but you must kiss me on the lips, for I love you."

"It is not to Egypt that I am going," said the swallow. "I am going to the House of Death. Death is the brother of sleep, is he not?"

And he kissed the Happy Prince on the lips, and fell down dead at his feet.

At that moment a curious crack sounded inside the statue, as if something had broken. The fact is that the leaden heart had snapped right in two.

Early the next morning the Mayor was walking in the square below in company with the town councillors. As they passed the column he looked up at the statue, "Dear me! How shabby the Happy Prince looks!" he said.

"How shabby, indeed!" cried the town councillors, who always agreed with the Mayor. And they went up to look at it.

"The ruby has fallen out of his sword, his eyes are gone, and he is golden no longer," said the Mayor. "In fact, he is little better than a beggar!"

"Little better than a beggar," said the town councillors.

"And here is actually a dead bird at his feet!" continued the Mayor. "We must really issue a proclamation that birds are not to be allowed to die here." And the town clerk made a note of the suggestion.

So they pulled down the statue of the Happy Prince. "As he is no longer beautiful he is no longer useful," said the art professor at the university.

Then they melted the statue in a furnace, and the Mayor held a meeting of the Corporation to decide what was to be done with the metal. "We must have another statue, of course," he said. "And it shall be a statue of myself."

"Of myself," said each of the town councillors, and they quarrelled. When I last heard of them they were quarrelling still.

"What a strange thing!" said the overseer of the workmen at the foundry. "This broken leaden heart will not melt in the furnace. We must throw it away."

So they threw it on a dust-heap where the dead swallow was also lying.

"Bring me the two most precious things in the city," said God to one of his angels. And the angel brought him the leaden heart and the dead bird.

"You have rightly chosen," said God. "For in my garden of paradise this little bird shall sing for evermore, and in my city of gold the Happy Prince shall praise me."

夜莺与玫瑰

"**她**说要是我能送她一些红玫瑰的话,她就与我共舞。"一个青年学生喊道,"可是我的整座花园,也找不着一朵红玫瑰呀。"

夜莺从冬青橡树的窝里听到了他的喊声,便透过片片树叶往外张望,甚感好奇。

"没有红玫瑰,我的整个花园都没有哇!"他哭喊道,美丽的双眼噙满了泪水。"啊,多么小的小东西,竟决定了有没有幸福!我通读所有圣贤之书,知晓全部哲学奥秘,然而就因为缺少一朵红玫瑰,我的生活就将不幸起来。"

"终于见着了一位真心真意的恋人。"夜莺说,"一个又一个夜晚,我都在歌唱着他,尽管我并不认识他;一个又一个夜晚,我都对星星讲述着他的故事,现在我终于见着他了。他的头发黑得如同盛开的风信子,嘴唇红如求之不得的玫瑰;然而满心痴情已使他的脸庞苍白如象牙,眉梢也挂满了忧愁。"

"王子明晚要开舞会,"青年学生喃喃地说,"我的心上人也会去。要是我送她一朵红玫瑰,她就会同我一起跳舞到天亮。要是我送她一朵红玫瑰,我便可以搂着她,让她依偎在我的肩头,紧紧握住她的手。但是没有一朵红玫瑰开在我的花园里啊,所以我只能孤零零地坐着,看着她从身边经过。她不会留意到我,我伤心欲绝啊。"

"这真是真心真意的恋人,"夜莺说,"我所歌唱的,却让他受尽磨难;令我欢欣的,却让他痛苦不堪。爱情真是让人叹为观止,比绿宝石还珍贵,比精美的猫眼石更昂贵。这爱,珍珠玛瑙换不来,市场上也找不着。这情,不可通过商人买到,也不能用天平称了换黄金。"

"乐师们将坐进专用的廊厢,"青年学生说,"拨动琴弦,我的心上人会随着竖琴和小提琴奏出的音乐翩翩起舞。她会跳得无比轻盈,双脚不着地似的,被身着华丽礼服的朝臣们簇拥着。但是我呢,她不会与我共舞,因为我没有一朵红玫瑰送给她。"说完,他就扑倒在草地上,双手蒙住脸,哭了起来。

"他为什么要哭呢?"一条绿色的小蜥蜴一边问,一边翘着尾巴从学生身边跑过。

"就是嘛,哭什么呢?"一只蝴蝶一边说,一边振翅追着阳光。

"就是嘛,哭什么呢?"一朵雏菊向周边同伴耳语,声音又柔又轻。

"他哭,是为了要一朵红玫瑰。"夜莺说。

"就为了一朵红玫瑰?"他们大声问道,"真是非常可笑!"小蜥蜴有些玩世不恭,直接哈哈大笑起来。

但是夜莺却明白了学生悲伤的隐情,她静静地坐在橡树上,思索着爱情的神秘之处。

突然,她张开褐色的双翅准备起飞,接着猛地冲向空中。她穿过小树丛,又像一道影子似的飞过花园。

草丛中央长着一棵美丽的玫瑰树,夜莺见着便飞了过去,栖在树梢上。

"送我一朵红玫瑰吧,"她喊道,"我会为你唱最甜美的歌。"

但玫瑰树摇了摇头。

"我的玫瑰花是白色的,"它

答道，"就像大海的浪花一样白，比山顶的积雪还要白。到老日晷旁找我的兄弟吧，兴许他会应你所求。"

于是，夜莺飞到长在老日晷旁的那棵玫瑰树上。

"送我一朵红玫瑰吧，"夜莺喊道，"我就为你唱最甜美的歌。"

但是玫瑰树摇了摇头。

"我的玫瑰花是黄色的，"玫瑰树答道，"就像琥珀宝座上美人鱼的头发一样黄，比割草人拿着镰刀到来之前草地上盛开的金水仙还要黄。到那学生窗下找我的兄弟吧，兴许他会应你所求。"

于是，夜莺飞到了长在那学生窗外的玫瑰树上。

"送我一朵红玫瑰吧，"夜莺喊道，"我就为你唱最甜美的歌。"

但是玫瑰树摇了摇头。

"我的玫瑰花是红色的，"玫瑰树答道，"就像鸽子的双脚一样红，比海底洞穴中随波荡漾的大珊瑚还要红。然而这个冬天冻僵了我的血管，寒霜摧毁了我的花蕾，风雨折断了我的枝丫，今年我一朵玫瑰花也开不了。"

"我只要一朵红玫瑰……"夜莺哭喊起来，"只要一朵红玫瑰！难道就没有办法让我得到它吗？"

"有一个办法，"玫瑰树答道，"但是太可怕了，我不敢告诉你。"

"告诉我吧，"夜莺说，"我不怕。"

"要是你想要一朵红玫瑰，"玫瑰树说道，"你就必须在月光下用歌声催生出来，然后用你心中的鲜血去染红它。你必须用胸脯顶着一根刺尖，为我唱歌。整个夜晚你都必须向着我唱歌，刺尖必须刺透你的心，你的生命之血必须流进我的血管，成为我的生命之血。"

"为了换得一朵红玫瑰，以死亡为代价确实很大，"夜莺喊道，"而且生命对谁都是非常珍贵的。活着多惬意呀，坐在绿林荫下，看完太阳驾着黄金马车，再望望月亮坐着珍珠马车。山楂树真香呀，藏于山谷的蓝铃花和在山坡上舞动的野生小花真美。然而爱情比生命更可贵，鸟心与人心相比，又算得了什么呢？"

于是，夜莺张开褐色的双翅准备起飞，接着猛地冲向空中。她穿过花园快得像一道影子，又像一道影子似的飞过小树丛。

那个青年学生仍旧躺在草地上，仍是她飞离时的地方，双眼仍然噙着泪水。

"高兴起来吧，"夜莺喊道，"快乐起来吧，你会得到你想要的红玫瑰。我要在月光下用歌声将它催生出来，然后用我心中的鲜血将它染红。我对你的所有要求就是，你要做一个真心真意的恋人，因为爱情比哲学更有智慧，尽管哲学是智慧之学；爱情比权力更加强大，尽管权力意味着强大。爱有像火焰般炽热的双翼，有像火焰般鲜红的身躯；爱之唇甜如蜂蜜，爱之气息香如乳香。"

青年从草丛中抬起头来，侧耳倾听，但他听不懂夜莺对他说了些什么，因为他只晓得书上写的事儿。

但是橡树听懂了，他觉得很伤心，因为他太喜欢这只小夜莺，这只把窝搭在自个儿枝头上的小夜莺了。

"最后再给我唱首歌吧，"橡树低声说道，"你离去后，我会感到无比寂寞。"

于是，小夜莺给橡树唱了起来，歌声犹如水从白银瓶里淙淙流出。

她唱完歌之后，学生便站起身来，从口袋里掏出一个记事本和一支铅笔。

"那只夜莺的确有范儿，"他一边自言自语，一边走过小树丛——

"这无可否认，但她有感情吗？怕是没有。说真的，她就像大多数从事艺术的人，有模有样但没有诚心。她不会为了别人而牺牲自己。她心里只有音乐，人人都知道艺术是自私的。不过，必须承认，她的歌声里确实有一些优美的旋律。可惜的是，那些旋律没有任何意义，也不能带来任何实际的好处！"他走进自己的房间，躺在小小的板床上，又想起自己的心上人，想着想着，就睡着了。

等月亮升到高空的时候，夜莺便飞向那棵玫瑰树，用胸脯顶着刺尖。整整一夜她都在用胸脯抵着刺尖歌唱，就连寒冷清澈的月亮也俯下身来倾听。整整一晚她都在歌唱，刺尖抵在胸口，越刺越深，她的生命之血也从身上渐渐流走。

最初她歌唱爱情之诞生，诞生于少男少女的心间。于是，在玫瑰树最顶端的枝头上，结出了一朵奇妙的玫瑰花蕾，伴随着一首接一首的歌，花瓣便一片接一片地绽放开来。花开时白白净净，一如笼罩在河面上的雾气——清白如曙光之脚，银白如黎明之翼。宛如银镜中的玫瑰花像，又如水塘里的玫瑰花影，这朵玫瑰花呀，就开在玫瑰树最顶端的枝头上。

然而，玫瑰树喊夜莺再抵紧些，刺得更深一些。"抵紧点，小夜莺，"树喊道，"不然，玫瑰花还没开成，天就亮啦。"

于是，夜莺对着刺尖抵得更紧，歌声也越发响亮，因为她在歌唱激情之诞生，诞生于成年男女的心灵。

玫瑰花的瓣儿呈现出一抹粉嫩的淡红色，宛如与新娘亲吻时新郎脸上泛起的红晕。但那根刺尖还没有刺进她的心，所以玫瑰花的心仍是白的，因为只有夜莺心中流淌出来的鲜血才能染红玫瑰花的心。

玫瑰树喊夜莺再抵紧些，刺得更深一些。"抵紧点，小夜莺，"树哭喊道，"不然，玫瑰花还没开成，天就亮啦。"

于是，夜莺紧紧插入那根刺，刺尖直刺她的心脏，一阵剧痛瞬间穿透全身。疼痛越来越剧烈，她就唱得越来越激昂，因为她在歌唱死亡才能成就之爱，歌唱坟中也能有不朽之情。

这朵奇妙的玫瑰花越来越红，仿佛东方破晓时空中的红霞。红色的层层花瓣啊，簇拥着红宝石般的深红色花心。

可是夜莺的歌声渐渐地微弱下去，小翅膀扑腾起来，双眼蒙上了一层薄膜。歌声模糊了，她感到有什么堵在了喉咙里似的。

然后，夜莺一展最后的歌喉。皎洁的月亮听到了，竟然忘了天已破晓，依然在天空里徘徊不归。红玫瑰听到了，喜出望外地浑身发颤，迎着清冷的晨风舒展开一层又一层的花瓣。山林仙女厄科把歌声带回自己所住的紫色山洞，唤醒了睡梦中的牧羊人。歌声飘荡到河畔的芦苇，芦苇遂将歌声情意捎给大海。

"看哪，看哪！"玫瑰树高声叫喊，"玫瑰花开好了！"可是夜莺没有回应，因为她死了，正躺在深深的草丛中，刺尖穿心而过。

到了中午，学生打开窗户，向外望去。

"怎么，多么好的运气啊！"他叫喊道，"这儿竟有一朵红玫瑰！我一生中从未见过这样的红玫瑰。这朵太美了，我敢肯定它有一个长之又长的拉丁名。"他探下身，摘下了这朵红玫瑰。

然后他戴上帽子，手捧红玫瑰向教授家跑去。

教授的女儿坐在门口，正往线轴上盘绕蓝色的丝线，脚边趴着她的小狗。

"你说过要是我送你一朵红玫瑰的话，你会同我共舞。"青年喊道，"这儿有一朵全世界最红的红玫瑰。今晚你就把它贴着心口戴上，我们一起跳舞时，这花便会告诉你我有多么爱你。"

但是女孩皱起了眉头。"我担心这朵玫瑰配不上我的裙子，"她答道，"而且，御前大臣的侄儿送了我一些真正的珠宝，人人都知道，珠宝的价格比花儿贵多了。"

"好吧，说实话，你真是无情无义。"青年恼羞成怒，把玫瑰扔到街上。花掉进了路边的水沟里,被一辆马车轱辘从身上碾了过去。

"无情无义!"女孩回应,"我也老实告诉你,你简直无理取闹;再说了,你是谁啊?不过是一个学生。怎么着,我就不信你的鞋上会有银扣儿,御前大臣的侄儿就有。"说完她从椅子上站起来,进屋去了。

"爱情,是一件多么愚蠢的东西啊!"青年边走边说,"它没有逻辑学的一半有用,因为它不能证明什么,反倒总是告诉人们一些不会发生的玩意儿,总是让人们相信一些虚无缥缈的玩意儿。说到底,爱情完全不切实际,况且这年月什么都得讲求实际。我还是回到哲学上,去研究形而上学吧。"

于是,他回到自己的房间,抽出一本落满灰尘的厚书,开始读起来。

THE NIGHTINGALE AND THE ROSE

"She said that she would dance with me if I brought her red roses," cried the young student. "But in all my garden there is no red rose."

From her nest in the holm oak tree the nightingale heard him, and she looked out through the leaves, and wondered.

"No red rose in my entire garden!" he cried, and his beautiful eyes filled with tears. "Ah, on what little things does happiness depend? I have read all that the wise men have written, and all the secrets of philosophy are mine, yet for want of a red rose is my life made wretched."

"Here at last is a true lover," said the nightingale. "Night after night have I sung of him, though I didn't know him: night after night have I told his story to the stars, and now I see him. His hair is dark as the hyacinth-blossom, and his lips are red as the rose of his desire; but passion has made his face like pale ivory, and sorrow has set her seal upon his brow."

"The Prince gives a ball tomorrow night," murmured the young student, "and my love will be of the company. If I bring her a red rose she will dance with me till dawn. If I bring her a red rose, I shall hold her in my arms, and she will lean her head upon my shoulder, and her hand will be clasped in mine. But there is no red rose in my garden, so I shall sit lonely, and she will pass me by. She will have no heed of me, and my heart will break."

"Here indeed is the true lover," said the nightingale. "What I sing of, he suffers: what is joy to me, to him is pain. Surely love is a wonderful thing. It is more precious than emeralds, and dearer than fine opals. Pearls and pomegranates cannot buy it, nor is it set forth in the marketplace. It may not be purchased of the merchants, nor can it be weighed out in the balance for gold."

"The musicians will sit in their gallery," said the young student, "and play upon their stringed instruments, and my love will dance to the sound of the harp and the violin. She will dance so lightly that her feet will not touch the floor, and the courtiers in their gay dresses will throng round her. But with me she will not dance, for I have no red rose to give her." And he flung himself down on the grass, and buried his face in his hands, and wept.

"Why is he weeping?" asked a little green lizard, as he ran past him with his tail in the air.

"Why, indeed?" said a butterfly, who was fluttering about after a sunbeam.

"Why, indeed?" whispered a daisy to his neighbour, in a soft, low voice.

"He is weeping for a red rose," said the nightingale.

"For a red rose?" they cried. "How very ridiculous!" and the little lizard, who was something of a cynic, laughed outright.

But the nightingale understood the secret of the student's sorrow, and she sat silent in the oak tree, and thought about the mystery of love.

Suddenly she spread her brown wings for flight, and soared into the air. She passed through the grove like a shadow, and like a shadow she sailed across the garden.

In the centre of the grassplot was standing a beautiful rose tree, and when she saw it she flew over to it, and lit upon a spray.

"Give me a red rose," she cried, "and I will sing you my sweetest song."

But the tree shook its head.

"My roses are white," it answered. "As white as the foam of the sea, and whiter than the snow upon the mountain. But go to my brother who grows round the old sundial, and perhaps he will give you what you want."

So the nightingale flew over to the rose tree that was growing round the old sundial.

"Give me a red rose," she cried. "And I will sing you my sweetest song."

But the tree shook its head.

"My roses are yellow," it answered. "As yellow as the hair of the mermaiden who sits upon an amber throne, and yellower than the daffodil that blooms in the meadow before the mower comes with his scythe. But go to my brother who grows beneath the student's window, and perhaps he will give you what you want."

So the nightingale flew over to the rose tree that was growing beneath the student's window.

"Give me a red rose," she cried. "And I will sing you my sweetest song."

But the tree shook its head.

"My roses are red," it answered. "As red as the feet of the dove, and redder than the great fans of coral that wave and wave in the ocean cavern. But the winter has chilled my veins, and the frost has nipped my buds, and the storm has broken my branches, and I shall have no roses at all this year."

"One red rose is all I want," cried the nightingale. "Only one red rose! Is there no way by which I can get it?"

"There is a way," answered the tree. "But it is so terrible that I dare not tell it to you."

"Tell it to me," said the nightingale. "I am not afraid."

"If you want a red rose," said the tree, "you must build it out of music by moonlight, and stain it with your own heart's blood. You must sing to me with your breast against a thorn. All night long you must sing to me, and the thorn must pierce your heart, and your life blood must flow into my veins, and become mine."

"Death is a great price to pay for a red rose," cried the nightingale. "And life is very dear to all. It is pleasant to sit in the green wood, and to watch the Sun in his chariot of gold, and the moon in her chariot of pearl. Sweet is the scent of the hawthorn, and sweet are the bluebells that hide in the valley, and the heather that blows on the hill. Yet love is better than life, and what is the heart of a bird compared to the heart of a man?"

So she spread her brown wings for flight, and soared into the air. She swept over the garden like a shadow, and like a shadow she sailed through the grove.

The young student was still lying on the grass, where she had left him, and the tears were not yet dry in his beautiful eyes.

"Be happy," cried the nightingale. "Be happy. You shall have your red rose. I will build it out of music by moonlight, and stain it with my own heart's blood. All that I ask of you in return is that you will be a true lover, for love is wiser than Philosophy, though he is wise, and mightier than power, though he is mighty. Flame-coloured are his wings, and coloured like flame is his body. His lips are sweet as honey, and his breath is like frankincense."

The student looked up from the grass, and listened, but he could not understand what the nightingale was saying to him, for he only knew the things that are written down in books.

But the oak tree understood, and felt sad, for he was very fond of the little nightingale who had built her nest in his branches.

"Sing me one last song," he whispered. "I shall feel very lonely when you are gone."

So the nightingale sang to the oak tree, and her voice was like water bubbling from a silver jar.

When she had finished her song, the student got up, and pulled a note book and a lead pencil out of his pocket.

"She has form," he said to himself, as he walked away through the grove— "that cannot be denied to her; but has she got feeling? I am afraid not. In fact, she is like most artists; she is all style without any sincerity. She would not sacrifice herself for others. She thinks merely of music, and everybody knows that the arts are selfish. Still, it must be admitted that she has some beautiful notes in her voice. What a pity it is that they do not mean anything, or do any practical good!" And he went into his room, and lay down on his little pallet-bed, and began to think of his love; and, after a time, he fell asleep.

And when the moon shone in the heavens the nightingale flew to the rose tree, and set her breast against the thorn. All night long she sang with her breast against the thorn, and the cold crystal moon leaned down and listened. All night long she sang and the thorn went deeper and deeper into her breast, and her life blood ebbed away from her.

She sang first of the birth of love in the heart of a boy and a girl. And on the top most spray of the rose tree there blossomed a marvellous rose, petal following petal, as song followed song. Pale was it, at first, as the mist that hangs over the river—pale as the feet of the morning, and silver as the wings of the dawn. As the shadow of a rose in a mirror of silver, as the shadow of a rose in a water pool, so was the rose that blossomed on the topmost spray of the tree.

But the tree cried to the nightingale to press closer against the thorn. "Press closer, little nightingale," cried the tree, "or the day will come before the rose is finished."

So the nightingale pressed closer against the thorn, and louder and louder grew her song, for she sang of the birth of passion in the soul of a man and a maid.

And a delicate flush of pink came into the leaves of the rose, like the flush in the face of the bridegroom when he kisses the lips of the bride. But the thorn had not yet reached her heart, so the rose's heart remained white, for only a nightingale's heart's blood can crimson the heart of a rose.

And the tree cried to the nightingale to press closer against the thorn. "Press closer, little nightingale," cried the tree, "or the day will come before the rose is finished."

So the nightingale pressed closer against the thorn, and the thorn touched her heart, and a fierce pang of pain shot through her. Bitter, bitter was the pain, and wilder and wilder grew her song, for she sang of the love that is perfected by death, of the love that dies not in the tomb.

And the marvellous rose became crimson, like the rose of the eastern sky. Crimson was the girdle of petals, and crimson as a ruby was the heart.

But the nightingale's voice grew fainter, and her little wings began to beat, and a film came over her eyes. Fainter and fainter grew her song, and she felt something choking her in her throat.

Then she gave one last burst of music. The white moon heard it, and she forgot the dawn, and lingered on in the sky. The red rose heard it, and it trembled all over with ecstasy, and opened its petals to the cold morning air. Echo bore it to her purple cavern in the hills, and woke the sleeping shepherds from their dreams. It floated through the reeds of the river, and they carried its message to the sea.

"Look, look!" cried the tree. "The rose is finished now." But the nightingale made no answer, for she was lying dead in the long grass, with the thorn in her heart.

And at noon the student opened his window and looked out.

"Why, what a wonderful piece of luck!" he cried. "Here is a red rose! I have never seen any rose like it in all my life. It is so beautiful that I am sure it has a long Latin name." And he leaned down and plucked it.

Then he put on his hat, and ran up to the professor's house with the rose in his hand.

The daughter of the professor was sitting in the doorway winding blue silk on a reel, and her little dog was lying at her feet.

"You said that you would dance with me if I brought you a red rose," cried the student. "Here is the reddest rose in all the world. You will wear it tonight next your heart, and as we dance together it will tell you how I love you."

But the girl frowned. "I am afraid it will not go with my dress," she answered. "And, besides, the Chamberlain's nephew has sent me some real jewels, and everybody knows that jewels cost far more than flowers."

"Well, upon my word, you are very ungrateful," said the student angrily. And he threw the rose into the street, where it fell into the gutter, and a cart-wheel went over it.

"Ungrateful!" said the girl. "I tell you what, you are very rude. And, after all, who are you? Only a student. Why, I don't believe you have even got silver buckles to your shoes as the Chamberlain's nephew has." And she got up from her chair and went into the house.

"What a silly thing love is!" said the student as he walked away. "It is not half as useful as logic, for it does not prove anything, and it is always telling one of things that are not going to happen, and making one believe things that are not true. In fact, it is quite unpractical, and, as in this age to be practical is everything, I shall go back to Philosophy and study Metaphysics."

So he returned to his room and pulled out a great dusty book, and began to read.

小气鬼巨人

每天下午，孩子们放学归来都会去巨人的花园里玩耍。花园又大又漂亮，绿草茵茵。草丛中到处开满了美丽的鲜花，宛如天上的繁星。园中还长着十二棵桃树，春天来临时便绽放出娇美的鲜花，有的粉红，有的洁白；到了秋天就会结出累累的硕果。小鸟坐在树梢放声歌唱，歌声是如此甜美，常常引得孩子们停下游戏来侧耳倾听。"我们在这里是多快乐啊！"他们互相欢呼着。

有一天，巨人回来了。之前他是去探访自己的朋友——康沃尔的食人魔，并在那里待了七年。七年后，巨人把要说的话都说完了，毕竟自个儿本来就没有多少话要说。他决定返回自己的城堡，到家时他发现孩子们正在花园里玩耍呢。

"你们在这里干什么？"他厉声呵道，一下子把孩子们全吓跑了。

"我自个儿的花园就是我自个儿的花园，"巨人说道，"这谁都能明白，除了我自己，我不允许任何人来这里玩耍。"于是，他修筑高墙把花园围了起来，并竖起一块告示牌"严禁擅入，违者必究"。

他是一个非常小气的巨人。

可怜的孩子们，现在没地方玩了。他们试图在路上玩，但路上尘土飞扬，又满是坚硬的石子，他们不喜欢。于是上课结束后，他们便时常围着高墙转悠，谈论着墙内的花园是多么漂亮。"过去我们在那里面玩得多快乐啊！"他们竞相感叹着。

接着春天来了，田野里到处都有小花盛开，处处都有小鸟飞跃。只是小气鬼巨人的花园依然停留在冬天。园内没有小孩，鸟儿就不愿飞来放歌，就连草木也忘了开花。偶尔有一朵美丽的鲜花从草丛中探出头来，当看到那块告示牌时禁不住怜惜起孩子们来，马上掉头又溜回地下，睡觉去了。唯独高兴的是雪和霜。"春天已经忘了这座花园，"她俩嚷道，"所以咱们可以在这里一整年一整年地住下去啦。"雪用她那巨大的白色斗篷盖住了青草，而霜则把所有的树木都涂成了银色。然后她们就邀请北风与自己同住，北风便应邀而来。北风裹着毛衣，整天在花园里咆哮着，还把烟囱管帽吹掉了。"这地方真是不错，"他说道，"我们应该请冰雹来参观参观。"于是冰雹如约而至。冰雹每天都要花三个小时来咔嗒咔嗒地撞击城堡的屋顶，击碎大部分瓦片之后，便以最快的速度在花园里跑上一圈又一圈。他穿着灰色的衣服，呼出来的气息像冰一样寒冷。

"我不明白，为什么春天迟迟不来呢，"小气鬼巨人端坐在窗前，往外望着他那座白茫茫、冷飕飕的花园，说道，"我希望天气会变好起来。"

但是春天一直没有来，夏天也没有来。秋天给每一座花园都送去了金黄的果实，可是巨人的花园她没有送，并说道："他太小气了。"因此，那里一直都是冬天，北风、冰雹、霜和雪一同在树丛中跳着舞。

一天早晨，巨人睁着眼躺在床上，忽然听到了动人的音乐。乐声甜美悦耳，这让他以为一定是国王的乐队从外面路过。其实呢，就是一只小小的朱顶雀在窗外唱歌，因为他很久都没有在自己的花园里听到鸟儿唱歌了，便觉得这似乎是天底下最优美的歌声了。接着，头顶上的冰雹收住舞步，北风也停止了咆哮，一股醉人的香气透过敞开的窗扉向他袭来。"我看，春天终于来啦！"巨人说着，跳下床，向外张望。

他看到了什么呢？

他看到了一幅最为奇妙的景象。孩子们从墙上的一个小洞钻了进来，然后爬上树枝坐着。在他能看到的每一棵树上，都坐着一个小孩。那些树都为孩子们的归来高兴得"鲜花怒放"，并伸开手臂在孩子们的头顶上轻轻挥舞。鸟儿们高兴地飞来飞去，叽叽喳喳地叫个不停；花儿们也透过绿茵茵的草丛抬头仰望，笑逐颜开。多么可爱的一幅场景啊，只是有一个角落还是冬天——那是花园最远处的角落，里面站着一个小男孩。

他太小了，够不着树枝，只得在树下转来转去，哭着鼻子抹着眼泪。那棵可怜的树依然浑身堆积着霜雪，头顶上北风又是怒吼又是咆哮。"爬上来吧！小家伙。"树一边说着，一边压低枝丫，拼命地弯下来，可是孩子的个头实在太小了。

巨人看到这幅场景，心也软了。"我先前太小气了！"他说，"现在我知道为什么春天不愿意来这里了。我要把那个可怜的小男孩抱到树上，然后把墙推倒，让我的花园成为孩子们的乐园，永远直到永远。"对自个儿先前的行为，他真是后悔极了。

于是，他蹑手蹑脚地下楼，轻轻地打开前门，往外走进花园。但是，当孩子们看到巨人的时候，一个个都吓得跑开了，花园再一次变成了冬天。只有那个小男孩没跑，因为他满眼都是泪水，没有看到巨人走来。巨人悄悄地来到他身后，轻轻地单手抱起他，然后把他放到树上。顿时树就开出了鲜花，引来鸟儿们在上面放声歌唱；小男孩伸出双手，一把搂住巨人的脖子，亲了起来。其余孩子看到巨人不再像以前那样凶，就都跑回来了，春天跟着他们也一起回来了。"这里现在就是你们的花园，小家伙们。"巨人说完，操起一把大斧头，砸掉了围墙。中午十二点人们一起去赶集时，看到巨人和孩子们正在园子里玩着，大家生平从未见过这么美丽的花园。

孩子们玩了一整天，傍晚时分跑来向巨人道别。

"可是你们的小伙伴在哪里呢，"巨人问道，"那个被我抱起放到树上的男孩？"巨人最疼他了，因为他亲过巨人。

"我们不知道啊，"孩子们答道，"他已经走了吧。"

"你们一定要告诉他，务必让他明天再来这儿。"巨人说。但是孩子们都说自个儿不知道他住哪儿，以前也从来没有见过他呢，对此巨人感到非常伤心。

每天下午放学后，孩子们都跑过来和巨人一起玩耍。但是巨人最爱的那个小男孩再也没有出现过。巨人对所有的孩子都很好，也一直想念着自己抱过的第一位小朋友。"我多么想见到他啊！"他常常叨念着。

年复一年，巨人很老了，身体也变得非常虚弱。他玩不动了，只能坐在一把巨大的扶手椅上，看看孩子们做游戏，再欣欣赏赏自个儿的花园。"我拥有许多美丽的花儿，"他说道，"但是最美丽的花儿还是这些孩子们。"

一个冬天的早晨，巨人起床穿衣服时望向窗外。他并不讨厌冬天了，因为他明白这只是春天在睡眠，花儿在休息罢了。

忽然，他惊奇地揉着双眼，看了又看。真是奇妙的一幕：在花园最远处的角落里有一棵树，树上开满了可爱的白花。金黄的枝条下，挂满了银白的果实，再下面就站着他最疼爱的那个小男孩。

巨人分外惊喜，跑下楼，冲进花园。他急忙穿过草地，跑近那个小男孩。挨近时，巨人带着愤怒，满脸涨得通红，问道："谁敢伤你？"因为孩子的两只手掌心上现出了两个钉痕，而且两只小脚上也有两个钉痕。

"谁敢伤你？"巨人大喊道，"告诉我，我就拿大刀，砍了他。"

"不!"孩子答道,"这些是爱的伤痕啊。"

"您是谁呢?"巨人问道,浑身感到一种奇怪的敬畏之情,便跪在了小孩面前。

小孩对巨人笑了笑,说道:"你让我在你的花园里玩过一次,今日你要跟我去我的花园,那里就是天堂啊。"

那天下午,孩子们跑进花园时,发现巨人躺在树下死去了,全身盖满了白花。

THE SELFISH GIANT

Every afternoon, as they were coming from school, the children used to go and play in the giant's garden.

It was a large lovely garden, with soft green grass. Here and there over the grass stood beautiful flowers like stars, and there were twelve peach trees that in the springtime broke out into delicate blossoms of pink and pearl, and in the autumn bore rich fruit. The birds sat on the trees and sang so sweetly that the children used to stop their games in order to listen to them. "How happy we are here!" they cried to each other.

One day the giant came back. He had been to visit his friend the Cornish ogre, and had stayed with him for seven years. After the seven years were over he had said all that he had to say, for his conversation was limited, and he determined to return to his own castle. When he arrived he saw the children playing in the garden.

"What are you doing here?" he cried in a very gruff voice, and the children ran away.

"My own garden is my own garden," said the giant. "Any one can understand that, and I will allow nobody to play in it but myself." So he built a high wall all round it, and put up a noticeboard.

He was a very selfish giant.

The poor children had now nowhere to play. They tried to play on the road, but the road was very dusty and full of hard stones, and they did not like it. They used to wander round the high wall when their lessons were over, and talk about the beautiful garden inside. "How happy we were there!" they said to each other.

Then the spring came, and all over the country there were little blossoms and little birds. Only in the garden of the selfish giant it was still winter. The birds did not care to sing in it as there were no children, and the trees forgot to blossom. Once a beautiful flower put its head out from the grass, but when it saw the noticeboard it was so sorry for the children that it slipped back into the ground again, and went off to sleep. The only people who were pleased were the snow and the frost. "Spring has forgotten this garden," they cried, "so we will live here all the year round." The snow covered up the grass with her great white cloak, and the frost painted all the trees silver. Then they invited the north wind to stay with them, and he came. He was wrapped in furs, and he roared all day about the garden, and blew the chimney pots down. "This is a delightful spot," he said. "We must ask the hail on a visit." So the hail came. Every day for three hours he rattled on the roof of the castle till he broke most of the slates, and then he ran round and round the garden as fast as he could go. He was dressed in grey, and his breath was like ice.

"I cannot understand why the spring is so late in coming," said the selfish giant, as he sat at the window and looked out at his cold white garden. "I hope there will be a change in the weather."

But the spring never came, nor the summer. The autumn gave golden fruit to every garden, but to the giant's garden she gave none. "He is too selfish," she said. So it was always winter there, and the north wind and the hail, and the frost, and the snow danced about through the trees.

One morning the giant was lying awake in bed when he heard some lovely music. It sounded so sweet to his ears that he thought it must be the King's musicians passing by. It was really only a little linnet singing outside his window, but it was so long since he had heard a bird sing in his garden that it seemed to him to be the most beautiful music in the world. Then the hail stopped dancing over his head, and the north wind ceased roaring, and a delicious perfume came to him through the open casement. "I believe the spring has come at last," said the giant. And he jumped out of bed and looked out.

What did he see?

He saw a most wonderful sight. Through a little hole in the wall the children had crept in, and they were sitting in the branches of the trees. In every tree that he could see there was a little child. And the trees were so glad to have the children back again that they had covered themselves with blossoms, and were waving their arms gently above the children's heads. The birds were flying about and twittering with delight, and the flowers were looking up through the green grass and laughing. It was a lovely scene, only in one corner it was still winter. It was the farthest corner of the garden, and in it was standing a little boy.

He was so small that he could not reach up to the branches of the tree, and he was wandering all round it, crying bitterly. The poor tree was still quite covered with frost and snow, and the north wind was blowing and roaring above it. "Climb up! Little boy," said the tree, and it bent its branches down as low as it could; but the boy was too tiny.

And the giant's heart melted as he looked out. "How selfish I have been!" he said. "Now I know why the spring would not come here. I will put that poor little boy on the top of the tree, and then I will knock down the wall, and my garden shall be the children's playground for ever and ever." He was really very sorry for what he had done.

So he crept downstairs and opened the front door quite softly, and went out into the garden. But when the children saw him they were so frightened that they all ran away, and the garden became winter again. Only the little boy did not run, for his eyes were so full of tears that he did not see the giant coming. And the giant stole up behind him and took him gently in his hand, and put him up into the tree. And the tree broke at once into blossom, and the birds came and sang on it, and the little boy stretched out his two arms and flung them round the giant's neck, and kissed him. And the other children, when they saw that the giant was not wicked any longer, came running back, and with them came the spring. "It is your garden now, little children," said the giant, and he took a great axe and knocked down the wall. And when the people were going to market at twelve o'clock they found the giant playing with the children in the most beautiful garden they had ever seen.

All day long they played, and in the evening they came to the giant to bid him good-bye.

"But where is your little companion?" he said. "The boy I put into the tree." The giant loved him the best because he had kissed him.

"We don't know," answered the children. "He has gone away."

"You must tell him to be sure and come here tomorrow," said the giant. But the children said that they did not know where he lived, and had never seen him before. And the giant felt very sad.

Every afternoon, when school was over, the children came and played with the giant. But the little boy whom the giant loved was never seen again. The giant was very kind to all the children, yet he longed for his first little friend, and often spoke of him. "How I would like to see him!" he used to say.

Years went over, and the giant grew very old and feeble. He could not play about any more, so he sat in a huge armchair, and watched the children at their games, and admired his garden. "I have many beautiful flowers," he said. "But the children are the most beautiful flowers of all."

One winter morning he looked out of his window as he was dressing. He did not hate the winter now, for he knew that it was merely the spring asleep, and that the flowers were resting.

Suddenly he rubbed his eyes in wonder and looked and looked. It certainly was a marvellous sight. In the farthest corner of the garden was a tree quite covered with lovely white blossoms. Its branches were all golden, and silver fruit hung down from them, and underneath it stood the little boy he had loved.

Downstairs ran the giant in great joy, and out into the garden. He hastened across the grass, and came near to the child. And when he came quite close his face grew red with anger, and he said, "Who has dared to wound you?" For on the palms of the child's hands were the prints of two nails, and the prints of two nails were on the little feet.

"Who has dared to wound you?" cried the giant. "Tell me, that I might take my big sword and slay him."

"No!" answered the child. "But these are the wounds of love."

"Who are you?" said the giant, and a strange awe fell on him, and he knelt before the little child.

And the child smiled on the giant, and said to him, "You let me play once in your garden, today you shall come with me to my garden, which is paradise."

And when the children ran in that afternoon, they found the giant lying dead under the tree, all covered with white blossoms.

忠诚的朋友

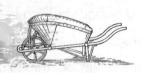

一天早晨，老水鼠把头从洞里探出来。他两颗珠子似的小眼睛闪闪发亮，颌下的灰色胡须稠密而又坚硬，尾巴像一条长长的黑橡皮带。小鸭子们正在池塘里游来游去，看上去就像一群金黄的金丝雀；鸭妈妈全身洁白，双腿纯红，正在努力教孩子们如何在水中倒立呢。

"如果不会倒立的话，你们永远也入不了上流社会。"鸭妈妈不停地对小鸭子们唠叨着，时而给他们示范一下怎么倒立。但是小鸭子们都不理她。他们太小了，根本不知道进入上流社会到底有什么好处。

"真是不听话的孩子！"老水鼠嚷道，"他们真该被淹死。"

"话不能这样说，"鸭妈妈答道，"万事开头难，做父母不够耐心怎么能行呢？"

"啊！天下父母心，这我可不了解，"老水鼠说，"毕竟我没有家室。实际上，我从来没有结过婚，也不打算结婚。爱情固然很棒，但友情要高出许多呢。确实，我知道世界上没有什么比忠诚的友情更崇高、更难得了。"

"那么，请问，依你之见一个忠诚的朋友该有怎样的职责呢？"一只绿色的朱顶雀端坐在旁边的一棵柳树上，听到这番对话后插嘴问道。

"没错，这正是我想知道的。"鸭妈妈一边说，一边游到池塘的尽头，然后倒立起来，以便给自己的孩子们做个好榜样。

"多傻的一个问题！"老水鼠喊道，"我当然希望我忠诚的朋友对我忠诚可靠。"

"那你会怎么回报呢？"那只小鸟一边追问，一边跳上一根银色的枝条，扇了扇自个儿的小翅膀。

"我没听明白你的意思。"老水鼠答道。

"让我给你讲一个关于友情的故事吧。"朱顶雀说。

"这个故事是关于我的吗？"老水鼠问道，"如果是的话，我倒是愿意听一听，因为我尤其喜欢虚构的故事。"

"故事与你挺般配的。"朱顶雀回答着，然后飞下来，落在池塘边，讲起了故事《忠诚的朋友》。

"从前，"朱顶雀说，"有一个忠诚的小家伙，名叫汉斯。"

"他很出众吗？"老水鼠问。

"不，"朱顶雀答道，"我觉得他一点儿也不出众，但他心地善良，圆圆的脸庞总是乐呵呵的，让人忍俊不禁。他独自住在一座很小的农舍里，每天都在花园里干活。在整个乡下的花园中就数他的花园最惹人喜爱了，那里有五彩石竹、桂竹香、荠菜和法国虎耳草。园内玫瑰有粉色的、黄色的，番红花有淡紫色的、金黄色的，堇菜有紫色的、白色的；那里还有耧斗菜和碎米荠、甘牛至和野兰香、莲香花和鸢尾花、黄水仙和康乃馨，他们逐月依着各自的花期次第绽放，一种接着另一种，所以园内总有美丽的鲜花，赏心悦目，总有怡人的清香扑鼻而来。

"小汉斯有很多朋友，但是最忠诚的朋友要数磨坊主休伊。确实，这个有钱的磨坊主对小汉斯是绝对忠诚可靠啦，每次路过汉斯的园子时，都少不了要挨着墙探身进去扯一大束鲜花，或捋一大把香草，要是遇上水果季节就干脆往自个儿的口袋满满地装些李子啊樱桃啊什么的。

"'真正的朋友应该分享一切，'磨坊主经常这么说。小汉斯听后也总是点头微笑，感到非常自豪，能有这样一位情操高尚的朋友。

"确实,有时候邻居们都觉得诧异,从来不见富有的磨坊主给过小汉斯任何回报,虽然他有上百袋面粉存在磨坊里,还有六头奶牛和一大群毛茸茸的绵羊。不过,汉斯从不为这些事情伤神,最让他高兴的事情莫过于听磨坊主高谈阔论,论说真正的友情都是无私的。

"就这样,小汉斯在自个儿的园子里接连忙活着。由春入夏,再到秋天,他都非常地快乐。然而,冬天来临时他若是采不到水果或鲜花拿到市场上去卖,他就得受冻挨饿了,日子会过得十分艰难;他时常连晚饭都吃不上,只能找几颗干梨或一些坚果来充饥,而后只得上床睡觉了。还有啊,冬天他非常地孤单,因为这期间磨坊主从不来看望他。

"'只要积雪还在,我去看小汉斯就没有什么好处,'磨坊主常常对妻子说,'毕竟人家遇到困难时,就该让他们清静点儿,别为来客所烦。反正这是我对友情的看法,我确信自己是对的。因此,我要等到春天来临时再去看望汉斯,他才能送我一大篮子报春花,从中他也会得到极大的快乐。'

"'你待人确实体贴入微。'妻子回应着,舒服地坐在扶手椅上,旁边的壁炉里松木烧得正旺。'真是体贴入微。听你谈论友情,真是一大享受。要我说,就是牧师本人也没你讲得这般美好,哪怕他确实住着三层的楼房,小指上还戴着金戒指。

"'可是我们不能邀请小汉斯过来吗?'磨坊主的小儿子问道,'要是可怜的汉斯有困难,我就把我的粥分一半给他,再领他看看我的小白兔。'

"'你真是个傻孩子!'磨坊主嚷道,'我真不明白送你上学有什么用!你好像什么也没学到。不是吗,如果小汉斯来这儿,看到咱们家温暖的炉火、丰盛的晚餐还有大桶的红酒,他会嫉妒的;嫉妒是最可怕的东西啦,它会损害人的品性。我当然不会允许汉斯的品性遭受损害。我是他最要好的朋友，我会始终照看他，免得遭受诱惑变坏。另外，要是汉斯来这儿，他会要我赊给他一点儿面粉，这我可不干。面粉是一回事儿，友情是另一回事儿，不能混为一谈的。不是吗，这两个词儿拼法不同，意思也截然不同，大家都能看得出来。'

"'你说得真好啊！'磨坊主的妻子说道，同时给她自个儿倒了一大杯热啤酒，'我真觉得晕晕忽忽了，就像在教堂一样。'

"'也有许多人做得好，'磨坊主回应，'但很少有人能说得很好。这表明，言行之中言比行难，当然言比行也好。'说着他严厉地瞪着桌子对面的小儿子，瞪得他羞愧地把脑袋耷拉下来，满脸通红，对着茶杯哭了起来。可是孩子那么小，怪不得他呀。"

"那就是故事的结局吗？"老水鼠问。

"当然不是，"朱顶雀答道，"那才是开始呢。"

"那你就落伍了，"老水鼠说道，"如今擅长讲故事的人，个个都是先从结局开始，然后讲到开场，最后再讲到中间。这是个新方法呢，是我那天从一个评论家那里听来的。那时，他正与一位年轻人绕着池塘漫步，长篇大论地谈起这事。我相信他肯定是对的，因为他戴着一副蓝色眼镜，头顶光秃秃的，只要年轻人发表意见他总是以'哑！'回应。不过，请你继续讲下去吧。我太喜欢那个磨坊主了。我自个儿也有一大堆美好心得，所以我们两人甚是惺惺相惜。"

"嗯，"朱顶雀单腿跳了起来，时而用这只，时而用那只，并继续说道，"冬天一过，报春花开始星星点点地绽放出淡黄淡黄的花儿，磨坊主就对他的妻子说自个儿要去看看小汉斯。

"'哎呀，你真是心地善良！'他的妻子高声说，'你总是念着别人。对了，记得带上那个大篮子，好把花儿装回来。'

"于是，磨坊主用一条结实的铁链把磨坊风车的叶帆绑紧，然后挎着篮子下山去了。

"'早上好，小汉斯，'磨坊主说。

"'早上好，'汉斯拄着铁锹，笑容满面地答道。

"'整个冬天你过得怎样啊？'磨坊主问。

"'呃，说真的，'汉斯大声回应，'你真好，还问起这个，真是个好人。只是这个冬天哪，我的日子着实难熬。不过现在春天来了，我非常开心，我的花儿都开得很好。'

"'冬天里，我们时常念叨你，汉斯，'磨坊主说，'还担心着你过得怎么样呢。'

"'你真是太好了，'汉斯说，'我倒是有点儿担心你忘了我呢。'

"'汉斯，你这么说就让我惊讶了，'磨坊主说，'友情是忘不了的。这就是友情的妙处，但我担心你不懂生活的诗意。对了，报春花看上去多可爱呀！'

"'它们开得可爱极了，'汉斯回答，'而且开了这么多，我真是幸运。我要把它们带到市场上卖给市长的女儿，然后用换得的钱赎回我的独轮手推车。'

"'赎回你的手推车？你不会是说，你把车卖了吧？这么干就是蠢到家了！'

"'呃，事实是，'汉斯说，'我不得不卖。你也明白，冬天的日子我真是难熬啊，身无分文，连面包都买不起。所以呢，我先是当掉了我礼拜天外衣上的银扣儿，接着是当银链子，又当大烟斗，最后才当手推车。但我现在要把它们全赎回来啦。'

"'汉斯，'磨坊主说，'我把自个儿的手推车送给你。车是不太好，确实，一侧的挡板没了，车轮的辐条也有点儿毛病。这些都不用管，我会把车送给你的。我心里明白，这么送人未免过于慷慨，而且许多人都会认为，我这么做无疑是愚蠢到家了，但我不跟他们一般见识。我认为，慷慨正是友情的精髓，再说，我已为自己添置了一辆新车。对了，你不要着急啊，我会把我的手推车送给你的。'

"'啊，真是，你真是大方，'小汉斯高兴得连滑稽的圆脸都熠熠发亮，说道，'我屋内就有块木板，很容易就能修好它。'

"'有块木板！'磨坊主说，'噢，我正想要块木板来修补仓顶呢，上面有一个大洞，要是不修麦子就要全潮了。真走运，你说有木板！说得千真万确，好心总有好报。我要把我的手推车送给你，现在你又要把你自个儿的木板送给我。当然，推车比木板值钱多了，可是真正的友情从不计较这样的事情。拜托你快些把板拿来，我今天就开始修补谷仓。'

"'好嘞，'小汉斯大声说着，就跑进棚屋，把木板拖了出来。

"'这块木板不是很大，'磨坊主看了看说，'我担心自己补完仓顶，就没什么剩下来给你修车用了。不过，这当然不能怪我。现在，我把手推车都送给了你，我敢肯定你会送我些花儿作为回报的。这儿有篮子，你要把它装得满满的。'

"'满满的？'小汉斯很是忧愁地说，毕竟那篮子实在太大了。他知道，要是装满了他就剩不了什么花去市场卖钱了，而他正急着要赎回自个儿的银扣呢。

"'是啊，就是，'磨坊主答道，'既然我都把自己的手推车送你了，我想让你送我些花儿不过分吧。我兴许错了，但我应能想到，友情，真正的友情，是来不得半点儿小气的。'

"'我亲爱的朋友，我最好的朋友，'小汉斯嚷道，'我园子里所有的花儿任你挑。我更愿尽快得到你的好评，至于我的银扣儿随便哪天赎回都行。'说完汉斯就跑去摘下所有漂亮的报春花，装满了磨坊主的大篮子。

"'再见，小汉斯。'磨坊主说完就肩扛木板，提起大篮子，向山上走去。

"'再见。'小汉斯说完就开心地挖土翻地，对那辆手推车真是太满意了。

"第二天,他正对着门廊钉上一些金银花,忽然听到路上传来磨坊主喊他的声音。于是他跳下梯子,跑过花园,往墙外看去。

"那儿站着磨坊主,背上扛着一大袋面粉。

"'亲爱的小汉斯,'磨坊主说,'你能不能替我把这袋面粉扛到市场上去呢?'

"'哦,真对不起,'汉斯回答,'我今天实在很忙。我要把所有藤蔓钉起来,把花全浇上水,把草都修剪完。'

"'嗯,真是的,'磨坊主说,'我倒是觉得,就凭我要送你手推车,你还拒绝帮我忙,就未免不讲交情了。'

"'哦,别这么说唉,'小汉斯嚷起来,'再怎么着我也不会不讲交情的。'说完他就跑去取帽子,扛起大袋面粉就吭哧吭哧地上路了。'

"这天热得要命,路上尘土飞扬,汉斯还没走到六英里就累得没法子了,只得坐下来歇口气。然而,他还是鼓足力气继续上路,最后终于赶到了市场。他在那里等了一段时间,将那袋面粉卖了个非常好的价钱,立马就往家赶,因为他担心停留太晚可能会在路上遇到强盗。

"'今天真是累得够呛,'小汉斯临上床睡觉前还自言自语,'不过我很开心自个儿没有拒绝磨坊主,毕竟他是我最好的朋友,再说,他还要把他的手推车送给我。'

"第二天一大早,磨坊主就下山来拿卖面粉的钱,但是小汉斯太累了,仍躺在床上呢。

"'我说真的,'磨坊主说,'你太懒了。真的,就凭我要把手推车送给你,我想你干活会更卖力的。懒散可是一桩大罪,我当然不喜欢我有哪个朋友游手好闲,拖拖拉拉。你千万别介意我对你直话直说。当然,要不是拿你当朋友,我就连做梦也不会这么说。但是,如果不能真话真说,那友情又有什么用呢?大家都知道说好听的话,溜须拍马，但真正的朋友总是说些难听的话，还不怕对方听了难受。的确如此，真正的朋友都会喜欢讲难听的话，因为他知道自个儿正在做好事。'

"'我真是抱歉，'小汉斯揉了揉双眼，脱下睡帽，说道，'可是我太累了，想在床上多躺一会儿呢，再听听鸟叫。你知不知道，我听了鸟叫后总会把活干得更好吗？'

"'嗯，我很高兴，'磨坊主拍着小汉斯的背，说道，'因为我要你穿好衣服就赶紧上山，来磨坊替我修补谷仓屋顶。'

"可怜的小汉斯正急着要去自个儿的花园干活，因为花儿已有两天没浇水了，但他不好意思拒绝磨坊主，毕竟磨坊主是他这么要好的朋友。

"'要是我说自己很忙，你会不会认为这么做不够交情？'汉斯小声询问，又是害羞又是胆怯。

"'嗯，真是的，'磨坊主答道，'我倒是觉得，就凭我要送你手推车，要你帮点儿忙也不过分。可当然啦，要是你不答应，那我就走了，我自己去干。'

"'哦！万万不可。'小汉斯大喊着跳下床，穿好衣服，上山去了谷仓。

"整整一天他都在那儿干活，直到太阳下山。太阳下山时磨坊主来了，看看他进展如何。

"'屋顶上的洞补好了吗，小汉斯？'磨坊主乐呵呵地大声喊起来。

"'都补好了。'小汉斯一边回答，一边顺着梯子爬下来。

"'啊!'磨坊主说,'为别人干活是世上最开心的事啦。'

"'听你说话真是一大福气,'小汉斯坐下来,揩着额头的汗,答道,'一份莫大的福气。只是,你这些美好想法,我恐怕永远也想不出来。'

"'哦!好想法会找上你的,'磨坊主说,'但你得多下些功夫啊。目前你只有友情的实践,总有一天你也会有友情的理论。'

"'你真相信我会吗?'小汉斯问。

"'这个我一点也不怀疑,'磨坊主答道,'但这会儿你已补好了屋顶,该回家去休息了,毕竟我还指望明天你能把我家羊群赶到山上去呢。'

"可怜的小汉斯听了,也不敢吭一声。第二天一早,磨坊主就把羊带到汉斯的小屋前,汉斯只得出发,赶着羊上山去。上山再下山费了整整一天的时间,汉斯到家时已是筋疲力尽,累得在椅子就呼呼睡着了,一直睡到天大亮。

"'真开心啊,能在我的园子里待会儿!'汉斯说完,立马就出去干活了。

"可是不知怎的,他根本就没能照料好自己的花儿,因为他那个磨坊主朋友总是过来找他,派他去干各种费力费时的活儿,或者叫他去磨坊帮忙。小汉斯有时非常苦恼,生怕他那些花儿会觉得他已把它们给忘了,但他还是自我安慰磨坊主是自个儿最要好的朋友。'而且,'汉斯时常说起,'他要把自己的手推车送我呢,这完全是一种不求回报的慷慨之举。'

"就这样,小汉斯没完没了地为磨坊主干活,而磨坊主则大谈特谈诸多关于友情的美好想法。这些高谈阔论汉斯都一一写在笔记本上,常常晚上拿出来温习,因为他非常好学。

"之后的一天晚上,小汉斯正坐在炉边取暖,忽然听到门口传来很大的拍击声。这天夜里天气坏透了,狂风绕着屋子吼得吓人,

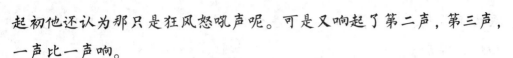

起初他还认为那只是狂风怒吼声呢。可是又响起了第二声,第三声,一声比一声响。

"'肯定是哪个可怜的赶路人。'小汉斯自言自语起来,并跑到门口。

"站在眼前的是磨坊主,一手提着灯笼,一手握着粗大的手杖。

"'亲爱的小汉斯,'磨坊主高喊,'我碰到大麻烦了。我家小孩从梯子上跌下来,摔伤了,我正要去找医生。可是医生住得太远,今晚天气又太坏,刚刚我突然想起,要是你代我去的话,那就好多了。你知道我就要把手推车送给你了,所以呢,你该为我做点什么作为回报,这才算天公地道。'

"'没问题,'小汉斯大声应答,'你来找我,我非常荣幸,马上就出发。可是你得把灯笼借给我呀,因为夜里太黑了,我怕会掉到沟里去。'

"'非常抱歉,'磨坊主答道,'这个灯笼是新的,要是有什么闪失,我的损失可就大了。'

"'好吧,不要紧,没灯也行,'小汉斯一边大声回应,一边取下自个儿的皮大衣和暖和的红帽子穿戴好,再绕着脖子系上围巾,紧接着就出发了。

"这晚的暴风雨真是可怕!天黑得让小汉斯几乎看不见,风也大得让他几乎站不稳。还好,他这个人非常勇敢,连续走了约莫三个小时后,终于来到了医生家,赶上前去敲门。

"'谁呀?'医生把头伸出卧室的窗户,大声问道。

"'小汉斯,医生。'

"'你有什么事儿,小汉斯?'

"'磨坊主的儿子从梯子上跌下来,摔伤了,磨坊主请你马上去看看。'

"'好的!'医生说完就吩咐备马,还有自个儿的大靴和灯笼。

医生下了楼,骑上马向着磨坊主住家方向奔去,而小汉斯则跌跌撞撞地走在后面。

"这场暴风雨越来越猛,大雨倾盆而下,小汉斯看不清自个儿要往哪儿走,也跟不上马儿的脚步。他最后迷路了,在一片沼泽地上转来又转去,转去又转来。那可是一个非常危险的地方,烂泥下面都是深坑,就是在那儿可怜的小汉斯被淹死了。第二天,几个牧羊人看到他的尸体漂浮在池塘的水面上,就捞起来送回他的农舍。

"大家都去参加了小汉斯的葬礼,毕竟他很有人缘,而磨坊主成了主祭。

"'既然我是他最好的朋友,'磨坊主说,'就该站在最佳位置,这样才算是天公地道。'于是,他走在了送葬队伍的最前面,披着一件长长的黑色斗篷,时而拿起一块大手帕抹抹双眼。

"'确实,小汉斯的走对每一个人而言都是一大损失,'铁匠评论。此时葬礼已经结束,大伙舒舒服服地都坐在客栈里,一边喝着香料酒,一边吃着甜糕点。

"'怎么说,对我都是一个巨大的损失,'磨坊主回应,'不是吗,我几乎快把自己的手推车送他了,到了现在我真不知道该拿这个手推车怎么办了。车摆在家里,还特别地碍手碍脚;拿去卖吧,破得不成样子,也卖不出什么价钱来。今后我一定要当心不再往外送东西了。人嘛,总是一慷慨就会吃亏。'"

"然后又怎么样了?"老水鼠等了好一会儿,问道。

"怎么样?故事结束啦。"朱顶雀说。

"可是,磨坊主后来又怎么样了?"老水鼠问。

"啊哈!这我真不知道了,"朱顶雀答道,"说实话,我也不关心。"

"那很明显,你天生一点怜悯心都没有。"老水鼠说。

"恐怕,你不太明白这个故事的寓意。"朱顶雀评论着。

"什么?"老水鼠尖叫道。

"寓意。"

"你是想说这个故事还有寓意吗？"

"当然。"朱顶雀说。

"好吧，真是的，"老水鼠气急败坏地说道，"我想你该在开讲之前就向我说清楚，这个故事有寓意。要是你说清楚了，我肯定不会听你的；说实话，我肯定会说'呸'，就像那个批评家一样。不过，我现在仍可以说。"于是，他把嗓门提到极限大叫道"呸"，然后尾巴一撬，又退回洞里去了。

"那你喜不喜欢老水鼠呢？"鸭妈妈吧嗒吧嗒地游了几分钟，前来问道。"他身上有一大堆优点，可我是个当妈的，身上自然有一位母亲的情感，我只要看到铁心不要的单身汉，就不会不掉眼泪。"

"我怕是惹他生气了，"朱顶雀答道，"其实呢，我只是给他讲了一个教人明辨是非、为人处世的故事。"

"啊！讲有寓意的故事，从来都是一种非常危险的举动。"鸭妈妈说。

我呢，非常赞同鸭妈妈的话。

THE DEVOTED FRIEND

One morning the old water rat put his head out of his hole. He had bright beady eyes and stiff grey whiskers and his tail was like a long bit of black india-rubber. The little ducks were swimming about in the pond, looking just like a lot of yellow canaries, and their mother, who was pure white with real red legs, was trying to teach them how to stand on their heads in the water.

"You will never be in the best society unless you can stand on your heads," she kept saying to them. And every now and then she showed them how it was done. But the little ducks paid no attention to her. They were so young that they did not know what an advantage it is to be in society at all.

"What disobedient children!" cried the old water rat. "They really deserve to be drowned."

"Nothing of the kind," answered the duck. "Every one must make a beginning, and parents cannot be too patient."

"Ah! I know nothing about the feelings of parents," said the water rat. "I am not a family man. In fact, I have never been married, and I never intend to be. Love is all very well in its way, but friendship is much higher. Indeed, I know of nothing in the world that is either nobler or rarer than a devoted friendship."

"And what, pray, is your idea of the duties of a devoted friend?" asked a green linnet, who was sitting in a willow tree hard by, and had overheard the conversation.

"Yes, that is just what I want to know," said the duck. And she swam away to the end of the pond, and stood upon her head, in order to give her children a good example.

"What a silly question!" cried the water rat. "I should expect my devoted friend to be devoted to me, of course."

"And what would you do in return?" said the little bird, swinging upon a silver spray, and flapping his tiny wings.

"I don't understand you," answered the water rat.

"Let me tell you a story on the subject," said the linnet.

"Is the story about me?" asked the water rat. "If so, I will listen to it, for I am extremely fond of fiction."

"It is applicable to you," answered the linnet; and he flew down, and alighting upon the bank, he told the story of *The Devoted Friend*.

"Once upon a time," said the linnet, "there was an honest little fellow named Hans."

"Was he very distinguished?" asked the water rat.

"No," answered the linnet, "I don't think he was distinguished at all, except for his kind heart, and his funny round good-humoured face. He lived in a tiny cottage all by himself, and every day he worked in his garden. In all the countryside there was no garden so lovely as his. Sweet William grew there, and gilly flowers, and Shepherds' purses, and fair maids of France. There were damask roses, and yellow roses, lilac crocuses and gold, purple violets and white. Columbine and lady's smock, marjoram and wild basil, the cowslip and the Flower-de-luce, the daffodil and the clove-pink bloomed or blossomed in their proper order as the months went by, one flower taking another flower's place, so that there were always beautiful things to look at, and pleasant odours to smell.

"Little Hans had a great many friends, but the most devoted friend of all was big Hugh the miller. Indeed, so devoted was the rich miller to little Hans, that he would never go by his garden without leaning over the wall and plucking a large nosegay, or a handful of sweet herbs, or filling his pockets with plums and cherries if it was the fruit season.

"'Real friends should have everything in common,' the miller used to say, and little Hans nodded and smiled, and felt very proud of having a friend with such noble ideas.

"Sometimes, indeed, the neighbours thought it strange that the rich miller never gave little Hans anything in return, though he had a hundred sacks of flour stored away in his mill, and six milch cows, and a large flock of woolly sheep; but Hans never troubled his head about these things, and nothing gave him greater pleasure than to listen to all the wonderful things the miller used to say about the unselfishness of true friendship.

"So little Hans worked away in his garden. During the spring, the summer, and the autumn he was very happy, but when the winter came, and he had no fruit or flowers to bring to the market, he suffered a good deal from cold and hunger, and often had to go to bed without any supper but a few dried pears or some hard nuts. In the winter, also, he was extremely lonely, as the miller never came to see him then.

"'There is no good in my going to see little Hans as long as the snow lasts,' the miller used to say to his wife. 'For when people are in trouble they should be left alone and not be bothered by visitors. That at least is my idea about friendship, and I am sure I am right. So I shall wait till the spring comes, and then I shall pay him a visit, and he will be able to give me a large basket of primroses, and that will make him so happy.'

"'You are certainly very thoughtful about others,' answered the wife, as she sat in her comfortable armchair by the big pinewood fire. 'Very thoughtful indeed. It is quite a treat to hear you talk about friendship. I am sure the clergyman himself could not say such beautiful things as you do, though he does live in a three-storied house, and wear a gold ring on his little finger.'

"'But could we not ask little Hans up here?' said the miller's youngest son. 'If poor Hans is in trouble I will give him half my porridge, and show him my white rabbits.'

"'What a silly boy you are!' cried the miller. 'I really don't know what is the use of sending you to school. You seem not to learn anything. Why, if little

Hans came up here, and saw our warm fire, and our good supper, and our great cask of red wine, he might get envious, and envy is a most terrible thing, and would spoil anybody's nature. I certainly will not allow Hans' nature to be spoiled. I am his best friend, and I will always watch over him, and see that he is not led into any temptations. Besides, if Hans came here, he might ask me to let him have some flour on credit, and that I could not do. Flour is one thing and friendship is another, and they should not be confused. Why, the words are spelt differently, and mean quite different things. Everybody can see that.'

"'How well you talk!' said the miller's wife, pouring herself out a large glass of warm ale. 'Really I feel quite drowsy. It is just like being in church.'

"'Lots of people act well,' answered the miller. 'But very few people talk well, which shows that talking is much the more difficult thing of the two, and much the finer thing also'. And he looked sternly across the table at his little son, who felt so ashamed of himself that he hung his head down, and grew quite scarlet, and began to cry into his tea. However, he was so young that you must excuse him."

"Is that the end of the story?" asked the water rat.

"Certainly not," answered the linnet. "That is the beginning."

"Then you are quite behind the age," said the water rat. "Every good storyteller nowadays starts with the end, and then goes on to the beginning, and concludes with the middle. That is the new method. I heard all about it the other day from a critic who was walking round the pond with a young man. He spoke of the matter at great length, and I am sure he must have been right, for he had blue spectacles and a bald head, and whenever the young man made any remark, he always answered 'Pooh!' But pray go on with your story. I like the miller immensely. I have all kinds of beautiful sentiments myself, so there is a great sympathy between us."

"Well," said the linnet, hopping now on one leg and now on the other. "As soon as the winter was over, and the primroses began to open their pale yellow stars, the miller said to his wife that he would go down and see little Hans.

"'Why, what a good heart you have!' cried his wife. 'You are always thinking of others. And mind you take the big basket with you for the flowers.'

"So the miller tied the sails of the windmill together with a strong iron chain, and went down the hill with the basket on his arm.

"'Good morning, little Hans,' said the miller.

"'Good morning,' said Hans, leaning on his spade, and smiling from ear to ear.

"'And how have you been all the winter?' said the miller.

"'Well, really,' cried Hans. 'It is very good of you to ask, very good indeed. I am afraid I had rather a hard time of it, but now the spring has come, and I am quite happy, and all my flowers are doing well.'

"'We often talked of you during the winter, Hans,' said the miller. 'And wondered how you were getting on.'

"'That was kind of you,' said Hans. 'I was half afraid you had forgotten me.'

"'Hans, I am surprised at you,' said the miller. 'Friendship never forgets. That is the wonderful thing about it, but I am afraid you don't understand the poetry of life. How lovely your primroses are looking, by-the-bye!'

"'They are certainly very lovely,' said Hans. 'And it is a most lucky thing for me that I have so many. I am going to bring them into the market and sell them to the Burgomaster's daughter, and buy back my wheelbarrow with the money.'

"'Buy back your wheelbarrow? You don't mean to say you have sold it? What a very stupid thing to do!'

"'Well, the fact is,' said Hans, 'that I was obliged to. You see the winter was a very bad time for me, and I really had no money at all to buy bread with. So I first sold the silver buttons off my Sunday coat, and then I sold my silver chain, and then I sold my big pipe, and at last I sold my wheelbarrow. But I am going to buy them all back again now.'

"'Hans,' said the miller. 'I will give you my wheelbarrow. It is not in very good repair; indeed, one side is gone, and there is something wrong with the wheel spokes; but in spite of that I will give it to you. I know it is very generous of me, and a great many people would think me extremely foolish for parting with it, but I am not like the rest of the world. I think that generosity is the essence of friendship, and, besides, I have got a new wheelbarrow for myself. Yes, you may set your mind at ease, I will give you my wheelbarrow.'

"'Well, really, that is generous of you,' said little Hans, and his funny round face glowed all over with pleasure. 'I can easily put it in repair, as I have a plank of wood in the house.'

"'A plank of wood!' said the miller. 'Why, that is just what I want for the roof of my barn. There is a very large hole in it, and the corn will all get damp if I don't stop it up. How lucky you mentioned it! It is quite remarkable how one good action always breeds another. I have given you my wheelbarrow, and now you are going to give me your plank. Of course, the wheelbarrow is worth far more than the plank, but true friendship never notices things like that. Pray get it at once, and I will set to work at my barn this very day.'

"'Certainly,' cried little Hans, and he ran into the shed and dragged the plank out.

"'It is not a very big plank,' said the miller, looking at it. 'And I am afraid that after I have mended my barn roof there won't be any left for you to mend the wheelbarrow with; but, of course, that is not my fault. And now, as I have given you my wheelbarrow, I am sure you would like to give me some flowers in return. Here is the basket, and mind you fill it quite full.'

"'Quite full?' said little Hans, rather sorrowfully, for it was really a very big basket, and he knew that if he filled it he would have no flowers left for the market, and he was very anxious to get his silver buttons back.

"'Well, really,' answered the miller. 'As I have given you my wheelbarrow, I don't think that it is much to ask you for a few flowers. I may be wrong, but I should have thought that friendship, true friendship, was quite free from selfishness of any kind.'

"'My dear friend, my best friend,' cried little Hans. 'You are welcome to all the flowers in my garden. I would much sooner have your good opinion than my silver buttons, any day.' And he ran and plucked all his pretty primroses, and filled the miller's basket.

"'Good-bye, little Hans,' said the miller, as he went up the hill with the plank on his shoulder and the big basket in his hand.

"'Good-bye,' said little Hans, and he began to dig away quite merrily, he was so pleased about the wheelbarrow.

"The next day he was nailing up some honeysuckle against the porch, when he heard the miller's voice calling to him from the road. So he jumped off the ladder, and ran down the garden, and looked over the wall.

"There was the miller with a large sack of flour on his back.

"'Dear little Hans,' said the miller, 'would you mind carrying this sack of flour for me to market?'

"'Oh, I am so sorry,' said Hans. 'But I am really very busy today. I have got all my creepers to nail up, and all my flowers to water, and all my grass to roll.'

"'Well, really,' said the miller. 'I think that, considering that I am going to give you my wheelbarrow, it is rather unfriendly of you to refuse.'

"'Oh, don't say that,' cried little Hans. 'I wouldn't be unfriendly for the whole world.' And he ran in for his cap, and trudged off with the big sack on his shoulders.

"It was a very hot day, and the road was terribly dusty, and before Hans had reached the sixth milestone he was so tired that he had to sit down and rest. However, he went on bravely, and at last he reached the market. After he had waited there some time, he sold the sack of flour for a very good price, and then he returned home at once, for he was afraid that if he stopped too late he might meet some robbers on the way.

"'It has certainly been a hard day,' said little Hans to himself as he was going to bed, 'but I am glad I did not refuse the miller, for he is my best friend, and, besides, he is going to give me his wheelbarrow.'

"Early the next morning the miller came down to get the money for his sack of flour, but little Hans was so tired that he was still in bed.

"'Upon my word,' said the miller, 'you are very lazy. Really, considering that I am going to give you my wheelbarrow, I think you might work harder. Idleness is a great sin, and I certainly don't like any of my friends to be idle or sluggish. You must not mind my speaking quite plainly to you. Of course I should not dream of doing so if I were not your friend. But what is the good of friendship if one cannot say exactly what one means? Anybody can say charming things and try to please and to flatter, but a true friend always says unpleasant things, and does not mind giving pain. Indeed, if he is a really true friend he prefers it, for he knows that then he is doing good.'

"'I am very sorry,' said little Hans, rubbing his eyes and pulling off his nightcap. 'But I was so tired that I thought I would lie in bed for a little time, and listen to the birds singing. Do you know that I always work better after hearing the birds sing?'

"'Well, I am glad of that,' said the miller, clapping little Hans on the back. 'For I want you to come up to the mill as soon as you are dressed and mend my barn roof for me.'

"Poor little Hans was very anxious to go and work in his garden, for his flowers had not been watered for two days, but he did not like to refuse the miller as he was such a good friend to him.

"'Do you think it would be unfriendly of me if I said I was busy?' he inquired in a shy and timid voice.

"'Well, really,' answered the miller. 'I do not think it is much to ask of you, considering that I am going to give you my wheelbarrow; but of course if you refuse I will go and do it myself.'

"'Oh! On no account,' cried little Hans. And he jumped out of bed, and dressed himself, and went up to the barn.

"He worked there all day long, till sunset, and at sunset the miller came to see how he was getting on.

"'Have you mended the hole in the roof yet, little Hans?' cried the miller in a cheery voice.

"'It is quite mended,' answered little Hans, coming down the ladder.

"'Ah!' said the miller, 'there is no work so delightful as the work one does for others.'

"'It is certainly a great privilege to hear you talk,' answered little Hans, sitting down and wiping his forehead. 'A very great privilege. But I am afraid I shall never have such beautiful ideas as you have.'

"'Oh! They will come to you,' said the miller. 'But you must take more pains. At present you have only the practice of friendship; some day you will have the theory also.'

"'Do you really think I shall?' asked little Hans.

"'I have no doubt of it,' answered the miller. 'But now that you have mended the roof, you had better go home and rest, for I want you to drive my sheep to the mountain tomorrow.'

"Poor little Hans was afraid to say anything to this, and early the next morning the miller brought his sheep round to the cottage, and Hans started off with them to the mountain. It took him the whole day to get there and back; and when he returned he was so tired that he went off to sleep in his chair, and did not wake up till it was broad daylight.

"'What a delightful time I shall have in my garden!' he said, and he went to work at once.

"But somehow he was never able to look after his flowers at all, for his friend the miller was always coming round and sending him off on long errands, or getting him to help at the mill. Little Hans was very much distressed at times, as he was afraid his flowers would think he had forgotten them, but he consoled himself by the reflection that the miller was his best friend. 'Besides,' he used to say, 'he is going to give me his wheelbarrow, and that is an act of pure generosity.'

"So little Hans worked away for the miller, and the miller said all kinds of beautiful things about friendship, which Hans took down in a notebook, and used to read over at night, for he was a very good scholar.

"Now it happened that one evening little Hans was sitting by his fireside when a loud rap came at the door. It was a very wild night, and the wind was blowing and roaring round the house so terribly that at first he thought it was merely the storm. But a second rap came, and then a third, louder than any of the others.

"'It is some poor traveller,' said little Hans to himself, and he ran to the door.

"There stood the miller with a lantern in one hand and a big stick in the other.

"'Dear little Hans,' cried the miller, 'I am in great trouble. My little boy has fallen off a ladder and hurt himself, and I am going for the doctor. But he lives so far away, and it is such a bad night, that it has just occurred to me that it would be much better if you went instead of me. You know I am going to give you my wheelbarrow, and so it is only fair that you should do something for me in return.'

"'Certainly,' cried little Hans, 'I take it quite as a compliment your coming to me, and I will start off at once. But you must lend me your lantern, as the night is so dark that I am afraid I might fall into the ditch.'

"'I am very sorry,' answered the miller. 'But it is my new lantern and it would be a great loss to me if anything happened to it.'

"'Well, never mind, I will do without it,' cried little Hans, and he took down his great fur coat, and his warm scarlet cap, and tied a muffler round his throat, and started off.

"What a dreadful storm it was! The night was so black that little Hans could hardly see, and the wind was so strong that he could scarcely stand. However, he was very courageous, and after he had been walking about three hours, he arrived at the doctor's house, and knocked at the door.

"'Who is there?' cried the doctor, putting his head out of his bedroom window.

"'Little Hans, doctor.'

"'What do you want, little Hans?'

"'The miller's son has fallen from a ladder, and has hurt himself, and the miller wants you to come at once.'

"'All right!' said the doctor; and he ordered his horse, and his big boots, and his lantern, and came downstairs, and rode off in the direction of the miller's house, little Hans trudging behind him.

"But the storm grew worse and worse, and the rain fell in torrents, and little Hans could not see where he was going, or keep up with the horse. At last he lost his way, and wandered off on the moor, which was a very dangerous place, as it was full of deep holes, and there poor little Hans was drowned. His body was found the next day by some goatherds, floating in a great pool of water, and was brought back by them to the cottage.

"Everybody went to little Hans' funeral, as he was so popular, and the miller was the chief mourner.

"'As I was his best friend,' said the miller, 'it is only fair that I should have the best place;' so he walked at the head of the procession in a long black cloak, and every now and then he wiped his eyes with a big pocket-handkerchief.

"'Little Hans is certainly a great loss to every one,' said the Blacksmith, when the funeral was over, and they were all seated comfortably in the inn, drinking spiced wine and eating sweet cakes.

"'A great loss to me at any rate,' answered the miller. 'Why, I had as good as given him my wheelbarrow, and now I really don't know what to do with it. It is very much in my way at home, and it is in such bad repair that I could not get anything for it if I sold it. I will certainly take care not to give away anything again. One always suffers for being generous.'"

"Well?" said the water rat, after a long pause.

"Well, that is the end," said the linnet.

"But what became of the miller?" asked the water rat.

"Oh! I really don't know," replied the linnet. "And I am sure that I don't care."

"It is quite evident then that you have no sympathy in your nature," said the water rat.

"I am afraid you don't quite see the moral of the story," remarked the linnet.

"The what?" screamed the water rat.

"The moral."

"Do you mean to say that the story has a moral?"

"Certainly," said the linnet.

"Well, really," said the water rat, in a very angry manner, "I think you should have told me that before you began. If you had done so, I certainly would not have listened to you; in fact, I should have said 'Pooh,' like the critic. However, I can say it now;" so he shouted out "Pooh" at the top of his voice, gave a whisk with his tail, and went back into his hole.

"And how do you like the water rat?" asked the duck, who came paddling up some minutes afterwards. "He has a great many good points, but for my own part I have a mother's feelings, and I can never look at a confirmed bachelor without the tears coming into my eyes."

"I am rather afraid that I have annoyed him," answered the linnet. "The fact is that I told him a story with a moral."

"Ah! That is always a very dangerous thing to do," said the duck.

And I quite agree with her.

了不起的火箭炮

国王的儿子要结婚了,举国上下一片欢腾。王子等了整整一年,终于等来了他的新娘。新娘是一位俄国公主,乘坐六头驯鹿拉的雪橇从芬兰一路赶了过来。雪橇像只金色的大天鹅,公主端坐在天鹅的两翅中间。公主一袭貂皮长袍,头上戴着一顶小巧的银丝帽子。她肤白如雪,像她长年居住的雪宫一样白,她的雪橇驶过街道时所有人都惊叹不已。"她就像一朵白玫瑰!"大家一边高呼,一边从阳台上朝她抛撒鲜花。

在城堡门口,王子正等着迎接公主呢。王子有一双漂亮的紫色眼睛和一头金黄色的秀发。他看见公主到来便单膝跪地,亲吻她的手。

"你的画像真美,"他轻声地说,"可是你本人比画像更美。"小公主一听脸红了起来。

"她刚才像一朵白玫瑰,"一个年轻侍从对旁边的人说道,"但是现在她又变成了一朵红玫瑰。"宫廷的人听了都很高兴。

接下来的三天里,人人都在念叨"白玫瑰,红玫瑰,红玫瑰,白玫瑰";国王下令,

那名侍从的薪俸翻倍。不过侍从根本没有领过什么薪俸，因此这道命令对他来说也没多大用处。不过这被视为莫大的荣耀，并理所当然地登上了《宫廷公报》。

三天后举行了婚礼庆典。仪式盛大而又壮观，新娘和新郎手牵手地走在绣有一粒粒小珍珠的紫色鹅绒华盖之下。接着是国宴，它持续了整整五个小时。王子和公主端坐在大厅的上首，端着透明的水晶杯喝酒。只有真心相爱的情侣才能用这对杯子喝酒，原因嘛，若是虚情假意，嘴唇一碰上，杯子就会变得灰暗无光。

"他们彼此真心相爱啊，这事儿一清二楚了，"那个小侍从说，"就像水晶一样透明清楚！"国王再次下令把他的薪俸翻倍。

"多么崇高的荣耀啊！"所有的朝臣一齐欢呼。

宴会之后举行舞会。新娘和新郎要一起跳玫瑰舞，国王早就许诺要吹长笛伴奏呢。他吹奏得很是差劲，可从未有人敢告诉他，因为他是一国之王。确实，他只知道两首曲子，而且从来都不甚清楚自己吹的是哪一首；但这都无关紧要，因为啊，不管他吹啥，人人都争着高呼："好听！好听！"

婚礼仪式的最后一项是盛大的烟花表演，燃放时间定于午夜十二点。小公主平生从未见过烟花，因而国王早就下令，公主婚庆日皇家烟花炮手务必到场伺候。

"烟花像什么样儿？"一天早晨公主在露天阳台上漫步时问王子。

"它们就像北极光，"尽管是提给别人的问题，国王总会抢着回答，"只是要自然得多。比起星星，我更喜欢烟花，因为你能确定它们什么时候出现。再说，它们就像我吹笛子一样令人陶醉啊！当然，你一定要好好欣赏。"

于是，一座燃放烟花的高台在王宫花园的尽头被搭了起来。待皇家烟花炮手把一切准备妥当后，各种烟花便聊了起来。

"这个世界确实太美了，"一个小爆竹大喊起来，"看看那些黄色郁金香吧。可不是嘛！如果它们是真正的爆竹，那就更加可爱了。很高兴我有旅行的经历，而旅行能大大地提高见识，并能消除所有的个人偏见。"

"国王的花园并非整个世界，你这个傻爆竹，"一支大大的罗马烛烟花筒说，"世界可大着呢，你要花三天时间才能看个遍。"

"任何一处，只要你一往情深，于你而言就是整个世界。"一只忧郁的转轮烟花若有所思地呼喊道。她早年痴恋一只陈旧的松木匣子，并常以这段伤心往事为荣。"可惜爱情已经不再时髦，叫那些诗人给绞杀了。他们写了过多的爱情诗篇，多得没人相信了，对此我也不感到奇怪。真正的爱情是痛苦，也是沉默。记得，我自己就曾经……但现在说也没有意义了。浪漫已成往事了。"

"胡说！"罗马烛回应，"浪漫永远不会消亡。它就像月亮一样，亘古长存。比方说那对新婚夫妇，就非常地相爱。这一切，都是我今天早晨从一个牛皮纸火药筒那儿听到的。这个火药筒正好跟我住同一个抽屉，他知晓宫内的最新消息。"

然而转轮烟花摇了摇头，喃喃地说："浪漫已死，浪漫已死，浪漫已死！"她相信同一件事只要说上多遍，到最后就会变成真的了。

突然，传来一阵刺耳的干咳，引得大家环顾四周。

干咳声来自一枚身材高大且神情傲慢的火箭炮。他被绑在一根长棍的顶端，开口说话前总会干咳几声，以引起大伙的注意。

"呃哼！呃哼！"他出声了，大伙都在听，唯独可怜的转轮烟花仍在摇着头，喃喃自语："浪漫已死！"

"肃静！肃静！"一个炮仗大声吆喝。他有些政客的派头，在地方选举中出尽风头，所以他懂得如何使用合适的政治用语。

"浪漫彻底死了，"转轮烟花嘀咕着，就沉入睡梦中去了。

全场刚一安静下来，火箭炮就赶紧咳了第三声，开始发言。他说得非常缓慢，吐字清晰，就像在口述自个儿的回忆录一样，目光总是越过听众的肩头，投向远方。说实在的，他的风度真是傲然不群。

"国王的儿子真是走运，"他说，"竟然赶在我燃放的日子成婚！说真的，即使是事先安排的，这对他来说也是再好不过的安排了。可王子们总是走好运。"

"我的天哪！"小爆竹说，"我原先的想法正好相反，燃放我们是为了给王子贺喜呢。"

"对你来说也许是这样，"火箭炮答道，"的确，我毫不怀疑对你是这样，但对我来说就不同了。我是一枚非凡的火箭炮，爸妈都非同凡响。我的妈妈是她那个年代最负盛名的转轮烟花，以优美舞姿驰名天下。她参加那场盛大公演时翻转了整整十九圈才熄灭，而且每翻转一圈都向空中抛出七颗粉红的星星。她的直径有三英尺半，选用最佳火药配制而成。我的爸爸和我一样也是火箭炮，拥有法国的高贵血统。他飞得可真高，高得大家都担心他不会下来了。然而他下来了，因为他心地善良，不愿让别人失望。他化作一阵黄金雨，非常耀眼地落了下来。对其表演各大报纸纷纷报道，言辞称颂有加、极尽恭维。确实，《宫廷公报》称赞他就是烟化艺术的成功典型。"

"烟花艺术，你是想说烟花艺术吧，"一个蓝色烟花说，"我知道的，应该是烟花才对，因为我看到这个词就写在我自个儿的药筒上呢。"

"哼，我说了是烟化。"火箭炮答道，语气甚为严厉，一下子镇住了蓝色烟花，而蓝色烟花则立马转身，开始欺负那些小爆竹，好显得自己还是个有头有脸的人物。

"我是说，"火箭炮继续讲，"我是说——我说的是什么来？"

"你是在说你自己。"罗马烛回答。

"当然，当然。我知道自个儿在讨论什么有趣的话题，就被这么粗鲁地打断了。我厌恶各种形式的粗鲁和无礼，因为我极其敏感。全世界没有谁比我更敏感了，对此我深信不疑。"

"一个敏感的人指什么人?"那个有些政客派头的炮仗问罗马烛。

"指那种人,如果自个儿脚上长了鸡眼,就总爱踩别人的脚趾。"罗马烛低声回答,炮仗听后笑得差点炸开了。

"请问,你在笑什么?"火箭炮质问,"我都没笑。"

"我笑,是因为我很高兴呀,"炮仗答道。

"这是个非常自私的理由。"火箭炮怒气冲冲地说,"你有什么权力高兴?你应该考虑别人。实际上,你应该想到我。我总是想到我自个儿,我希望别人也都能这样。这就是所说的同情心。同情心则是一种极美的美德,而我的同情心已是登峰造极。比方说,要是今晚我出了什么意外,那对每个人来说将是多么不幸啊!王子和公主将永远不再幸福,他们的整个婚姻生活都将毁于一旦;至于国王嘛,我清楚他是过不了这个坎的。真的,我一想到自己所处的重要地位,几乎要感动得流泪了。"

"如果你想给别人带来快乐,"罗马烛嚷起来,"你最好别流眼泪弄湿自己。"

"当然喽,"蓝色烟花这会儿精神好多了,大声附和,"这是最起码的常识。"

"常识,一点不假!"火箭炮愤愤不平地说,"你们可别忘了,我本来就不同寻常,也是非同凡响。不是吗,任何人都能明白常识,没有想象力也行。但是我有想象力啊,因为我从不把事情想成实际的模样,而是总把它们想得不同寻常。至于说我不要把自个儿弄湿嘛,显然在座的没有哪一位能体会欣赏多情之心。幸运的是,我自己没拿这当回事。唯一能够支撑人一生的,就是意识到比起自己来别人个个都差得很远呢。这种感觉,我一直都在培养。但你们全没心没肺,在这里大声欢笑、尽情欢乐,就像不知道王子和公主刚刚成婚似的。"

"咳,真的,"一盏小小的孔明灯大声说道,"干吗不呢?这可是一个大喜的日子，等我飞上天空时，我要把这一切说给星星听。你会看到星星一闪一闪地眨着眼睛，那就是我在跟他们诉说新娘是多么地漂亮呢。"

"啊！多么肤浅的人生观啊！"火箭炮说，"但这不过是我意料想之中的。你们啊，腹中空空。不是吗，也许王子和公主会移居一个地方，那儿有一条很深的河；也许他们会有一个独生子，是个金发碧眼的小男孩，跟王子长得一模一样；也许有一天小男孩会跟他的保姆一起出去散步；也许保姆会到一棵古老的大树下睡着了；也许小男孩会掉进深河里淹死。多可怕的不幸啊！可怜的人儿，痛失独子！真是太可怕了！我会伤心死的！"

"但是他们并没有失去自己的独生子，"罗马烛说，"他们根本没有遭受什么不幸啊。"

"我从没说他们已经有过，"火箭炮答道，"刚才我只是说他们可能会有。如果他们已经失去了独生子的话，再谈这事就没什么用了。我讨厌那些为打翻的牛奶而哭泣的人。但是一想到他们可能会痛失独子，我真是伤心极了。"

"你当然是！"蓝色烟花喊道，"事实上，你还是我见过的最装腔作势的人。"

"你是我见过的最粗鲁无礼的人，"火箭炮反驳道，"你还不理解我对王子的友情。"

"什么，你压根儿就不认识他。"罗马烛低声吼道。

"我从未说过我了解他，"火箭炮回答，"我敢说，如果我了解他，我压根儿就不应成为他的朋友。尝试去了解自己的朋友可是非常危险的举动。"

"说真的，你最好不要把自己弄湿，"孔明灯说，"这可重要了。"

"对你来说非常重要，这我丝毫不怀疑，"火箭炮答道，"不过，我想哭就会哭起来。"说着他还真声泪俱下了，泪水像雨滴一样顺着绑他的长棍流了下来，差点淹死了两只小甲虫。这两只小虫刚想合伙做窝，正在寻找宜居的干爽处呢。

"他的天性一定很浪漫，"转轮烟花说，"根本没有什么可哭的时候他竟然哭起来了。"她深深地叹了一口气，不禁想起来了自个儿痴恋的那个松木匣子。

但是罗马烛和蓝色烟花都非常地气愤，不停地高声叫起来："骗局！骗局！"他们都极其务实，当遇上不能苟同的事情时，就叫它"骗局"。

接着，月亮升起来，就像一个美不可言的银盘；星星次第闪耀，宫殿里传来了一阵音乐声。

王子和公主正在领舞。他们的舞姿是如此优美，引得身材高挑的白色百合凑到窗前偷看，大朵的红色罂粟则频频颔首，应节而舞。

随后十点的钟声敲响了，接着是十一点钟，再接着是十二点钟。当午夜的最后一下钟声敲响时，人们都来到露天阳台上，国王派人去请皇家烟花炮手。

"开始烟花表演吧。"国王说道。皇家烟花炮手深深地鞠了一躬，便大踏步走下阳台，径直走向花园的尽头。他带了六个助手，每个助手都举着长杆，顶端各绑着一个点燃的火把。

这无疑是一场盛大而又壮观的表演。

飕！飕！转轮烟花响了起来，转了一圈又一圈。轰！轰！罗马烛烟花筒响起来了。然后，小爆竹到处欢舞，蓝色烟花又把一切映得通红。"再见了，"孔明灯大声告别，腾空高飞时也不忘撒下小小的蓝色火星。砰！砰！大炮仗也跟着响起来，尽情地玩耍。大伙表演得都很成功，只剩下那枚非凡的火箭炮了。他哭得浑身湿漉漉的，根本无法点燃。他身上最好的东西是火药，而火药已被泪水泡成了废物。他要么不愿搭理，要么冷嘲热讽那些穷亲戚，而亲戚们却个个犹如美不胜收的金花直冲云霄，伴随着炽烈的火焰。好哇！好哇！王宫上下高声欢呼，小公主也高兴地笑个不停。

"我猜，他们留着我，准是为了哪个盛典用的，"火箭炮说，"肯定就是这个意思。"他的神情比以往更加傲慢了。

第二天，工人们过来打扫。"来的显然是一个代表团，"火箭炮说，"我接见他们时应该表现出威严来。"于是他翘起鼻子，紧锁眉头，像正在思索什么非常重要的问题。但是，工人们压根儿就没有注意到他；直到收工要走时，其中的一个工人才瞥见他。"喂！"他叫道，"火箭炮真差！"工人拎起他扔向墙外的水沟。

"火箭炮真差？火箭炮真差？"他一边翻着跟头，一边说道，"不可能！'火箭炮真大'，这才是那人说的。'差'和'大'的读音听起来很像。"说完他就一头栽进了稀泥里。

"这儿并不舒服，"他说道，"但这无疑是一处时髦的矿泉疗养地，他们送我来疗养，恢复健康。当然，我的神经受到了极大的伤害，我需要休养。"

接下来有一只小青蛙游到他的跟前，他长着一对宝石般明亮的眼睛，穿着一件绿色的斑纹外衣。

"看来，是一个新来的！"青蛙说，"嗯，毕竟什么东西都比不上泥巴。要是再有雨天和沟渠，我就万分地高兴了。你看下午会下雨么吗？我当然希望下，可是这天空蔚蓝，万里无云。真是遗憾！"

"呃哼！呃哼！"火箭炮一边说，一边开始咳起来。

"你的嗓音真动听！"青蛙大声叫起来，"真的很像呱呱叫，青蛙呱呱叫起来当然是世界上最悦耳的声音啦。你今晚就会听到我们合唱团的表演。我们坐在古老的养鸭塘里，就在那间农舍旁，月亮一露脸我们就开始演唱。歌声醉人哪，人人都躺在床上听我们唱歌。事实上，就在昨天我还听说，农夫的妻子对她的妈妈说自个儿晚上一刻都没合眼就是因为我们在唱。看到自己这么走红，我真是开心极了。"

"呃哼！呃哼！"火箭炮生气地咳起来。他非常恼火，自己竟然插不进话。

"动听的嗓音，千真万确！"青蛙继续说，"我希望你能光临鸭塘。我得找我的女儿去了。我有六个漂亮的女儿，真担心她们会碰上梭鱼。梭鱼可是个彻头彻尾的怪物，会毫不犹豫地拿她们当早点呢。好啦，再见！说真的，我很开心与你对话。"

"对话，果如其言！"火箭炮说，"你自个儿从头到尾一直说个不停，这可不叫对话。"

"总得要有人听，"青蛙回应，"我喜欢自个儿一人包揽两人的所有谈话。这样既节省时间，又避免了争论。"

"可是我喜欢争论。"火箭炮说。

"但愿你别这样，"青蛙得意地说道，"争论太庸俗了，毕竟在一个好的社会，人人都持有完全一致的意见。再次说声再见了，我看到我的女儿在那边呢。"说完小青蛙就游走了。

"你这个家伙很烦人哪，"火箭炮说，"而且很没教养。我讨厌那些只顾谈自己的人，就像你，要知道此时别人也想说说话呀，比如我。这就是我所说的自私，而自私则是最可恶的行为，对于有我这种性情的人来说尤其如此，因为我有同情心是出了名的。说实在的，你应该以我为榜样；你不可能找到更好的榜样了。既然你有这机会，你最好好好把握，因为我马上就要返回宫中了。在宫中我可是大受欢迎的宠儿，实际上王子和公主昨日成婚是在恭喜我呢。当然，这些事你一无所知，毕竟你是个外来的。"

"跟他说话没用啦，"一只蜻蜓坐在一株高大的棕色菖蒲顶端，插话说，"一点儿用也没有，因为他已经游走了。"

"是吗，那损失的是他，不是我。"火箭炮答道，"不会仅仅因为他不听，我就要停止对他说话。我喜欢听自个儿说话，这是我的一大乐趣。我经常独自一人说上一大堆话，还有啊我是多么的聪明，甚至有时自个儿讲的话一句也不明白。"

"那么你真该去讲授哲学了。"蜻蜓说完，便张开轻纱般可爱的双翼朝高空飞去了。

"他不留在这儿，多傻啊！"火箭炮说，"我敢打包票，他可不是经常有这种提高自己心智的机会。不过，我一点儿也不介意。像我这样的天才，总有一天会被人赏识的。"他在稀泥里又往下陷得更深了一点儿。

过了一会儿，一只大白鸭游到他面前。她双腿金黄，脚上带蹼，走起路来身姿摇曳，是大伙眼里的大美人。

"嘎！嘎！嘎！"她说道，"你这模样真是古怪！请问，你是天生如此呢，还是意外事故造成的？"

"很明显，你一直生活在乡下，"火箭炮答道，"否则，你会知道我是谁。不过，我原谅你的孤陋寡闻。指望别人和自个儿一样非同凡响，难免不公平。待你听说我能一飞冲天，并能化作一阵黄金雨降落下来，你肯定会大吃一惊的。"

"我倒不看重那个，"鸭子说，"因为我看不出那对谁有什么用处。现在，要是你能像牛一样耕田，像马一样拉车，或者像牧羊犬一样看守羊群，那就有能耐了。"

"好家伙，"火箭炮大声嚷起来，语气甚是傲慢，"你原来属于下等人，我算是看明白了。有我这种身份的人，从来都不会派上什么实际用场。我们学有所长，那就绰绰有余了。对任何所谓的勤劳，我都看不上眼，更别提你似乎在赞赏的那些勤劳了。没错，我一直认为，苦力活不过是那些无事可做之人的避难所罢了。"

"好吧，好吧，"回话的鸭子性格十分随和，从不和任何人争吵，"每个人都有不同的品位。我希望，不管如何，你要在这儿把家安下来才是。"

"哦！不，亲爱的，"火箭炮大叫道，"我只是一个游客，显赫的游客。事实是，我觉得这地方太乏味了。这儿既没有社交活动，也不能归隐独处，事实上压根儿就是郊野一隅。我多半会回到宫里去，因为我明白我命中注定要轰动这个世界。"

"我自个儿也曾有过念头，要投身于公共事业，"鸭子评论起来，"可要改革的事情太多了。没错，以前我就担任过一次会议的主席，我们还通过了一些决议，谴责我们不喜欢的任何事情。不过，那些决议好像也没什么效果。眼下，我一心转向家庭生活，专心照顾好家人。"

"我就是为公共事业而生，"火箭炮说，"我所有的亲戚，甚至包括他们中地位卑微的，都是这样。只要我们一出场，就会引来万众瞩目。我自个儿么，倒还没有真正地出过场，但轮到我出场时那将会无比壮观。至于家庭生活嘛，它会让人老得快，并让人分心，不再追求更高的目标。"

"啊！更高的生活目标，该是多么美好啊！"鸭子说，"这倒提醒了我，我真的好饿。"大白鸭顺流游走了，一路叫着："嘎！嘎！嘎！"

"回来！回来！"火箭炮尖叫道，"我有一大堆话要对你说呢。"然而，鸭子并没有理会他。"她走了，真让我高兴，"火箭炮自言自语，"她无疑是平庸之辈。"他又往稀泥里陷得更深了一点儿，开始想起天才的落寞境遇，忽然从沟边跑过来两个小男孩，身上套着白色罩衫，手里拿着一把水壶和几根柴火。

"这次来的肯定是代表团了吧，"火箭炮说着，努力摆出无比庄严的架势。

"喂！"其中的一个男孩喊道，"看看这根破棍子！真弄不明白，它怎么会掉进这里呢。"男孩把火箭炮从阴沟里拾了上来。

"破棍子！"火箭炮说，"不可能！'金棍子'才是他刚才说的。'金棍子'倒是十分中听。原来，他误认为我是王公权贵了！"

"咱们把它扔进火里去吧！"另一个男孩说道，"好让水烧开。"

于是他俩把柴火堆积在一起，火箭炮搁在最上面，然后生起火来。

"这下可棒了，"火箭炮高声嚷起来，"他俩要在大白天燃放我，好让大家都能看到我。"

"我们现在去躺一会儿，"他们说，"等我们醒来时水就烧开了。"他们躺在草地上，闭上了眼睛。

火箭炮浑身湿透，所以烤干花了很长时间。不过，最终火苗还是点燃了他。

"现在我要燃放啦！"他呼喊着，把身体挺得笔直。"我肯定会一飞冲天，远远地高过星星，远远地高过月亮，远远地高过太阳。实际上，我会飞得高到——"

嘶！嘶！嘶！他直冲云霄。

"真开心，"他叫道，"我要永远地像这样飞下去。我真是太成功了！"

但是谁也没有看到他。

然后，他开始感到一阵奇怪的刺痛袭遍全身。

"现在我要爆炸啦，"他大喊着，"我要点燃整个世界，还要发出巨大轰鸣，让世人在接下来的一整年里只够谈论我的表演。"接着他当真爆炸了。砰！砰！砰！火药爆开了。这下千真万确。

但是谁都没有听到他的动静，就连那两个小男孩也没有，因为他俩正睡得香呢。

这之后，他只剩下那根棍子，跌落下来，打在了正在水沟边散步的鹅背上。

"天哪！"那只鹅惊呼起来，"天要下棍子雨了。"于是她赶忙跳进水里。

"我就知道我肯定要引起巨大轰动。"火箭炮喘着气，说完就熄灭了。

THE REMARKABLE ROCKET

The King's son was going to be married, so there were general rejoicings. He had waited a whole year for his bride, and at last she had arrived. She was a Russian Princess, and had driven all the way from Finland in a sledge drawn by six reindeer. The sledge was shaped like a great golden swan, and between the swan's wings lay the little Princess herself. Her long ermine cloak reached right down to her feet, on her head was a tiny cap of silver tissue, and she was as pale as the snow palace in which she had always lived. So pale was she that as she drove through the streets all the people wondered. "She is like a white rose!" they cried, and they threw down flowers on her from the balconies.

At the gate of the castle the Prince was waiting to receive her. He had dreamy violet eyes, and his hair was like fine gold. When he saw her he sank upon one knee, and kissed her hand.

"Your picture was beautiful," he murmured, "but you are more beautiful than your picture." And the little Princess blushed.

"She was like a white rose before," said a young page to his neighbour, "but she is like a red rose now." And the whole court was delighted.

For the next three days everybody went about saying, "White rose, red rose, red rose, white rose." And the King gave orders that the Page's salary was to be doubled. As he received no salary at all this was not of much use to him, but it was considered a great honour, and was duly published in *the Court Gazette*.

When the three days were over the marriage was celebrated. It was a magnificent ceremony, and the bride and bridegroom walked hand in hand under a canopy of purple velvet embroidered with little pearls. Then there was a state banquet, which lasted for five hours. The Prince and Princess sat at the top of the Great Hall and drank out of a cup of clear crystal. Only true lovers could drink out of this cup, for if false lips touched it, it grew grey and dull and cloudy.

"It is quite clear that they love each other," said the little Page, "as clear as crystal!" And the King doubled his salary a second time.

"What an honour!" cried all the courtiers.

After the banquet there was to be a ball. The bride and bridegroom were to dance the rose-dance together, and the King had promised to play the flute. He played very badly, but no one had ever dared to tell him so, because he was the King. Indeed, he knew only two airs, and was never quite certain which one he was playing. But it made no matter, for, whatever he did, everybody cried out, "Charming! Charming!"

The last item on the programme was a grand display of fireworks, to be let off exactly at midnight. The little Princess had never seen a firework in her life, so the King had given orders that the royal pyrotechnist should be in attendance on the day of her marriage.

"What are fireworks like?" she had asked the Prince, one morning, as she was walking on the terrace.

"They are like the Aurora Borealis," said the King, who always answered questions that were addressed to other people. "Only much more natural. I prefer them to stars myself, as you always know when they are going to appear, and they are as delightful as my own flute-playing. You must certainly see them."

So at the end of the King's garden a great stand had been set up, and as soon as the royal pyrotechnist had put everything in its proper place, the fireworks began to talk to each other.

"The world is certainly very beautiful," cried a little squib. "Just look at those yellow tulips. Why! if they were real crackers they could not be lovelier. I am very glad I have travelled. Travel improves the mind wonderfully, and does away with all one's prejudices."

"The King's garden is not the world, you foolish squib," said a big Roman candle. "The world is an enormous place, and it would take you three days to see it thoroughly."

"Any place you love is the world to you," exclaimed the pensive Catherine Wheel, who had been attached to an old deal box in early life, and prided herself on her broken heart. "But love is not fashionable any more, the poets have killed it. They wrote so much about it that nobody believed them, and I am not surprised. True love suffers, and is silent. I remember myself once— But it is no matter now. Romance is a thing of the past."

"Nonsense!" said the Roman candle. "Romance never dies. It is like the moon, and lives forever. The bride and bridegroom, for instance, love each other very dearly. I heard all about them this morning from a brown paper cartridge, who happened to be staying in the same drawer as myself, and he knew the latest court news."

But the Catherine Wheel shook her head. "Romance is dead, Romance is dead, Romance is dead," she murmured. She was one of those people who think that, if you say the same thing over and over a great many times, it becomes true in the end.

Suddenly, a sharp, dry cough was heard, and they all looked round.

It came from a tall, supercilious-looking rocket, who was tied to the end of a long stick. He always coughed before he made any observation, so as to attract attention.

"Ahem! Ahem!" he said, and everybody listened except the poor Catherine Wheel, who was still shaking her head, and murmuring, "Romance is dead."

"Order! Order!" cried out a cracker. He was something of a politician, and had always taken a prominent part in the local elections, so he knew the proper Parliamentary expressions to use.

"Quite dead," whispered the Catherine Wheel, and she went off to sleep.

As soon as there was perfect silence, the rocket coughed a third time and began. He spoke with a very slow, distinct voice, as if he was dictating his memoirs, and always looked over the shoulder of the person to whom he was talking. In fact, he had a most distinguished manner.

"How fortunate it is for the King's son," he remarked, "that he is to be married on the very day on which I am to be let off! Really, if it had been arranged beforehand, it could not have turned out better for him; but Princes are always lucky."

"Dear me!" said the little squib. "I thought it was quite the other way, and that we were to be let off in the Prince's honour."

"It may be so with you," he answered. "Indeed, I have no doubt that it is, but with me it is different. I am a very remarkable rocket, and come of remarkable parents. My mother was the most celebrated Catherine Wheel of her day, and was renowned for her graceful dancing. When she made her great public appearance she spun round nineteen times before she went out, and each time that she did so she threw into the air seven pink stars. She was three feet and a half in diameter, and made of the very best gunpowder. My father was a rocket like myself, and of French extraction. He flew so high that the people were afraid that he would never come down again. He did, though, for he was of a kindly disposition, and he made a most brilliant descent in a shower of golden rain. The newspapers wrote about his performance in very flattering terms. Indeed, *the Court Gazette* called him a triumph of Pylotechnic art."

"Pyrotechnic, Pyrotechnic, you mean," said a Bengal light. "I know it is Pyrotechnic, for I saw it written on my own canister."

"Well, I said Pylotechnic," answered the rocket, in a severe tone of voice, and the Bengal light felt so crushed that he began at once to bully the little squibs, in order to show that he was still a person of some importance.

"I was saying," continued the rocket. "I was saying—What was I saying?"

"You were talking about yourself," replied the Roman candle.

"Of course; I knew I was discussing some interesting subject when I was so rudely interrupted. I hate rudeness and bad manners of every kind, for I am extremely sensitive. No one in the whole world is so sensitive as I am, I am quite sure of that."

"What is a sensitive person?" said the cracker to the Roman candle.

"A person who, because he has corns himself, always treads on other people's toes," answered the Roman candle in a low whisper; and the cracker nearly exploded with laughter.

"Pray, what are you laughing at?" inquired the rocket. "I am not laughing."

"I am laughing because I am happy," replied the cracker.

"That is a very selfish reason," said the rocket angrily. "What right have you to be happy? You should be thinking about others. In fact, you should be thinking about me. I am always thinking about myself, and I expect everybody else to do the same. That is what is called sympathy. It is a beautiful virtue, and I possess it in a high degree. Suppose, for instance, anything happened to me tonight, what a misfortune that would be for every one! The Prince and Princess would never be happy again, their whole married life would be spoiled; and as for the King, I know he would not get over it. Really, when I begin to reflect on the importance of my position, I am almost moved to tears."

"If you want to give pleasure to others," cried the Roman candle, "you had better keep yourself dry."

"Certainly," exclaimed the Bengal light, who was now in better spirits. "That is only common sense."

"Common sense, indeed!" said the rocket indignantly. "You forget that I am very uncommon, and very remarkable. Why, anybody can have common sense, provided that they have no imagination. But I have imagination, for I never think of things as they really are; I always think of them as being quite different. As for keeping myself dry, there is evidently no one here who can at all appreciate an emotional nature. Fortunately for myself, I don't care. The only thing that sustains one through life is the consciousness of the immense inferiority of everybody else, and this is a feeling I have always cultivated. But none of you have any hearts. Here you are laughing and making merry just as if the Prince and Princess had not just been married."

"Well, really," exclaimed a small fire balloon. "Why not? It is a most joyful occasion, and when I soar up into the air I intend to tell the stars all about it. You will see them twinkle when I talk to them about the pretty bride."

"Ah! What a trivial view of life!" said the rocket. "But it is only what I expected. There is nothing in you; you are hollow and empty. Why, perhaps the Prince and Princess may go to live in a country where there is a deep river, and perhaps they may have one only son, a little fair-haired boy with violet eyes like the Prince himself; and perhaps some day he may go out to walk with his nurse; and perhaps the nurse may go to sleep under a great elder-tree; and perhaps the little boy may fall into the deep river and be drowned. What a terrible misfortune! Poor people, to lose their only son! It is really too dreadful! I shall never get over it."

"But they have not lost their only son," said the Roman candle. "No misfortune has happened to them at all."

"I never said that they had," replied the rocket. "I said that they might. If they had lost their only son there would be no use in saying anything more about the matter. I hate people who cry over spilt milk. But when I think that they might lose their only son, I certainly am much affected."

"You certainly are!" cried the Bengal light. "In fact, you are the most affected person I ever met."

"You are the rudest person I ever met," said the rocket, "and you cannot understand my friendship for the Prince."

"Why, you don't even know him," growled the Roman candle.

"I never said I knew him," answered the rocket. "I dare say that if I knew him I should not be his friend at all. It is a very dangerous thing to know one's friends."

"You had really better keep yourself dry," said the fire balloon, "that is the important thing."

"Very important for you, I have no doubt," answered the rocket, "but

I shall weep if I choose." And he actually burst into real tears, which flowed down his stick like raindrops, and nearly drowned two little beetles, who were just thinking of setting up house together, and were looking for a nice dry spot to live in.

"He must have a truly romantic nature," said the Catherine Wheel, "for he weeps when there is nothing at all to weep about." And she heaved a deep sigh and thought about the deal box.

But the Roman candle and the Bengal light were quite indignant, and kept saying, "Humbug! Humbug!" at the top of their voices. They were extremely practical, and whenever they objected to anything they called it humbug.

Then the moon rose like a wonderful silver shield; and the stars began to shine, and a sound of music came from the palace.

The Prince and Princess were leading the dance. They danced so beautifully that the tall white lilies peeped in at the window and watched them, and the great red poppies nodded their heads and beat time.

Then ten o'clock struck, and then eleven, and then twelve, and at the last stroke of midnight every one came out on the terrace, and the King sent for the Royal Pyrotechnist.

"Let the fireworks begin," said the King. And the royal pyrotechnist made a low bow, and marched down to the end of the garden. He had six attendants with him, each of whom carried a lighted torch at the end of a long pole.

It was certainly a magnificent display.

Whizz! Whizz! Went the Catherine Wheel, as she spun round and round. Boom! Boom! Went the Roman candle. Then the squibs danced all over the place, and the Bengal lights made everything look scarlet. "Good-bye," cried the Fire-balloon as he soared away, dropping tiny blue sparks. Bang! Bang! Answered the crackers, who were enjoying themselves immensely. Every one was a great success except the remarkable rocket. He was so damp with crying that he could not go off at all. The best thing in him was the gunpowder, and that was so wet with tears that it was of no use. All his poor relations, to whom he would never speak, except with a sneer, shot up into the sky like wonderful golden flowers with blossoms of fire. Huzza! Huzza! cried the court; and the little Princess laughed with pleasure.

"I suppose they are reserving me for some grand occasion," said the rocket. "No doubt that is what it means," and he looked more supercilious than ever.

The next day the workmen came to put everything tidy. "This is evidently a deputation," said the rocket. "I will receive them with becoming dignity": so he put his nose in the air, and began to frown severely as if he were thinking about some very important subject. But they took no notice of him at all till they were just going away. Then one of them caught sight of him. "Hallo!" he cried. "What a bad rocket!" and he threw him over the wall into the ditch.

"Bad rocket? Bad rocket?" he said, as he whirled through the air. "Impossible! Grand rocket that is what the man said. Bad and grand sound very much the same, indeed they often are the same." And he fell into the mud.

"It is not comfortable here," he remarked, "but no doubt it is some fashionable watering place, and they have sent me away to recruit my health. My nerves are certainly very much shattered, and I require rest."

Then a little frog, with bright jewelled eyes, and a green mottled coat, swam up to him.

"A new arrival, I see!" said the frog. "Well, after all there is nothing like mud. Give me rainy weather and a ditch, and I am quite happy. Do you think it will be a wet afternoon? I am sure I hope so, but the sky is quite blue and cloudless. What a pity!"

"Ahem! Ahem!" said the rocket, and he began to cough.

"What a delightful voice you have!" cried the frog. "Really it is quite like a croak, and croaking is of course the most musical sound in the world. You will hear our glee club this evening. We sit in the old duck pond close by the farmer's house, and as soon as the moon rises we begin. It is so entrancing that everybody lies awake to listen to us. In fact, it was only yesterday that I heard the farmer's wife say to her mother that she could not get a wink of sleep at night on account of us. It is most gratifying to find oneself so popular."

"Ahem! Ahem!" said the rocket angrily. He was very much annoyed that he could not get a word in.

"A delightful voice, certainly," continued the frog. "I hope you will come over to the duck-pond. I am off to look for my daughters. I have six beautiful daughters, and I am so afraid the Pike may meet them. He is a perfect monster, and would have no hesitation in breakfasting off them. Well, good-bye: I have enjoyed our conversation very much, I assure you."

"Conversation, indeed!" said the rocket. "You have talked the whole time yourself. That is not conversation."

"Somebody must listen," answered the frog, "and I like to do all the talking myself. It saves time, and prevents arguments."

"But I like arguments," said the rocket.

"I hope not," said the frog complacently. "Arguments are extremely vulgar, for everybody in good society holds exactly the same opinions. Good-bye a second time; I see my daughters in the distance." And the little frog swam away.

"You are a very irritating person," said the rocket, "and very ill-bred. I hate people who talk about themselves, as you do, when one wants to talk about oneself, as I do. It is what I call selfishness, and selfishness is a most detestable thing, especially to any one of my temperament, for I am well known for my sympathetic nature. In fact, you should take example by me; you could not possibly have a better model. Now that you have the chance you had better avail yourself of it, for I am going back to court almost immediately. I am a great favourite at court; in fact, the Prince and Princess were married yesterday in my honour. Of course you know nothing of these matters, for you are a provincial."

"There is no good talking to him," said a dragonfly, who was sitting on the top of a large brown bulrush. "No good at all, for he has gone away."

"Well, that is his loss, not mine," answered the rocket. "I am not going to stop talking to him merely because he pays no attention. I like hearing myself talk. It is one of my greatest pleasures. I often have long conversations all by myself, and I am so clever that sometimes I don't understand a single word of what I am saying."

"Then you should certainly lecture on Philosophy," said the dragonfly, and he spread a pair of lovely gauze wings and soared away into the sky.

"How very silly of him not to stay here!" said the rocket. "I am sure that he has not often got such a chance of improving his mind. However, I don't care a bit. Genius like mine is sure to be appreciated some day." And he sank down a little deeper into the mud.

After some time a large white duck swam up to him. She had yellow legs, and webbed feet, and was considered a great beauty on account of her waddle.

"Quack, quack, quack," she said. "What a curious shape you are! May I ask were you born like that, or is it the result of an accident?"

"It is quite evident that you have always lived in the country," answered the rocket, "otherwise you would know who I am. However, I excuse your ignorance. It would be unfair to expect other people to be as remarkable as oneself. You will no doubt be surprised to hear that I can fly up into the sky, and come down in a shower of golden rain."

"I don't think much of that," said the duck, "as I cannot see what use it is to anyone. Now, if you could plough the fields like the ox, or draw a cart like the horse, or look after the sheep like the collie-dog that would be something."

"My good creature," cried the rocket in a very haughty tone of voice, "I see that you belong to the lower orders. A person of my position is never useful. We have certain accomplishments, and that is more than sufficient. I have no sympathy myself with industry of any kind, least of all with such industries as you seem to recommend. Indeed, I have always been of opinion that hard work is simply the refuge of people who have nothing whatever to do."

"Well, well," said the duck, who was of a very peaceable disposition, and never quarrelled with any one. "Everybody has different tastes. I hope, at any rate, that you are going to take up your residence here."

"Oh! Dear, no," cried the rocket. "I am merely a visitor, a distinguished visitor. The fact is that I find this place rather tedious. There is neither society here, nor solitude. In fact, it is essentially suburban. I shall probably go back to court, for I know that I am destined to make a sensation in the world."

"I had thoughts of entering public life once myself," remarked the duck. "There are so many things that need reforming. Indeed, I took the chair at a meeting some time ago, and we passed resolutions condemning everything that we did not like. However, they did not seem to have much effect. Now I go in for domesticity, and look after my family."

"I am made for public life," said the rocket, "and so are all my relations, even the humblest of them. Whenever we appear we excite great attention. I have not actually appeared myself, but when I do so it will be a magnificent sight. As for domesticity, it ages one rapidly, and distracts one's mind from higher things."

"Ah! The higher things of life, how fine they are!" said the duck. "And that reminds me how hungry I feel." And she swam away down the stream, saying, "Quack, quack, quack."

"Come back! Come back!" screamed the rocket. "I have a great deal to say to you." But the duck paid no attention to him. "I am glad that she has gone," he said to himself. "She has a decidedly middle-class mind." And he sank a little deeper still into the mud, and began to think about the loneliness of genius, when suddenly two little boys in white smocks came running down the bank, with a kettle and some faggots.

"This must be the deputation," said the rocket, and he tried to look very dignified.

"Hallo!" cried one of the boys. "Look at this old stick! I wonder how it came here." And he picked the rocket out of the ditch.

"Old stick!" said the rocket. "Impossible! Gold stick, that is what he said. Gold stick is very complimentary. In fact, he mistakes me for one of the court dignitaries!"

"Let us put it into the fire!" said the other boy. "It will help to boil the kettle."

So they piled the faggots together, and put the rocket on top, and lit the fire.

"This is magnificent," cried the rocket. "They are going to let me off in broad daylight, so that everyone can see me."

"We will go to sleep now," they said, "and when we wake up the kettle will be boiled." And they lay down on the grass, and shut their eyes.

The rocket was very damp, so he took a long time to burn. At last, however, the fire caught him.

"Now I am going off!" he cried, and he made himself very stiff and straight. "I know I shall go much higher than the stars, much higher than the moon, much higher than the sun. In fact, I shall go so high that—"

Fizz! Fizz! Fizz! and he went straight up into the air.

"Delightful," he cried, "I shall go on like this for ever. What a success I am!"

But nobody saw him.

Then he began to feel a curious tingling sensation all over him.

"Now I am going to explode," he cried. "I shall set the whole world on fire, and make such a noise that nobody will talk about anything else for a whole year." And he certainly did explode. Bang! Bang! Bang! Went the gunpowder. There was no doubt about it.

But nobody heard him, not even the two little boys, for they were sound asleep.

Then all that was left of him was the stick, and this fell down on the back of a goose who was taking a walk by the side of the ditch.

"Good heavens!" cried the goose. "It is going to rain sticks." And she rushed into the water.

"I knew I should create a great sensation," gasped the rocket, and he went out.

少年国王

加冕典礼的前一天晚上，少年国王独自坐在他那间漂亮的房间里。大臣们按照当时的礼仪惯例，以伏地叩拜的方式向他告退；他们都退至王宫的大殿，接受礼仪官最后的一些培训，因为他们中间有一些人举止仍十分随意。不消说，随意的举止出现在大臣身上，就是非常严重的过失了。

这个少年国王——他还只是一个少年，才十六岁呢——巴不得大臣们都离去。他如释重负地长叹一声，猛地把背靠向刺绣卧榻的软垫上。他躺在了那里，双眼怒视，嘴巴大张，就像褐色的林中牧神法翁，也像刚被猎人捕获的林中幼兽。

确实，先前还真是猎人找回了他，也几乎是碰巧遇上了他。他光着脚丫，手拿笛子，正跟在一个穷苦牧人的羊群后面。这个牧羊人从小把他养大，少年也总以为自个儿就是牧羊人的儿子。其实呢，他原是老国王独生女的孩子，他的母亲偷偷地嫁给了一个地位低很多的人——有些人传言，他是一个外乡人，能把鲁特琴弹得出神入化，借此赢得了年轻公主的芳心；其他人则传说，他是一位来自意大利海港里米尼的画家，公主对其宠爱有加。兴许是宠爱过度，结果那人突然从城中消失了，连在大教堂画的画都没画完。少年出生仅仅一周，就被人趁母亲熟睡时从她身边偷偷抱走，交由膝下无子的一对普通农民抚养。他们则住在森林的深处，骑马过去需要一天多的时间。可能是悲伤过度，或如王宫御医所宣布的瘟疫，或如一些人所传言的香料酒中被人下了意大利烈性毒药，总之那个生下他的白皙女子，醒来不到一小时就气绝身亡了。被委以重任的信使带着那个婴儿跨上马鞍跑了，当其从跑得疲惫不堪的马背上俯身去敲牧人的柴门时，公主的尸首正被人埋进一处敞开的墓穴里。墓穴在城门外一片荒废的教堂墓地内，是事先被挖好了的；传说，那墓穴内还躺着一具尸首，是个英俊帅气的外国小伙子，双手被一根绳子反绑于背后，胸被刺中并留有许多殷红的伤口。

那些传言不知真假，至少是人们互相窃窃私语的闲言碎语。可以肯定的是，老国王在临终前，要么是因后悔自己所犯下的滔天罪行而动了恻隐之心，要么只是希望王位不要旁落于外人，他派人把由那个婴儿长成的少年接了回来，并当着王公大臣的面，宣布少年为继承人。

似乎就从身份得到认可的那一刻起，少年就表现出了对美的非凡激情，这注定要对他的人生产生巨大的影响。在专用套间伺候少年的那些人常常讲起，当少年看到为自己准备的精美服装和贵重珠宝时，情不自禁地从双唇间迸出快乐的欢呼声，又欣喜若狂地甩掉身上的粗革皮衣和粗羊皮斗篷。确实，他有时会怀念自己在林中生活时的那种怡然自得，动不动就对每天占用大量时间的繁琐宫廷仪式大发脾气。但是这座瑰丽无比的宫殿——欢乐宫，他们这样称呼它——他现在发现自己已成为它的主人，这对他来说它又似乎是一个全新的世界，只讨他的欢心。一旦能从会议厅或接待室脱身出来，少年就会直奔那宽大气派的楼梯，沿着镀金的铜狮雕塑和明亮的斑岩台阶跑下来，从一个房间游走到另一个房间，从一条走廊游走到另一条走廊，好像一个人正在努力寻寻觅觅，以从美中找到一副止疼的妙药，找到一种治病的良方。

　　踏上发现之旅，他是这么称呼的——对他来说，确实算是真正的奇境漫游——他身边有时会伴有几位身材高挑、头发金黄的宫廷侍从，他们身上的斗篷随风招展，艳丽的绶带甚是飘逸；但更多的时候，他会独自一人，某种几近先知先觉的机敏本能让他感到，艺术的秘密最好是在秘密中学习，而美呢，与智慧一样，只喜欢独自前来的崇拜者。

　　这一时期许多有关这个少年的奇闻怪事不胫而走。据传言，一位胖乎乎的镇长来到宫里，要代表全城的市民陈述一篇语言华丽的献辞，他意外地看到少年无比虔诚地跪拜在一幅刚从威尼斯带来的巨画跟前，这似乎预示着对某些新神的崇拜。还有一次，少年一连几个小时都无影无踪，大伙费了好大劲才在王宫北面塔楼的一间小屋里找到了他。只见他正如痴如醉地凝视着一块希腊宝石，上面雕着美少年阿多尼斯的画像。还有传言，有人亲眼看见少年用温热的双唇紧贴着一尊大理石古雕像的前额，那雕像是建造石桥时在河床上发现的，上面刻着罗马皇帝哈德良的俾斯尼亚奴仆——美少年安提诺斯的名字。他整夜不睡，用来观察月光照在月亮女神所钟情的美貌牧羊人恩底弥翁的一尊银像上，会有怎样的效果。

　　所有珍稀而昂贵的物品无疑都会让他心醉神迷。他迫不及待地都想搜罗到手。于是，他派出了许多商人：有些人前往北方海域，从粗犷的渔民手里买走琥珀；有些人前往埃及，搜寻只有法老陵墓中才有的珍奇绿玉，这些碧玉传说具有魔力；有些人前往波斯，购置丝绸地毯和彩绘陶器；还有些人前往印度，采购薄纱和彩绘象牙、月亮宝石和翡翠镯子、檀香木和蓝色珐琅器皿，以及细羊毛披肩。

然而，最让他上心的是他要在加冕典礼上穿的一件王袍，需用金线织成，还有一顶镶满红宝石的王冠，外加一根缀满一串串珍珠的权杖。事实上，这就是少年今晚所思量的事儿，其时他正躺在豪华的卧榻上，凝望着大块的松木在敞开的壁炉里渐渐燃尽。这件王袍的设计出自当时最负盛名的艺术家之手，早在数月之前就已送他过目。他命工匠昼夜赶制，并下令搜遍天下也要得到能够配得上王袍的珠宝。恍惚中，他仿佛看到自己身着精美的王袍站上了大教堂高耸的圣坛，而后他那充满稚气的唇边长时间地浮现出一丝微笑，宛如深邃密林的乌黑眼睛放射出明亮的光芒。

过了一会儿他从座位上站起来，斜靠着壁炉烟囱的雕花庇檐，环顾灯火幽暗的房间。四周的墙壁上悬挂着富丽的织锦画，展示的是"美神得胜"。一个镶嵌着玛瑙和琉璃的大衣橱占满了一个墙角，对着窗户的地方立着一个做工奇特的洒金水漆面屉柜，柜的上方则摆着一些精致的威尼斯玻璃高脚杯和一个黑纹玛瑙杯。丝绸床罩上绣着浅白的罂粟花，仿佛刚从睡神疲倦的双手中滑落下来；一根根长长的刻有凹槽的象牙柱撑起了天鹅绒华盖，上面饰有一大簇一大簇的鸵鸟毛，宛如一团团白色的泡沫，一直延伸到哑银雕饰的回纹天花板。美少年纳西瑟斯的青铜像笑容可掬，把一面磨得锃亮的镜子举过自己的头顶。桌上端放着一个平底盆，由紫水晶制成。

往外，少年能看到大教堂的巨型圆顶，像个大气泡般隐隐约约地浮现在影影绰绰的屋宇上方；河边的露台上雾气重重，疲惫的哨兵正在来回踱步。再远处是一片果园，一只夜莺正在放声歌唱。一缕淡淡的茉莉花香从敞开的窗户飘了进来。他把棕色的卷发从前额往后拂去，拿起一把鲁特琴，用手指漫不经心地拨弄着琴弦。他眼皮发沉，头耷拉了下来，一股莫名的倦意向他袭来。他从未这么真切地，或者说这么强烈地感受到美好事物的神奇与神秘。

钟楼传来午夜钟声时少年摇了摇唤人的铃铛，于是他的侍从走进来，礼仪繁杂地为他脱去衣袍，往他手上喷了些玫瑰香水，还往他的枕头上撒了些鲜花。待侍从退出房间后，不一会他就睡着了。

沉睡中少年做了一个梦，梦是这样的：

他觉得自个儿正站在一间又长又矮的阁楼里，四周尽是织布机运转的飕飕声和咔咔声。微弱的光线透过格栅窗照射进来，他看见了织工们俯身弯腰地在织布机台上劳作时的枯槁身影。粗大的织布机横梁上蜷缩着一个小孩，脸色苍白，面带病容。每当梭子飞快地穿过经纱时，他们要拉起沉重的筘座；一旦梭子停下时，他们就得放下筘座，将纬线压紧。他们的脸上露出饥饿难忍的痛苦表情，瘦弱的双手一直在哆嗦发抖。一些面黄肌瘦的妇人坐在一张桌旁，埋头做着针线活。这个地方充斥着一股恶臭，空气污秽又沉闷，墙壁潮湿，滴水成流。

少年国王走向一个织工，站在一边看着他。

那个织工愤怒地看着他，说道："你为什么盯着我？莫非是主人派来监视我们的密探？"

"你们的主人是谁？"少年国王问道。

"我们的主人！"织工痛苦地喊道，"他也是一个人，跟我没什么两样。实际上，我们之间只有一点不同——他穿着绫罗绸缎，而我褴褛衣衫；我饿得要死，而他撑得难受。"

"这是个自由的国度，"少年国王说，"你也不是谁的奴隶。"

"在战争年代，"织工答道，"强者把弱者变成奴隶，而在和平年代富人则把穷人变成奴隶。我们得做工活命，而他们给的工钱却少得让我们没法活命。我们为他们整日劳作，他们的金库堆满黄金，但我们的孩子没等长大就逐个夭亡了，我们所爱戴的人却面露冷漠和凶狠。我们采榨葡萄酿酒，却是他人端杯喝酒；我们播种谷物，自家饭桌却空无一物；我们身戴锁链，却没人看见；我们实为奴隶，却被说成人身自由。"

"所有人都是这样吗？"少年问道。

"所有人都是这样，"织工答道，"无论老年人还是青年人，无论男人还是女人，无论小孩还是年迈体弱的老者。商人压榨我们，我们却一定要听从他们的指使。牧师骑马跑过，只管数着自个儿的念珠，就是没有人管我们的死活。贫穷转着饥饿的眼睛，悄悄地爬进我们那暗无天日的陋巷，罪孽则一脸冷漠地紧随其后。苦难在早晨把我们唤醒，羞耻则在夜晚伴我们入睡。可是，这些与你何干呢？你又不是我们中的一员。你看起来太快乐了。"说着他就满脸愤怒地转过头，把梭子朝织布机那边扔了过去，少年国王方才看到，梭子上穿的是一根金线。

少年大惊失色，对织工说道，"你正在织的这件，是什么袍子？

"小国王加冕要用的袍子，"他回应道，"这与你何干呢？"

少年国王大叫一声，醒了过来。瞧！他在自个儿的卧室呢，透过窗子还能看见蜜黄色的大月亮，高悬在朦胧的夜空中。

少年再次睡着后又做了一个梦，梦是这样的：

他觉得自个儿正躺在一艘巨型帆船的甲板上，一百个奴隶正在奋力划着桨。他身边的一块地毯上，坐着帆船的船长。船长黑得像根乌木，裹着条深红色的丝巾，肥厚的耳垂挂着硕大的银耳坠，双手拿着一架象牙天平。

奴隶们浑身赤裸，只围着一块破烂的腰布；每个奴隶都与旁边的人用铁链锁在一起。太阳热辣辣地直射在他们身上，一些黑人沿着过道跑来跑去，挥着皮鞭抽打他们。他们伸出瘦削的胳膊，划着水中沉重的船桨，桨板上飞溅起咸咸的水花。

最后，他们来到一个小海湾，开始探测水深。一阵微风从岸边吹过来，给甲板和大三角帆蒙上了一层红色的浮尘。三个阿拉伯人骑着野驴跑过来，向他们投掷长矛。船主伸手拈弓搭箭，射中了其中一个阿拉伯人的喉咙。那人重重地摔入海浪中，同伴们便飞快地跑走了。一个蒙着黄色面纱的女子，骑着骆驼缓缓地跟在后面，时不时地回头看看那具尸体。

　　黑人抛下锚，收起帆，便纷纷走进舱底，拖上来一条长长的绳梯，上面系着沉甸甸的铅坠。船长将绳梯扔过船舷，并将梯两边的上端牢牢地拴在两根铁桩上。接下来，黑人抓住其中最年轻的一个奴隶，打开他的镣铐，再用蜡灌封他的鼻孔和耳朵，还要在他的腰部绑上一块大石头。那名奴隶有气无力地爬下绳梯，消失在海里，沉下去的地方冒出来几个水泡。其他奴隶中有几个好奇地盯着海面。船头上坐着一个驱鲨人，单调地连续敲着鼓。

　　过了一会儿，那个潜水的奴隶浮出水面，气喘吁吁地攀梯而上，右手还攥着一颗珍珠。黑人从他手中一把夺过珍珠，又把他推回海里。奴隶们靠在桨旁都一一睡着了。

　　他一次又一次地浮上来，每次都带上来一颗美丽的珍珠。船长把珍珠过秤后，装进一个绿色皮革的小袋子里。

　　少年国王想说点什么，可是他的舌头好像跟上颚黏在了一起，嘴唇也不听使唤了。黑人们相互喋喋不休，开始为一串明亮的珠子争吵起来。两只白鹤绕着帆船飞了一圈又一圈。

　　接着，潜水的奴隶最后一次浮出水面，带上来的珍珠比霍尔木兹的所有珍珠都要美，因为它形如满月，亮过启明星。然而，他的脸色异常苍白，一头栽倒在甲板上，鲜血从耳朵和鼻孔里迸射而出。

他颤抖了一下,然后就僵直不动了。黑人耸了耸肩,把尸体扔过船舷,落入海里。

船长大笑着,伸手抄起了那颗珍珠。待看清珍珠的模样后,他把珍珠按在额头,鞠躬致意。"它将,"他宣布说,"用在少年国王的权杖上。"他向黑人打了个手势,吩咐起锚开船。

听到这话,少年国王大喊一声,醒了过来。透过窗子,他看见黎明伸出纤长的灰白手指,正在摘去渐渐暗淡的群星。

少年再次睡着后,又做了一个梦,梦是这样的:

他觉得自个儿正穿越一片昏暗的树林,林间到处都是奇怪的果实,还有美丽而有毒的鲜花。一条条小毒蛇在他经过时冲他咝咝吐信,一只只鲜亮的鹦鹉在枝条间尖叫着飞来飞去。大大的乌龟躺在暖烘烘的烂泥中昏睡。树上挤满了猿猴和孔雀。

他走啊走啊,一直走到树林的边缘,看到了一大群人正在一条干涸的河床上劳作。他们就像蚂蚁一样蜂拥在巨石周围。他们在地下挖出一个个深坑,然后便跳进去。他们中有些人用大斧劈开石块,其余人则在沙砾中摸索着什么。

他们将仙人掌连根拔起,将猩红的花朵踩在脚下。他们忙这忙那,奔走相告,谁也没有闲着。

死亡和贪婪从洞穴的阴暗处紧盯着那些人。死亡开口说:"我等烦了;你把三分之一的人分给我,让我走吧。"然而,贪婪摇了摇头。"他们可是我的仆人。"她答道。

死亡问她:"你手里拿的是什么呢?"

"我有三粒谷,"她答道,"这于你何干?"

"给我一粒,"死亡大声喊道,"种在我的园子里;只要一粒,我就走了。"

"我不会给你任何东西。"贪婪说着,就把手藏进长袍的褶皱里面。

死亡大笑起来，拿出一只杯子，浸入池水中，接着从杯子里冒出来了疟疾。疟疾穿过人群，其中三分之一的人倒地而亡。死亡身后卷起一股寒气，身旁游荡着一群水蛇。

贪婪看到人都死了三分之一，就捶胸痛哭起来。她捶打着自个儿干瘪的胸脯，大声哀号。"你杀了我三分之一的仆人！"她喊叫道，"你快走。鞑靼地区的山里正在打仗，每一方的国王都在呼唤你去。阿富汗人杀了祭神的黑牛，正在奔赴战场。他们用戈矛敲击着自己的盾牌，还戴上了铁盔。我的山谷与你何干，要你待着不走？你快走，别再来了。"

"不，"死亡答道，"你不给我一粒谷，我就赖着不走。"

但是贪婪一听就握起拳头，咬紧牙关。"我不会给你任何东西。"她喃喃地说道。

死亡哈哈大笑，拿起一块黑石，扔进了森林，接着从一大片野毒芹中冒出来身着火焰长袍的热病。热病穿过人群，去触摸他们，凡是被她摸到的人都死了。她穿过时脚下踏过的青草都枯萎了。

贪婪颤抖起来，把灰撒到头上。"你太残忍了，"她喊叫道，"你太残忍了。印度的好多城池正在闹饥荒，撒马尔罕的蓄水池都干了。埃及的好多城池正在闹饥荒，蝗虫也从沙漠袭来。尼罗河洪水还没漫出堤岸，僧侣们诅咒着神祇伊西斯和奥西里斯。你赶快去那些需要你的地方吧，把我的仆人给我留下。"

"不，"死亡答道，"不给我一粒谷，我就赖着不走。"

"我不会给你任何东西。"贪婪说。

死亡又哈哈大笑起来，捻着手指打了个唿哨，接着从空中飞出来一个女子。她的额头上写着"瘟疫"字样，身边盘旋着一群瘦骨嶙峋的秃鹫。她展翅罩住整个山谷，没有留下一个活人。

贪婪尖叫着穿过森林，逃之夭夭；死亡跳上他的红马飞奔而去，跑得比风还快。

从谷底的烂泥中爬出无数条恶龙和长有鳞甲的骇人怪物，豺狼沿着沙地一路小跑过来，抬头嗅着空气。

少年国王哭着问道："这些人是谁，他们在找什么东西呢？"

"在为一位国王找王冠上的红宝石。"站在他身后的一个人答道。

少年国王吓了一跳，转过头来，看见一个朝圣者模样打扮的男子，手里拿着一面银镜。

他的脸色变得苍白，追问道："为哪位国王？"

朝圣者答道："看看这面镜子，你就会看见他。"

他往镜子里看了看，当看清自个儿的面孔时，他大叫一声，醒了过来，只见明媚的阳光水一般地倾泻进房间，在外面花园和游乐园的树上，鸟儿正在放声歌唱。

御前大臣和朝中重臣前来向少年国王行礼，侍从们送来了金丝王袍，并把王冠和权杖摆放在他的面前。

少年国王看着这些东西，确实美，比他见过的任何东西都要美。可是，他想起自个儿做过的梦。于是，他对他的大臣们说："把这些东西拿走，因为我不想用它们了。"

群臣都感到惊讶，甚至有几个还大笑起来，因为他们觉得，少年国王是在开玩笑。

但是少年再次对着他们开口，口气十分严厉："把这些东西拿走，别再让我看见。虽然今天是我加冕的日子，但是我也不想用。因为，这件王袍是由痛苦用苍白无力的双手在悲伤这台织布机上织成的，红宝石的心是由鲜血染红的，珍珠的心中有死亡的阴影。"接着他就把自个儿做的三个梦告诉了他们。

朝臣们听完后面面相觑，窃窃私语："他肯定疯了，梦不就是梦，幻象不就是幻象么？它们又不是真的，用不着放心上。再说，那些为我们干活的人活得怎样又与我们何干呢？难道一个人没跟种麦的见过面就不能吃面包，没跟种葡萄的说过话也不能喝葡萄酒么？"

御前大臣对少年国王说:"陛下,臣恳请您抛下这等忧伤之念,穿上这件华美的王袍,再戴上这顶王冠。因为您若不穿上国王的衣袍,子民又如何知悉您是国王呢?"

少年国王看着他。"果真这样么?"他质问道,"如果我不穿国王的衣袍,他们会不认我这个国王吗?"

"他们会认不出您的,陛下。"御前大臣大声说。

"我原以为真有那么一些人天生是帝王之相,"他回答,"但也有可能如你所说。不过,我还是不会穿这件王袍,也不会戴这顶王冠;我要按进宫时的穿戴,走出宫去。"

于是少年吩咐他们通通退下,只留下一个总是跟他做伴的侍从,比他自个儿还小一岁呢。他把这个侍从留下来伺候自己,等他用清水洗过澡,就打开一个彩绘大箱,从中取出当初在山坡上放羊时穿的粗革皮衣和粗羊皮斗篷。少年把这些穿在身上,拿起他那根未经打磨的牧羊杖。

小侍从看呆了,瞪着大大的蓝眼睛,笑着对他说:"陛下,我看见您的王袍和权杖了,可您的王冠在哪里呢?"

少年国王随手扯下一条攀附着阳台的野刺藤,把它弄弯,做成一个圆环,戴在他自个儿的头上。

"这就是我的王冠。"他答道。

这般穿戴后,少年走出自个儿的房间来到大殿,贵族们正在那里恭候着。

贵族们一看就乐了,有人向他大声地喊道:"陛下,您的子民在等着朝见他们的国王,而陛下却让他们看到了一个乞丐。"其余的人则愤怒地说道:"他让我们的国家丢脸,不配做我们的主。"然而,少年一句话都没有回答他们,只顾往前走,走下锃亮的斑岩楼梯,穿过一道道青铜门,然后纵身上马,向大教堂骑去,小侍从则跟在他身旁跑着。

百姓们哈哈大笑起来，纷纷说道："是国王的弄臣骑马跑过来了。"他们对他是百般嘲笑。

少年拉住缰绳，说道："错了，我就是国王。"接着他就给他们讲他自个儿做的三个梦。

这时，从人群中走出来一个男子，痛苦地对他说："陛下，莫非您不知道，穷人的生计来自于富人的奢华吗？依赖富人的铺张我们得以活命，是富人的恶习让我们得到了面包。为一个苛刻的主子干活固然苦，但没有主子要我们干活就会更苦。您以为乌鸦会养活我们吗？您有什么良方能应对这些难题吗？难道您会对买主说'你们要付这么多钱来买'，又会对卖主说'你们要以这个价钱去卖'吗？我以为您不会。所以，回您的王宫去，穿上您那件高贵的紫袍吧。您与我们何干，您与我们所受的苦难又有何干？"

"难道富人和穷人不是兄弟吗？"少年国王问道。

"是兄弟，"那人答道，"那个有钱的兄弟名叫该隐（即《圣经》中杀害弟弟的人）。"

少年国王双眼噙满泪水，继续策马前行，穿过嘀嘀咕咕的人群。那个小侍从害怕起来，就离开了他。

少年来到大教堂的大门前，士兵们横戟一拦，喝道："你来此地找什么？除了国王，任何人不得入内。"

少年气得满脸通红，对他们说："我就是国王。"接着，他推开他们的戟，径直走了进去。

看见牧人装束的少年走进来，年迈的主教惊讶地从宝座上起身，走上前去迎接，对他说道："孩子呀，这是一位国王的穿戴吗？我该拿什么王冠给你加冕，该把什么权杖交到你的手中呢？当然，对你来说，这该是个快乐的日子，而非一个负屈受辱的日子。"

"快乐非要用愁苦来装门面吗？"少年国王说。然后，他告诉主教自己做的三个梦。

主教听完三个梦后，紧锁眉头，说道："孩子，我是一个老人，已到风烛残年，我也知道世界之大，有着许许多多坏人坏事。凶恶的盗匪从山上冲下来，掳走无数年幼的孩童，卖给摩尔人；狮子伏击商队，扑咬骆驼；野猪拱翻谷底的庄稼，狐狸啃咬山上的葡萄藤；海盗把海滨村镇夷为废墟，烧毁渔民的船只，夺走他们的渔网；在盐碱地的沼泽中住着麻风病人，他们编织芦苇搭建棚屋，谁也不愿意去靠近他们；乞丐在城中四处流浪，与狗争食。难道你能让这些事情不发生吗？难道你愿意与麻风病人同床共眠，与乞丐同桌共餐吗？狮子会听你的吩咐，野猪会听你的安排吗？难道制造苦难的上帝不比你聪明吗？因而，我不会赞美你的所作所为，相反我要你骑马回宫，面带喜色，穿上与一位国王相配的衣袍，我会用黄金王冠为你加冕，我会把珍珠权杖放到你的手中。至于你做的梦么，不要再去想了。世间的负担太重，不是一个人能挑得起的；世间的忧愁太沉，不是一颗心能承受得了的。"

"在教堂里你还说得出这些话？"少年国王说着，便阔步走过主教的身旁，登上祭坛的台阶，站在了基督像的面前。

少年站在基督像的前面，右手边和左手边满是绝妙的黄金盘、盛着黄色葡萄酒的圣餐杯以及装着圣油的小瓶子。他跪在基督像下，一支支大型蜡烛在珠光宝气的神龛旁燃出明亮的火光，焚香飘出的烟雾化作一圈圈蓝色的轻烟在穹顶下缭绕。他低头祈祷着，穿着笔挺法衣的那些牧师悄悄地离开了祭坛。

突然，从外面的大街上传来一阵喧嚣声，一群羽缨乱颤的贵族闯了进来，手握出鞘的宝剑和锃亮的钢盾。"那个做梦的人在哪里？"他们大声嚷道，"那个装扮得像一个乞丐的国王——这个让我们的国家丢脸的孩子在哪里？我们一定要杀了他，他不配统治我们。"

少年国王再次低下头，继续祈祷，他念完祷词后转过身来，悲伤地看着他们。

瞧！透过彩绘的窗户，阳光倾泻而下照在少年的身上，缕缕光线围着他织出一件金丝长袍，比那件为取悦他而编织的王袍更加华美；手中那根牧羊杖开花了，开出的朵朵百合比珍珠还要白；他戴在头上的干瘪的野刺藤也开花了，开出的朵朵玫瑰比红宝石还要红。比优等珍珠更白的是百合，花茎由白银制成；比上等红宝石更红的是玫瑰，它们的叶子是由金箔制成的。

少年穿着国王的衣袍站在那里，珠光宝气的神龛飞快地开启，璀璨的水晶圣体匣射出一道奇妙而神秘的光芒。他身着王者的衣袍站在那里，上帝的荣光照满了整座教堂，雕刻壁龛里的圣徒们似乎都动起来了。他身着华美的王袍站在他们面前，管风琴奏起了音乐，号手们吹响了小号，唱诗班的孩子们也齐声歌唱起来。

臣民们敬畏地跪伏在地；贵族们收剑入鞘，向少年国王行礼；主教脸色发白，双手颤抖不已。"一位比我更伟大的人为您加冕了。"他高声喊着，跪倒在国王的面前。

少年国王走下高高的圣坛上，穿过人群，向家走去。但是，没有人敢抬头看他的脸，因为他有着天使一般的圣颜。

THE YOUNG KING

It was the night before the day fixed for his coronation, and the young King was sitting alone in his beautiful chamber. His courtiers had all taken their leave of him, bowing their heads to the ground, according to the ceremonious usage of the day, and had retired to the Great Hall of the palace, to receive a few last lessons from the Professor of Etiquette; there being some of them who had still quite natural manners, which in a courtier is, I need hardly say, a very grave offence.

The lad—for he was only a lad, being but sixteen years of age—was not sorry at their departure, and had flung himself back with a deep sigh of relief on the soft cushions of his embroidered couch, lying there, wild-eyed and open-mouthed, like a brown woodland Faun, or some young animal of the forest newly snared by the hunters.

And, indeed, it was the hunters who had found him, coming upon him almost by chance as, bare-limbed and pipe in hand, he was following the flock of the poor goatherd who had brought him up, and whose son he had always fancied himself to be. The child of the old King's only daughter by a secret marriage with one much beneath her in station—a stranger, some said, who, by the wonderful magic of his lute-playing, had made the young Princess love him; while others spoke of an artist from Rimini, to whom the Princess had shown much, perhaps too much honour, and who had suddenly disappeared from the city, leaving his work in the cathedral unfinished—he had been, when but a week old, stolen away from his mother's side, as she slept, and given into the charge of a common peasant and his wife, who were without children of their own, and lived in a remote part of the forest, more than a day's ride from the town. Grief, or the plague, as the court physician stated, or, as some suggested, a swift Italian poison administered in a cup of spiced wine, slew, within an hour of her wakening, the white girl who had given him birth, and as the trusty messenger who bare the child across his saddle-bow stooped from his weary horse and knocked at the rude door of the goatherd's hut, the body of the Princess was being lowered into an open grave that had been dug in a deserted churchyard, beyond the city gates, a grave where it was said that another body was also lying, that of a young man of marvellous and foreign beauty, whose hands were tied behind him with a knotted cord, and whose breast was stabbed with many red wounds.

Such, at least, was the story that men whispered to each other. Certain it was that the old King, when on his deathbed, whether moved by remorse for his great sin, or merely desiring that the kingdom should not pass away from his line, had had the lad sent for, and, in the presence of the council, had acknowledged him as his heir.

And it seems that from the very first moment of his recognition he had shown signs of that strange passion for beauty that was destined to have so great an influence over his life. Those who accompanied him to the suite of rooms set apart for his service, often spoke of the cry of pleasure that broke from his lips when he saw the delicate raiment and rich jewels that had been prepared for him, and of the almost fierce joy with which he flung aside his rough leathern tunic and coarse sheepskin cloak. He missed, indeed, at times the fine freedom of his forest life, and was always apt to chafe at the tedious court ceremonies that occupied so much of each day, but the wonderful palace—Joyeuse, as they called it—of which he now found himself lord, seemed to him to be a new world fresh-fashioned for his delight; and as soon as he could escape from the council-board or audience-chamber, he would run down the great staircase, with its lions of gilt bronze and its steps of bright porphyry, and wander from room to room, and from corridor to corridor, like one who was seeking to find in beauty an anodyne from pain, a sort of restoration from sickness.

Upon these journeys of discovery, as he would call them—and, indeed, they were to him real voyages through a marvellous land, he would sometimes be accompanied by the slim, fair-haired court pages, with their floating mantles, and gay fluttering ribands; but more often he would be alone, feeling through a certain quick instinct, which was almost a divination, that the secrets of art are best learned in secret, and that beauty, like wisdom, loves the lonely worshipper.

Many curious stories were related about him at this period. It was said that a stout Burgo-master, who had come to deliver a florid oratorical address on behalf of the citizens of the town, had caught sight of him kneeling in real adoration before a great picture that had just been brought from Venice, and that seemed to herald the worship of some new gods. On another occasion he had been missed for several hours, and after a lengthened search had been discovered in a little chamber in one of the northern turrets of the palace gazing, as one in a trance, at a Greek gem carved with the figure of Adonis. He had been seen, so the tale ran, pressing his warm lips to the marble brow of an antique statue that had been discovered in the bed of the river on the occasion of the building of the stone bridge, and was inscribed with the name of the Bithynian slave of Hadrian. He had passed a whole night in noting the effect of the moonlight on a silver image of Endymion.

All rare and costly materials had certainly a great fascination for him, and in his eagerness to procure them he had sent away many merchants, some to traffic for amber with the rough fisher-folk of the north seas, some to Egypt to look for that curious green turquoise which is found only in the tombs of kings, and is said to possess magical properties, some to Persia for silken carpets and painted pottery, and others to India to buy gauze and stained ivory, moonstones and bracelets of jade, sandalwood and blue enamel and shawls of fine wool.

But what had occupied him most was the robe he was to wear at his coronation, the robe of tissued gold, and the ruby-studded crown, and the sceptre with its rows and rings of pearls. Indeed, it was of this that he was thinking tonight, as he lay back on his luxurious couch, watching the great pinewood log that was burning itself out on the open hearth. The designs, which were from the hands of the most famous artists of the time, had been submitted to him many months before, and he had given orders that the artificers were to toil night and day to carry them out, and that the whole world was to be searched for jewels that would be worthy of their work. He saw himself in fancy standing at the high altar of the cathedral in the fair raiment of a king, and a smile played and lingered about his boyish lips, and lit up with a bright lustre his dark woodland eyes.

After some time he rose from his seat, and leaning against the carved penthouse of the chimney, looked round at the dimly-lit room. The walls were hung with rich tapestries representing the Triumph of Beauty. A large press, inlaid with agate and lapis-lazuli, filled one corner, and facing the window stood a curiously wrought cabinet with lacquer panels of powdered and mosaiced gold, on which were placed some delicate goblets of Venetian glass, and a cup of dark-veined onyx. Pale poppies were broidered on the silk coverlet of the bed, as though they had fallen from the tired hands of sleep, and tall reeds of fluted ivory bare up the velvet canopy, from which great tufts of ostrich plumes sprang, like white foam, to the pallid silver of the fretted ceiling. A laughing Narcissus in green bronze held a polished mirror above its head. On the table stood a flat bowl of amethyst.

Outside he could see the huge dome of the cathedral, looming like a bubble over the shadowy houses, and the weary sentinels pacing up and down on the misty terrace by the river. Far away, in an orchard, a nightingale was singing. A faint perfume of jasmine came through the open window. He brushed his brown curls back from his forehead, and taking up a lute, let his fingers stray across the cords. His heavy eyelids drooped, and a strange languor came over him. Never before had he felt so keenly, or with such exquisite joy, the magic and the mystery of beautiful things.

When midnight sounded from the clock-tower he touched a bell, and his pages entered and disrobed him with much ceremony, pouring rosewater over his hands, and strewing flowers on his pillow. A few moments after that they had left the room, he fell asleep.

And as he slept he dreamed a dream, and this was his dream.

He thought that he was standing in a long, low attic, amidst the whir and clatter of many looms. The meagre daylight peered in through the grated windows, and showed him the gaunt figures of the weavers bending over their cases. Pale, sickly-looking children were crouched on the huge crossbeams. As the shuttles dashed through the warp they lifted up the heavy battens, and when the shuttles stopped they let the battens fall and pressed the threads together. Their faces were pinched with famine, and their thin hands shook and trembled. Some haggard women were seated at a table sewing. A horrible odour filled the place. The air was foul and heavy, and the walls dripped and streamed with damp.

The young King went over to one of the weavers, and stood by him and watched him.

And the weaver looked at him angrily, and said, "Why are you watching me? Are you a spy set on us by our master?"

"Who is your master?" asked the young King.

"Our master!" cried the weaver, bitterly. "He is a man like myself. Indeed, there is but this difference between us—that he wears fine clothes while I go in rags, and that while I am weak from hunger he suffers not a little from overfeeding."

"The land is free," said the young King, "and you are no man's slave."

"In war," answered the weaver, "the strong make slaves of the weak, and in peace the rich make slaves of the poor. We must work to live, and they give us such mean wages that we die. We toil for them all day long, and they heap up gold in their coffers, and our children fade away before their time, and the faces of those we love become hard and evil. We tread out the grapes, and another drinks the wine. We sow the corn, and our own board is empty. We have chains, though no eye beholds them; and are slaves, though men call us free."

"Is it so with all?" he asked,

"It is so with all," answered the weaver, "with the young as well as with the old, with the women as well as with the men, with the little children as well as with those who are stricken in years. The merchants grind us down, and we must do their bidding. The priest rides by and tells his beads, and no man has care of us. Through our sunless lanes creeps Poverty with her hungry eyes, and Sin with his sodden face follows close behind her. Misery wakes us in the morning, and Shame sits with us at night. But what are these things to you? You are not one of us. Your face is too happy." And he turned away scowling, and threw the shuttle across the loom, and the young King saw that it was threaded with a thread of gold.

And a great terror seized upon him, and he said to the weaver, "What robe is this that you are weaving?"

"It is the robe for the coronation of the young King," he answered. "What is that to you?"

And the young King gave a loud cry and woke, and lo! He was in his own chamber, and through the window he saw the great honey-coloured moon hanging in the dusky air.

And he fell asleep again and dreamed, and this was his dream.

He thought that he was lying on the deck of a huge galley that was being rowed by a hundred slaves. On a carpet by his side the master of the galley was seated. He was black as ebony, and his turban was of crimson silk. Great earrings of silver dragged down the thick lobes of his ears, and in his hands he had a pair of ivory scales.

The slaves were naked, but for a ragged loin-cloth, and each man was chained to his neighbour. The hot sun beat brightly upon them, and the Negroes ran up and down the gangway and lashed them with whips of hide.

They stretched out their lean arms and pulled the heavy oars through the water. The salt spray flew from the blades.

At last they reached a little bay, and began to take soundings. A light wind blew from the shore, and covered the deck and the great lateen sail with a fine red dust. Three Arabs mounted on wild asses rode out and threw spears at them. The master of the galley took a painted bow in his hand and shot one of them in the throat. He fell heavily into the surf, and his companions galloped away. A woman wrapped in a yellow veil followed slowly on a camel, looking back now and then at the dead body.

As soon as they had cast anchor and hauled down the sail, the Negroes went into the hold and brought up a long rope ladder, heavily weighted with lead. The master of the galley threw it over the side, making the ends fast to two iron stanchions. Then the Negroes seized the youngest of the slaves and knocked his gyves off, and filled his nostrils and his ears with wax, and tied a big stone round his waist. He crept wearily down the ladder, and disappeared into the sea. A few bubbles rose where he sank. Some of the other slaves peered curiously over the side. At the prow of the galley sat a shark-charmer, beating monotonously upon a drum.

After some time the diver rose up out of the water, and clung panting to the ladder with a pearl in his right hand. The Negroes seized it from him, and thrust him back. The slaves fell asleep over their oars.

Again and again he came up, and each time that he did so he brought with him a beautiful pearl. The master of the galley weighed them, and put them into a little bag of green leather.

The young King tried to speak, but his tongue seemed to cleave to the roof of his mouth, and his lips refused to move. The Negroes chattered to each other, and began to quarrel over a string of bright beads. Two cranes flew round and round the vessel.

Then the diver came up for the last time, and the pearl that he brought with him was fairer than all the pearls of Ormuz, for it was shaped like the full moon, and whiter than the morning star. But his face was strangely pale, and as he fell upon the deck the blood gushed from his ears and nostrils. He quivered for a little, and then he was still. The Negroes shrugged their shoulders, and threw the body overboard.

And the master of the galley laughed, and, reaching out, he took the pearl, and when he saw it he pressed it to his forehead and bowed. "It shall be," he said, "for the sceptre of the young King," and he made a sign to the Negroes to draw up the anchor.

And when the young King heard this he gave a great cry, and woke. And through the window he saw the long grey fingers of the dawn clutching at the fading stars.

And he fell asleep again, and dreamed, and this was his dream.

He thought that he was wandering through a dim wood, hung with strange fruits and with beautiful poisonous flowers. The adders hissed at him as he went by, and the bright parrots flew screaming from branch to branch. Huge tortoises lay asleep upon the hot mud. The trees were full of apes and peacocks.

On and on he went, till he reached the outskirts of the wood, and there he saw an immense multitude of men toiling in the bed of a dried-up river. They swarmed up the crag like ants. They dug deep pits in the ground and went down into them. Some of them cleft the rocks with great axes; others grabbled in the sand.

They tore up the cactus by its roots, and trampled on the scarlet blossoms. They hurried about, calling to each other, and no man was idle.

From the darkness of a cavern Death and Avarice watched them, and Death said, "I am weary; give me a third of them and let me go." But Avarice shook her head. "They are my servants," she answered.

And Death said to her, "What do you have in your hand?"

"I have three grains of corn," she answered. "What is that to you?"

"Give me one of them," cried Death, "to plant in my garden; only one of them, and I will go away."

"I will not give you anything," said Avarice, and she hid her hand in the fold of her raiment.

And Death laughed, and took a cup, and dipped it into a pool of water, and out of the cup rose Ague. She passed through the great multitude, and a third of them lay dead. A cold mist followed her, and the water snakes ran by her side.

And when Avarice saw that a third of the multitude was dead she beat her breast and wept. She beat her barren bosom, and cried aloud. "You have slain a third of my servants," she cried, "get you gone. There is war in the mountains of Tartary, and the kings of each side are calling to you. The Afghans have slain the black ox, and are marching to battle. They have beaten upon their shields with their spears, and have put on their helmets of iron. What is my valley to you, that you should tarry in it? Get you gone, and come here no more."

"No," answered Death, "but till you hast given me a grain of corn I will not go."

But Avarice shut her hand, and clenched her teeth. "I will not give you anything," she muttered.

And Death laughed, and took up a black stone, and threw it into the forest, and out of a thicket of wild hemlock came Fever in a robe of flame. She passed through the multitude, and touched them, and each man that she touched died. The grass withered beneath her feet as she walked.

And Avarice shuddered, and put ashes on her head. "You are cruel," she cried. "You are cruel. There is famine in the walled cities of India, and the cisterns of Samarcand have run dry. There is famine in the walled cities of Egypt, and the locusts have come up from the desert. The Nile has not overflowed its banks, and the priests have cursed Isis and Osiris. Get you gone to those who need you, and leave me my servants."

"No," answered Death, "but till you hast given me a grain of corn I will not go."

"I will not give you anything," said Avarice.

And Death laughed again, and he whistled through his fingers, and a woman came flying through the air. Plague was written upon her forehead, and a crowd of lean vultures wheeled round her. She covered the valley with her wings, and no man was left alive.

And Avarice fled shrieking through the forest, and Death leaped upon his red horse and galloped away, and his galloping was faster than the wind.

And out of the slime at the bottom of the valley crept dragons and horrible things with scales, and the jackals came trotting along the sand, sniffing up the air with their nostrils.

And the young King wept, and said, "Who were these men, and for what were they seeking?"

"For rubies for a king's crown," answered one who stood behind him.

And the young King started, and, turning round, he saw a man habited as a pilgrim and holding in his hand a mirror of silver.

And he grew pale, and said, "For what king?"

And the pilgrim answered, "Look in this mirror, and you should see him."

And he looked in the mirror, and, seeing his own face, he gave a great cry and woke, and the bright sunlight was streaming into the room, and from the trees of the garden and pleasaunce the birds were singing.

And the Chamberlain and the high officers of State came in and made obeisance to him, and the pages brought him the robe of tissued gold, and set the crown and the sceptre before him.

And the young King looked at them, and they were beautiful. More beautiful were they than aught that he had ever seen. But he remembered his dreams, and he said to his lords, "Take these things away, for I will not wear them."

And the courtiers were amazed, and some of them laughed, for they thought that he was jesting.

But he spoke sternly to them again, and said, "Take these things away, and hide them from me. Though it be the day of my coronation, I will not wear them. For on the loom of sorrow, and by the white hands of pain, has this my robe been woven. There is blood in the heart of the ruby, and death in the heart of the pearl." And he told them his three dreams.

And when the courtiers heard them they looked at each other and whispered, saying, "Surely he is mad. For what is a dream but a dream, and a vision but a vision? They are not real things that one should heed them. And what have we to do with the lives of those who toil for us? Shall a man not eat bread till he has seen the sower, nor drink wine till he has talked with the vinedresser?"

And the Chamberlain spoke to the young King, and said, "My lord, I pray you set aside these black thoughts of yours, and put on this fair robe, and set this crown upon your head. For how shall the people know that you are a king, if you have not a king's raiment?"

And the young King looked at him. "Is it so, indeed?" he questioned. "Will they not know me for a king if I have not a king's raiment?"

"They will not know you, my lord," cried the Chamberlain.

"I had thought that there had been men who were kinglike," he answered, "but it may be as you say. And yet I will not wear this robe, nor will I be crowned with this crown, but even as I came to the palace so will I go forth from it."

And he bade them all leave him, save one page whom he kept as his companion, a lad a year younger than himself. Him he kept for his service, and when he had bathed himself in clear water, he opened a great painted chest, and from it he took the leathern tunic and rough sheepskin cloak that he had worn when he had watched on the hillside the shaggy goats of the goatherd. These he put on, and in his hand he took his rude shepherd's staff.

And the little page opened his big blue eyes in wonder, and said smiling to him, "My lord, I see your robe and your sceptre, but where is your crown?"

And the young King plucked a spray of wild briar that was climbing over the balcony, and bent it, and made a circlet of it, and set it on his own head.

"This shall he my crown," he answered.

And thus attired he passed out of his chamber into the Great Hall, where the nobles were waiting for him.

And the nobles made merry, and some of them cried out to him, "My lord, the people wait for their king, and you show them a beggar," and others were wroth and said, "He brings shame upon our state, and is unworthy to be our master." But he answered them not a word, but passed on, and went down the bright porphyry staircase, and out through the gates of bronze, and mounted upon his horse, and rode towards the cathedral, the little page running beside him.

And the people laughed and said, "It is the King's fool who is riding by," and they mocked him.

And he drew rein and said, "No, but I am the King." And he told them his three dreams.

And a man came out of the crowd and spoke bitterly to him, and said, "Sir, don't you know that out of the luxury of the rich comes the life of the poor? By your pomp we are nurtured, and your vices give us bread. To toil for a hard master is bitter, but to have no master to toil for is bitter still. Do you think that the ravens will feed us? And what cure have you for these things? Will you say to the buyer, 'You shall buy for so much,' and to the seller, 'You shall sell at this price'? I don't believe. Therefore go back to your palace and put on your purple and fine linen. What have you to do with us, and what we suffer?"

"Are not the rich and the poor brothers?" asked the young King.

"Ay," answered the man, "and the name of the rich brother is Cain."

And the young King's eyes filled with tears, and he rode on through the murmurs of the people, and the little page grew afraid and left him.

And when he reached the great portal of the cathedral, the soldiers thrust their halberts out and said, "What do you seek here? None enters by this door but the King."

And his face flushed with anger, and he said to them, "I am the King," and waved their halberts aside and passed in.

And when the old Bishop saw him coming in his goatherd's dress, he rose up in wonder from his throne, and went to meet him, and said to him, "My son, is this a king's apparel? And with what crown shall I crown you, and what sceptre shall I place in your hand? Surely this should be to you a day of joy, and not a day of abasement."

"Shall Joy wear what grief has fashioned?" said the young King. And he told him his three dreams.

And when the Bishop had heard them he knit his brows, and said, "My son, I am an old man, and in the winter of my days, and I know that many evil things are done in the wide world. The fierce robbers come down from the mountains, and carry off the little children, and sell them to the Moors. The lions lie in wait for the caravans, and leap upon the camels. The wild boar roots up the corn in the valley, and the foxes gnaw the vines upon the hill. The pirates lay waste the sea coast and burn the ships of the fishermen, and take their nets from them. In the salt-marshes live the lepers; they have houses of wattled reeds, and none may come nigh them. The beggars wander through the cities, and eat their food with the dogs. Can you make these things not to be? Will you take the leper for your bedfellow, and set the beggar at your board? Shall the lion do your bidding, and the wild boar obey you? Is not He who made misery wiser than you are? Wherefore I praise you not for this that you have done, but I bid you ride back to the Palace and make your face glad, and put on the raiment that beseemeth a king, and with the crown of gold I will crown you, and the sceptre of pearl will I place in your hand. And as for your dreams, think no more of them. The burden of this world is too great for one man to bear, and the world's sorrow too heavy for one heart to suffer."

"Do you say that in this house?" said the young King, and he strode past the Bishop, and climbed up the steps of the altar, and stood before the image of Christ.

He stood before the image of Christ, and on his right hand and on his left were the marvellous vessels of gold, the chalice with the yellow wine, and the vial with the holy oil. He knelt before the image of Christ, and the great candles burned brightly by the jewelled shrine, and the smoke of the incense curled in thin blue wreaths through the dome. He bowed his head in prayer, and the priests in their stiff copes crept away from the altar.

And suddenly a wild tumult came from the street outside, and in entered the nobles with drawn swords and nodding plumes, and shields of polished steel. "Where is this dreamer of dreams?" they cried. "Where is this King who is apparelled like a beggar—this boy who brings shame upon our state? Surely we will slay him, for he is unworthy to rule over us."

And the young King bowed his head again, and prayed, and when he had finished his prayer he rose up, and turning round he looked at them sadly.

And lo! Through the painted windows came the sunlight streaming upon him, and the sun beams wove round him a tissued robe that was fairer than the robe that had been fashioned for his pleasure. The dead staff blossomed, and bare lilies that were whiter than pearls. The dry thorn blossomed, and bare roses that were redder than rubies. Whiter than fine pearls were the lilies, and their stems were of bright silver. Redder than male rubies were the roses, and their leaves were of beaten gold.

He stood there in the raiment of a king, and the gates of the jewelled shrine flew open, and from the crystal of the many-rayed monstrance shone a marvellous and mystical light. He stood there in a king's raiment, and the Glory of God filled the place, and the saints in their carven niches seemed to move. In the fair raiment of a king he stood before them, and the organ pealed out its music, and the trumpeters blew upon their trumpets, and the singing boys sang.

And the people fell upon their knees in awe, and the nobles sheathed their swords and did homage, and the Bishop's face grew pale, and his hands trembled. "A greater than I have crowned you," he cried, and he knelt before him.

And the young King came down from the high altar, and passed home through the midst of the people. But no man dared look upon his face, for it was like the face of an angel.

公主的生日

这天是公主的生日。她刚满十二岁,阳光明媚地照耀着王宫的座座花园。

她是一位真正的皇家千金,一位西班牙公主,但是就像穷苦人家的孩子一样,每年也只有一个生日。因此她过生日那一天要有真正的好天气,这被全国人民视为一件重要的大事。确实,那天的天气也真是好。一株株斑纹郁金香昂首挺直花茎,仿佛一排排士兵,傲视着草地那边的玫瑰,说道:"到眼下,我们可跟你们一样美啦!"一只只紫色的蝴蝶翩翩起舞,依次探访每一朵鲜花,翅膀上沾着金灿灿的花粉;小蜥蜴从墙缝里爬出,躺着沐浴在日光下;日头晒得石榴纷纷裂开,露出里面的红心来。就连一串串淡黄色的柠檬,沿着阴阴郁郁的拱廊从陈旧欲坠的棚架上悬挂下来,在明媚的阳光中仿佛也平添了些许亮色;玉兰树也打开一朵朵硕大的象牙色球状花苞,空气中弥漫着浓浓的芳香。

小公主和同伴们在露台上走来走去,围着石花瓶和长满青苔的古老石雕玩起了捉迷藏。平日里,她只许与其身份相当的孩子一起玩耍,所以她总是只能自个儿玩。但是她生日这天是个例外,国王已经下令,她可以邀请任何她喜欢的小伙伴一起玩。那些身材颀长的西班牙孩子四处溜达时透露出一种高贵的优雅，男孩们头戴大羽帽，身上披着迎风飘拂的短斗篷，女孩们提起锦缎长裙的下摆，举着黑银双色的大扇子以遮挡刺眼的阳光。然而，所有孩子中公主殿下是最优雅的，穿着也是最有品位的，遵循着当下多少有点儿烦冗的时尚。她穿着银灰色的绸缎长袍，裙摆和宽大的泡泡袖上密密麻麻地绣满了银线花，坚挺的胸衣上镶着一排排精美的珍珠。她走起路来，裙子下面就会探出两只小小的拖鞋，上面饰有大朵大朵的粉红色玫瑰花结。她手拿粉红兼珍珠白的大纱扇，整齐的发髻硬挺在白净的小脸蛋周围，宛如淡金色的光环，上面还别着一朵美丽的白玫瑰。

从王宫的一扇窗户里看着他们的是那位忧郁的国王。国王身后站着他所憎恨的兄弟，他是阿拉贡省的堂·佩德罗；身旁则坐着听他忏悔的神父，来自格拉纳达城的大宗教裁判官。国王甚至比往常更加伤心，因为公主带着孩子气认真地向宫中朝臣鞠躬回礼，或是以扇掩面嘲笑总是陪她左右且满脸阴郁的阿尔布开克公爵夫人，让他不由得想起了年轻的王后，也就是公主的母亲：在他看来，她仿佛就在不久前刚从法兰西这个欢乐浪漫的国度嫁过来，就在西班牙阴郁又堂皇的宫廷中枯萎凋零了，撒手人寰时孩子才六个月大；王后都没来得及再次看到果园里的杏花盛开，也没赶得上从如今杂草丛生的庭院中央那棵疙疙瘩瘩的老树再次采摘无花果。国王爱她爱得如此之深，甚至不能容忍坟墓将她掩埋起来。于是，他吩咐一名摩尔人医生对她的尸身进行了防腐处理，为此还饶其一命，因为大家都在传言这位摩尔人因信邪教行巫术已被宗教裁判所判处死刑；直到现在王后的尸身仍安躺在王宫的黑色大理石礼拜堂中铺着织锦的灵床上，一如近十二年前那个狂风大作的三月天里僧侣们抬放进去时的模样。国王每月都会来一次，身披一件黑色的斗篷，手提一盏幽暗的灯笼，走进礼堂就跪倒在她的身边，大声呼唤："我的王后！我的王后啊！"有时他会不顾在西班牙生活事无巨细乃至国王哀恸都得受其规限的正式礼节，万分悲痛地紧抓她那戴满珠宝的苍白双手，疯狂地亲吻她那妆容整齐的冰冷脸颊，想唤醒她。

今天国王似乎又见到她了，就像他在巴黎枫丹白露城堡与她初次相见时那样。那时他才十五岁，而她就更年少了。就在那次相遇期间，由罗马教廷驻巴黎特使主持，他俩正式订婚，法兰西国王和全体朝臣出席了仪式。而后，他就返回西班牙王宫埃斯库里亚尔去了，怀揣着一小束金黄的头发，外加一份甜蜜的回忆：在他即将踏入马车告别之际，她俯身用稚气的双唇亲吻他的手。后来，他俩在两国边境的小镇布尔戈斯匆匆举行了婚礼，随即返回京城马德里公开举办盛大庆典，遵循惯例在拉·阿托查教堂做了大弥撒，还有一场远比平常庄严的火刑处决——近三百名异教徒，其中许多都是英国人，被刽子手烧死在火刑柱上。

确实，国王爱王后爱得走火入魔，乃至许多人认为因此而毁了国运，因为当时西班牙正在与英国为争夺新世界的美洲而交战。国王几乎从不放王后离开自己的视线，为了她国王似乎都忘记了所有重大国事。另外，激情会让人变得无比盲目，因此他没能察觉到，为取悦王后而举办的诸多繁琐仪式反而加重了她的怪病。王后去世之后，他一度就像个完全失去理智的人。说真的，若非担心小公主会落入他弟弟的掌控，国王无疑会正式退位并遁入格拉纳达的特拉普派大修道院，那时他已是那儿的名誉院长了。他那位兄弟生性残暴，在西班牙可谓臭名昭著。甚至许多人怀疑是他害死了王后。传言王后到访他在阿拉贡的城堡时，是他呈上了一副有毒的手套。王后去世后，国王曾下令王国的所有属地都要公开哀悼三年，即使哀悼期满，他也无法忍受大臣们提及续弦联姻的事儿。神圣的罗马皇帝曾亲自派来使节，为他的侄女波希米亚大公妃提亲，但是国王提请使节回禀皇帝：西班牙国王已娶"悲伤"为妻，即便"悲伤"不能生养子嗣，他却爱"悲伤"不爱美人。这一席回话让他的王国失去了富饶的尼德兰诸省，因为不久之后这些省份在罗马皇帝的煽动下造反，领头的就是新教改革派的一些狂热分子。

今天，当国王看着小公主在露台上玩耍时，往日的婚姻生活仿佛回到眼前。他的整个婚姻生活，有炽烈如火的狂喜，也有戛然而止的剧痛。公主继承王后所有可爱的神态，同样倔强又固执的摆头姿势，同样弯曲又傲慢的美丽嘴唇，同样漂亮又迷人的微笑——正宗的法兰西微笑——公主时不时地朝国王这边的窗户望上一眼，或者伸出小手让显贵的西班牙绅士们亲吻。然而，孩子们尖锐的笑声，他听着刺耳，明媚无情的阳光又嘲笑着他的哀伤。一股奇怪香料的沉闷气味，就像防腐医生使用的香料，似乎弄脏了早晨的清新空气——或许是自己的幻觉吧？国王用双手捂住脸，等公主再次抬头望窗户时窗帘已经拉下，国王已经走了。

公主失望地噘了噘小嘴，耸了耸双肩。当然，国王本该陪她过生日的。那些无聊的国事有什么要紧呢？或许他是去了那间死气沉沉的礼拜堂了吧？那儿灯火长明，但从未让公主进去过。看这里阳光多么明媚，大伙儿个个都这么开心，他走开真是太傻了啊！再说，人扮斗牛比赛的号角已经吹响，他肯定会错过观看啦，更不用说还会错过木偶戏和其他精彩的表演了。她的叔叔和大裁判官可聪明多了。他们都走出来，来到露台上向她说了些好听的祝福语。于是，她甩了甩小脑瓜，拉着堂·佩德罗的手，缓缓地走下台阶，朝着搭在花园尽头的那座紫绸长亭走去，其余小孩则紧跟在她后面，严格地按照先后顺序，谁的名字最长，谁就走在最前面。

一队贵族男孩装扮成斗牛士，衣着光鲜地出来迎接公主。年少的努瓦伯爵是个约摸十四岁光景的美少年，他优雅地向公主弯腰脱帽致敬，并庄重地引领她进入斗牛场，走到斗牛场上方的看台上，然后坐到一把镀金的小象牙椅上。孩子们围成一圈在四周坐下，一边舞动着大扇子，一边相互窃窃私语；堂·佩德罗和大裁判官则笑呵呵地站在入口处。就连那位面貌凶恶，人称"侍从女总管"的女公爵，看上去也不像平常那么乖戾了，动作中透露着与生俱来的贵族气度，一抹冷冷的笑容掠过她那布满皱纹的脸庞，牵动着她那毫无血色的薄薄嘴唇。

　　这真是一场精彩的斗牛表演，在公主看来要远远胜过在帕尔马公爵拜访她父亲时，大家带她去塞维利亚现场观看的那场真正的斗牛比赛。此时一些男孩骑上披挂华丽的假马四处奔跑，手中舞着长枪，枪上还系着鲜艳的缎带。其余男孩则徒步而行，冲着"公牛"挥着猩红的大氅，等它攻上来时就轻身一跳跃到栅栏外面。至于"公牛"么，就跟一头活牛一模一样，尽管它只是一个蒙了层牛皮的柳枝架子。它有时还会后腿站立起来满场跑动，这是任何一头活牛做梦都想不到的。这头"公牛"斗得也非常出彩，孩子们看着都兴奋得不得了，纷纷站到长凳上，挥舞着手中的手绢高声大喊"好样的，斗牛，好样的，斗牛"，那劲头就像他们已经长大成人了。一番鏖战中，有几匹木马被"公牛"顶穿了一次又一次，马背上的骑手也纷纷被掀了下来；最终，年少的努瓦伯爵用膝盖镇住"公牛"，在征得公主允许给牛致命的一击后，挥起木剑猛地刺入"公牛"的脖子，用力太猛使得牛头直接掉了下来，却露出了满脸笑容的德洛林小公子，他是法兰西驻马德里大使的儿子。

　　随着一阵热烈的掌声，斗牛场迅速被清理完毕，几匹战死的木马被两名身穿黄黑两色制服的摩尔人侍从庄严肃穆地拖出去了。短暂的幕间休息期间穿插了一名法兰西体操师走钢丝的表演。然后，在特地搭建的木偶戏小剧场的舞台上，一些意大利木偶开始表演半古典的悲剧《索芙妮丝芭》。木偶表演非常出色，举手投足极其自然，以至于接近结束之际公主双眼都让泪水模糊了。事实上，有些孩子真的哭了起来，大人们只好用糖果来安慰他们；连大检察官都感动不已，禁不住对堂·佩德罗说他自个儿都不忍心看下去了，这些小玩意儿只是用木块和彩蜡做成的,在几根丝线的牵引下机械地动来动去的东西,竟然会表现得如此悲伤,也会遭遇这么恐怖的不幸。

接着上场的是一个非洲杂耍艺人,提着一个扁平的大篮子,上面盖着一块红布。艺人把篮子放在场地中央,然后从自个儿的包头巾里取出一根怪异的簧管,吹了起来。不一会儿,只见红布开始动起来,随着管声越吹越尖,两条金绿色的蛇从布下探出古怪的楔形脑袋,缓缓地升起来,并随着音乐摇来摆去,宛如水草在河水中摇摆。然而,孩子们看到斑斑点点的蛇头和迅速吐进吐出的蛇信子时,倒是有些害怕;等艺人从沙中变出一株小小的橘子树,进而开出漂亮的白花、结出成簇的果实时,孩子们就高兴多了;当艺人拿起拉斯—托雷斯侯爵小女儿的扇子将其变成一只蓝色的小鸟,绕着亭子飞来飞去并鸣啭不停时,孩子们又是兴奋又是惊讶,真是没的说了。随后,皮拉尔圣母大教堂舞蹈班的男孩们表演了庄严肃穆的小步舞曲,这也同样引人入胜。这种美妙的舞蹈仪式,每年五月为纪念圣母都会在那座高高的圣母祭坛前上演,公主却从未见过;事实上,自从有个疯子牧师(许多人都推测他被收买了),企图诱使阿斯图里亚斯王子吃下有毒的圣饼之后,西班牙的王室成员再也没有踏入过萨拉戈萨大教堂。因而,公主先前只是道听途说地知道了所谓的"圣母之舞",现在观看才知道这支舞确实很精彩。男孩们身着老式的白色天鹅绒宫廷礼服,头戴奇特的三角帽,帽檐镶着银边,帽顶插着大簇的鸵鸟羽毛。他们在阳光下翩翩起舞,那身耀眼的白色服饰在黝黑脸庞和乌黑长发的衬托下更加炫目。他们穿梭于错综的队形,繁复的舞步尽显庄重尊严,徐缓的手势和洒脱的鞠躬极尽精致优雅,大伙个个看得如痴如醉。孩子们表演结束时,脱下插有羽毛的大帽子向小公主致敬。她十分恭谨地答谢,并许诺要向皮拉尔圣母的神龛敬献一支大蜡烛,以报答圣母恩赐给她的欢乐。

然后,一群英俊的埃及人——那个年代把吉卜赛人称为埃及人——走入场中,盘腿席地而坐,围成了一圈,便开始轻轻地弹起齐特琴,伴着琴调轻舞腰身并尽可能低声地哼唱,轻柔如梦。他们看到堂·佩德罗时却面露愠色,有几个看上去甚是恐惧,因为在几个星期前佩德罗下令,把他们部落中的两个人绞死在了塞维尔的街市上,罪名是行巫术。然而,漂亮可人的小公主把他们迷住了,当时公主往后一仰,蓝色的大眼睛偷偷地从扇子上方望过来,他们便确信像公主这般可爱的人儿绝不会残忍地对待任何人。于是,他们继续轻柔地弹奏,又长又尖的指甲不停地轻触琴弦,头开始点起来,仿佛正要入睡似的。突然,爆出一声尖叫,孩子们都吓了一跳,佩德罗一把握住自个儿匕首的玛瑙柄,只见表演者一跃而起,绕着场地疯狂地转起圈来,一边敲打手鼓,一边使用他们那种喉音粗沉的古怪语言唱起了狂放的情歌。然后,随着另一声信号他们又都扑倒在地,静静地躺在那儿,场内顿时一片沉寂,唯余单调的齐特琴声。如此这般重复几次之后,他们就消失了一会儿,待回来时则用铁链牵着一头皮毛蓬乱的棕熊,肩上还扛着几只北非的巴巴利猴子。棕熊颇有气势地倒立起来,瘦骨伶仃的猴子则与两个似乎是其主人的吉卜赛男孩耍起了各种逗乐的把戏,拿着小剑厮杀,又用火枪射击,还完成了一整套正规军的操练,就像国王的卫队那样。说实话,吉卜赛人表演得非常成功。

但是,整个上午的娱乐活动中最有趣的无疑要数小矮人跳舞了。小矮人跌跌撞撞地冲上场,摇摇摆摆地迈着罗圈腿,左右晃荡着超大的畸形头,孩子们高兴得大喊大叫起来。小公主也哈哈大笑起来,弄得那位侍从女总管不得不提醒她:西班牙有过不少国王千金在与其出身相当的人面前哭泣的先例,却从来没见过哪位王室公主在比其出身要低的人面前乐成这等模样。然而,小矮人委实让人忍俊不禁,即使是一向以对恐怖事物深有雅癖而著称的西班牙宫廷,如此奇异的这么一个小怪物也是前所未见。小矮人自己嘛,也是首次出场，毕竟前一天才被发现。那时，两名贵族正在城镇周边的一大片栓皮栎林中打猎，来到一个偏僻的角落时就看见了正在林中狂奔的小矮人，于是就把他带进宫来，作为献给小公主的一份惊喜。小矮人的父亲是个穷得可怜的烧炭翁，巴不得打发掉这么个丑不拉几又不中用的孩子。也许小矮人身上最逗人的地方就是他对自个儿的奇形怪相一无所知。的确，他看起来非常开心，整个人显得精神饱满。孩子们大笑时，他也跟着大笑起来，笑得跟他们一样无拘无束，一样欢天喜地。每支舞曲行将结束之际他都会向每一个孩子鞠一个最滑稽的躬，微笑着向他们逐一点头，仿佛他自个儿真的就是他们中的一员呢，并非大自然出于调侃而造出来供人耍笑的小怪物。至于公主么，小矮人完全被她迷住了。小矮人双眼一直盯着她，仿佛专为她一个人跳舞似的。表演行将结束时，公主想起自己见过宫中贵妇是如何把一束束花抛向加法奈里的——他是教皇从自己的礼拜堂选派到马德里的意大利著名男高音，希望他甜美的歌喉会治好国王的忧伤；想到这儿她便从头上取下那朵美丽的白玫瑰，连同自己最甜美的微笑一起抛向场中的小矮人，半是为了打趣，半是为了戏弄那个侍从女总管。小矮人很把这当回事，一手拿起花贴上粗糙的嘴唇，另一只手按在心上，单膝朝着公主跪下；他满脸堆笑，嘴巴咧到了耳根，明亮的小眼睛射出喜悦的光芒。

这下彻底地击垮了公主的矜持。她在小矮人跑出场好长一段时间，都一直乐呵呵地笑个不停，并向叔叔表示这样的舞蹈应该马上再演一遍。然而，侍从女总管声称日头正紧，认为公主殿下最好还是立即回宫，那里已经为她准备了一场盛宴，包括一个真正的生日蛋糕，上面布满了用彩色砂糖撒成公主姓名的首字母，一杆可爱的银色小旗在顶部飘舞。于是，公主庄严地站起来，吩咐小矮人要在她午休后再来献舞，继而向年少的努瓦伯爵道谢，感谢他的盛情款待，然后起驾回宫，孩子们则按来时的顺序尾随而出。

小矮人听说自个儿要去公主面前再次献舞，而且还是公主亲自下令的，他真是得意万分。他一头冲进花园，欣喜若狂地对着白玫瑰亲个不停，并乐不可支地做出各种极其粗俗且笨拙的举动。

看到小矮人竟敢擅闯自己的美丽家园，花儿们已是义愤填膺，再看到他在走道上来回蹦跶，还十分可笑地把胳膊举过头顶摆来摆去，它们再也按捺不住胸中的怒火。

"他实在是太丑了，丑得绝不能让他在我们所待的任何地方玩耍。"郁金香大声喊道。

"他应该喝些罂粟汁，然后睡上一千年才好。"红色的大百合花说道，一朵朵气得怒火万丈。

"他就是个十足的恐怖鬼！"仙人掌尖叫起来，"不是吗，他七歪八扭、又矮又肥，头大得与腿完全不相称。说实话，见着他我浑身就像针刺般不舒服，要是他走近我，我就拿刺扎他。"

"还有，他还拿着我最美的一朵花，"白玫瑰树惊呼道，"那朵花可是我今天早上亲手送给公主作为生日礼物的，而他竟从公主那儿偷走了。"说着她拼命地大叫起来："小偷，小偷，小偷！"

就连那几株红天竺葵吧，素来性子随和，而且大伙都知道他们家有一大帮子穷亲戚。可是，他们在看见小矮人时也都厌恶地蜷起了身子。紫罗兰们温和地插了一句，小矮人肯定是普通得要命，但他自个儿也无可奈何。对此，天竺葵理直气壮地群起反驳，那就是他最大的缺陷了，而且没有理由因为一个人无可救药就该去恭维他。确实，一些紫罗兰自个儿也觉得，小矮人的丑陋大都是有意矫揉造作出来的，要是他流露出些许悲伤，至少是些许忧思，而不是这么兴冲冲地上蹿下跳，并搞出这么荒诞不经、怪里怪气的姿态来，那就显得品位高多了。

至于老日晷么，他可是一位极有来头的人物，曾经只向查理五世陛下本人报告每天的时间，就连他见到小矮人的模样时也惊呆了，带影子的长手指僵在那儿，差不多忘了要去标记整整两分钟的时间。他还情不自禁地对正在栏杆上晒太阳的乳白色大孔雀说，谁都知道国王的孩子会是国王，烧炭工的孩子会是烧炭工，假装否认实是荒谬之举。孔雀完全同意这种说法，还真的尖叫起来："当然，当然。"声音既响亮又刺耳，惊得金鱼纷纷从清凉的喷泉池里探出水面，向巨雕人身鱼尾的海神特里同们打听到底发生了什么事情。

然而，不知怎的鸟儿们却喜欢小矮人。过去它们经常在森林里看到小矮人，他像精灵一般追着风中飞旋的树叶舞来舞去，或是蜷缩在某棵老橡树的树洞里把坚果分享给松鼠。鸟儿们不嫌弃他长得丑陋，一点儿也不嫌弃。不是吗，毕竟连夜莺自己长得也没那么耐看，尽管她夜间在橘子林里唱歌唱得那么甜美，甚至月亮有时都会俯下身来聆听。再说，小矮人对它们也很好。有那么一个可怕的寒冬，树上没有果子，地面冻得像铁块似的，狼群也饿得下山到城门口觅食物，小矮人并没有忘记过鸟儿们，相反总会从他那一小块黑面包中掰点儿分给它们，不管他用的早餐有多么差，有多么少，都会分给它们。

于是鸟儿们围着小矮人飞呀飞，飞过他的身边时就用双翅蹭蹭他的脸颊。它们叽叽喳喳地嚷着笑着，小矮人可高兴啦，忍不住拿出那朵美丽的白玫瑰展示给它们看，并告诉它们这是公主亲手送给他的，因为公主爱上了他。

小矮人说的话，鸟儿们一句也听不懂。不过，听不懂也不要紧，因为它们把头歪到一边，显得很聪明的样子，这就跟听懂什么差不多了，而且比听懂要容易得多。

蜥蜴们也对小矮人颇有好感。当小矮人跑来跑去，跑累了就趴在草地上休息的时候,他们就爬到他身上玩啊闹啊,想尽一切好办法去逗他开心。"不是每个人都能长得像我们蜥蜴一样美的,"他们嚷道,"那种要求未免太高了。还有啊,这么说听上去荒诞不经,但他毕竟真的没有那么丑,当然,前提是大家闭上眼睛,不看他就行了。"蜥蜴们天生就有极高的哲学天赋,当无事可做或遇上雨天出不了门时,就经常坐在一起思考,一个小时接着一个小时地连续思考。

然而,蜥蜴们和鸟儿们的举动都让花儿们大为恼火。"这只是说明,"它们说,"不消停地到处跑啊飞啊,是多么败坏风气!有教养的人,总会和我们一样规规矩矩地待在一个地方。从未有人见过我们在走道上来回蹦跶,或是疯疯癫癫地冲过草丛追着蜻蜓跑。当我们确实想换一换空气的时候,我们就让人请来园丁,再由他把我们送到另一个花圃去。这样有尊严,也就应该这样。但是鸟儿和蜥蜴压根儿不知道什么叫安宁,事实上鸟儿甚至连个固定的住地都没有。他们不过是流浪汉罢了,就像吉卜赛人一样,所以真该拿对待流浪汉的态度来对付它们。"于是,花儿们鼻孔朝天,趾高气扬。过了一会儿,看到小矮人手忙脚乱地从草地上蹿起来,穿过露台,朝王宫奔去,它们可高兴极啦。

"他真应该被关在室内,终老一生,"花儿们说道,"瞧瞧他那驼背,还有那弯曲的腿。"说完它们就嗤嗤地笑了起来。

然而小矮人对此一无所知。他可喜欢小鸟和蜥蜴了,觉得花儿在整个世界上最为美好,当然喽,公主得除外。但是她却把美丽的白玫瑰送给了他,她爱他,这就大不一样了。他多么希望自个儿能够挽着她一同回去啊!她一定会将右手边让给他坐,对着他微笑;他也一刻都不会离开她的身边,还会让她做自个儿的玩伴,教给她各式各样的好玩把戏。因为啊,他虽然从未进过王宫,却知道了许许多多了不起的事。他会用灯芯草编出小小的笼子,好把蚱蜢关在里面唱歌；还会用细长有节的竹子做成排箫，吹起来就连牧神潘也爱听。他听得懂每种鸟的叫声，可以把椋鸟从树梢上唤下来，也可以把苍鹭从湖中叫上来。他识得每一种动物的踪迹，能顺着纤小的脚印寻觅野兔，也能循着踩过的落叶追踪野猪。所有野外之舞他都能跳，秋日红裳之狂舞，麦田蓝色凉鞋之轻舞，冬季白雪花环之舞，春天果园鲜花之舞。他知道斑鸠在哪里筑巢，有一次捕鸟人捕走了雏鸟的爸爸和妈妈，他就亲手把一窝雏鸟养大，还找了棵修去顶枝的榆树，在树缝里为他们盖了一间小小的鸟巢。他们一直很温顺，每天早上都会从他的掌心吃食。公主肯定会喜欢它们，也会喜欢那些在深深的蕨菜丛中蹦蹦跳跳的兔子，那些长着坚硬羽毛的黑嘴松鸦，那些能把自个儿蜷缩成刺球的刺猬，还有聪明的大乌龟，慢吞吞地爬来爬去，摇头晃脑地啃着嫩叶。没错，公主一定要来森林，和他一起玩喽。他会把自个儿的小床让给公主，会在窗外守候到天亮，不让野牛伤着她，也不让骨瘦如柴的豺狼溜进小屋。天亮时分，他会轻轻敲击百叶窗唤醒她，然后他们一块儿出去跳舞，一跳就是一整天。说实话，森林里一点儿也不寂寞。有时，一个主教骑着白骡子经过，边走边读一本有彩图的书。有时，头戴天鹅绒绿帽、身着鹿皮短上衣的驯鹰人路过，腕上擎着蒙有头罩的猎鹰。葡萄成熟酿酒时节就会迎来踩榨葡萄的人，他们手脚都被染成紫的了，戴着鲜亮常春藤编织的头冠，还拿着正滴着葡萄酒的皮囊；烧炭工晚上坐在大火盆的周围，一边看着干燥的原木在火中慢慢地烧成炭，一边把板栗埋进余烬中烘烤，此时有些盗贼从藏身的山洞里蹿出来，和他们一起说笑逗乐。还有一次，小矮人看见一支华丽的队伍蜿蜒地走向托莱多城，漫漫长路，尘土飞扬。走在队伍前面的是一些僧侣们，一边唱着悦耳的歌，一边举着鲜艳的旗幡和黄金十字架，然后走上来的是身着银色盔甲、手拿火绳枪和长矛的士兵，其中还有三个赤脚行走的男人，身上穿的奇怪黄袍画满了奇妙的图案，手里则拿着点燃的蜡烛。当然，森林里还有许许多多的东西都值得一看，公主玩累了，小矮人就会为她找一块覆满青苔的柔软坡地，或者就把她抱在怀里，因为他力气很大，尽管他知道自个儿个头不高。他会用泻根果给公主串一条红项链，就跟她佩戴在裙子上的那些白色浆果一样漂亮；公主戴厌了就可一扔了事。小矮人还会给她找来别的什么。他会给她找来橡果壳和带着露珠的银莲花，还有小小的萤火虫，放在她那淡淡的金发上，会像星星那样忽闪忽闪的。

　　可是公主在哪里呢？小矮人问那朵白玫瑰，白玫瑰默而不答。整个王宫殿似乎都睡着了，就连没有关上百叶窗的地方，也都拉下了厚厚的窗帘，遮住了窗户，也就挡住了炽烈的阳光。他四处转悠，寻找可以进去的地方，终于瞅见一扇小小的便门正敞开着。他溜了进去，发现自己来到一座华丽的大厅，依他自个儿的感觉，恐怕比整座森林还要华丽得多；厅内处处金光闪闪，就连地面都是用五颜六色的大石块铺成的，一块块拼接成了一种几何图案。然而小公主并不在那儿，只有一些美妙的白色雕像从绿玉基座上俯视着他，双眼尽显忧伤和茫然，唇边泛起诡异的微笑。

　　在大厅的尽头悬挂着一幅绣得富丽堂皇的黑天鹅绒帷幔，上面绣着太阳和繁星，绣的也是国王最喜爱的颜色。兴许公主就藏在那后面？无论如何，他都要去看个究竟。

　　于是，小矮人蹑手蹑脚地潜了过去，把帷幔拉到一边。没人；

后面只不过是另一个房间罢了，虽然在他眼里要比他刚才离开的那个还要漂亮。墙壁上挂着一幅针织绿壁毯，描绘的是多人狩猎的场景，那是一些欧洲佛兰德艺术家花了七年多时间才完成的作品。这房间一度是人称"傻子胡安"的寝室。这个疯子国王甚是痴迷于狩猎，在精神错乱时常常试图跨上画中那些扬起前蹄的高头大马，扳倒大猎犬正在围攻的成年牝鹿，吹响自个儿的行猎号角，拔剑去刺那头飞奔中的白鹿。如今这个房间成了议事厅，中央的桌子上面摆着各位大臣的红色文件夹，上面印有象征西班牙的金郁金香徽记，还有哈布斯堡王室的纹章和徽标。

小矮人惊奇地四下里张望，心里有些怕了，不敢再往前走。画中那些奇怪的默不作声的骑手，策马飞快地驰过长长的林中空地却无任何声响，在他看来就像先前听烧炭工说的那些可怕的幽灵——善于捉人的怪物康普拉乔，只在夜间行猎，要是遇上人，就会先把人变成牝鹿，然后追杀。可是他想起了漂亮可人的公主，便鼓起了勇气。他想趁公主身边没人时找到她，好向她表白。兴许她就在再往前的那个房间里呢。

他从柔软的摩尔地毯上跑过去，打开了前面的门。没人！她也不在这儿呢。眼前的房间空无一人。

这是一间御用会客厅，用于接待外国使臣，要是国王同意亲自接见他们的话，只是后来不常用了。许多年以前，就是在这一间房内，英国的使臣曾商讨安排他们女王的婚事，那时英国女王还是属于欧洲天主教的君主之一，嫁的是神圣罗马帝国皇帝的长子。房内挂着由西班牙科尔多瓦皮革做成的烫金帷幔，黑白相间的天花板上悬着一盏沉重的镀金枝形吊灯，金枝架上可插三百支蜡烛。房内还有用金布做成的一个大华盖，华盖上面饰有由一粒粒小珍珠连缀而成的狮子和卡斯蒂利亚的塔楼图案，华盖下方立着的正是御座本身，座上盖着一块华贵的黑色天鹅绒罩，上面点缀着朵朵银质郁金香，并精巧地搭配着银和珍珠穗子。御座往下的第二级台阶上摆着公主的跪凳,凳子的软垫由银线织布包着;再往下,已处于华盖能够覆盖的范围之外,放着教皇特使帕帕尔·努西奥的椅子。只有教皇特使才有资格在任何公共仪式上当着国王的面坐着,他那缠绕着猩红色帽缨的枢机主教帽就放在椅子前方的紫色小凳上。御座对面的墙上挂着一幅真人大小的查理五世画像,身着猎装,身边有一头大獒犬;另一面墙的中心位置则挂着一幅腓力二世的画像,画上的腓力二世正在接受尼德兰诸省的拜谒。两扇窗户之间立着一只黑色的乌木陈列柜,柜中镶着一块块象牙做成的嵌板,板上雕刻着德国画家霍尔拜因《死亡之舞》组画中的人物——有人说,正是由那位著名大师亲手雕刻而成。

然而,小矮人才不管这些奇珍异宝呢。即便用华盖上的所有珍珠,也换不走他的白玫瑰;就是用御座本身,也换不得他那白玫瑰的一片花瓣儿。他想要的,就是赶在公主去长亭之前见她一面,然后待自己跳完舞就邀请公主一起走。王宫里面空气既沉又闷,但森林中风儿自由往来,阳光则浮动着扭转黄金手掌,拨开瑟瑟轻颤的叶片。林中也有花,或许没有御花园里的花那么艳丽,但气味倒是更加芬芳。林中有早春开遍的风信子,浪花般地连成一片紫,淹没了清幽凉爽的峡谷和绿草茵茵的山丘;还有黄色的报春花簇拥在多节瘤的橡树根周围;还有亮艳的白屈菜、蓝色的婆婆纳、淡紫色和金黄色的鸢尾花。榛树枝头挂着一条条褐黄色的柔荑花,吊钟花扛着一串串蜜蜂经常光顾的斑驳花朵,不胜重负地低着头。栗树花开,犹如亮白的繁星,聚集成一座座塔尖;山楂花开宛如苍白的美人,簇拥成一轮轮明月。没错,公主肯定会愿意,只要能找到她就行!公主会跟他一块儿去美丽的森林,他会整天地跳舞,逗她开心。想到这儿,一抹笑意点亮了他的双眼,于是他就走进了下一个房间。

所有房间之中,就数这间最亮、最美了。四周的墙壁上蒙着粉红色的意大利卢卡花缎，上面织有鸟的图案，并星星点点地穿插着精致的银花；家具都是用纯银打制的，上面镶着鲜艳的花环和纵身前跃的爱神丘比特像；两个大壁炉前立着大幅屏风，上面绣着鹦鹉和孔雀；地板由海绿色的彩纹玛瑙铺成，似乎向远方一直延伸到尽头。房内也不是只有他一个人！在门口的暗影下，他还看到在房间最远的那一端有个小小的人影也正在看着他。他心里咯噔了一下，唇间迸发出一声欢呼，于是他走上前，从暗处来到有阳光的亮处。他这般走动时，那个人影也上前走到了亮处，这下他看得清清楚楚了。

公主啊！不，那是个怪物，是他平生所见过的最怪的怪物。怪物不像其他人长得有模有样，而是驼背，扭胳膊曲腿，畸形大头往下耷拉着，黑色长发乱如鬃鬣。小矮人皱起眉头，怪物也皱起眉头。他笑了，它也跟着他笑了，并把两手放到腰间，就像他自个儿叉腰一样。他挖苦地对它鞠了一躬，它也对他俯身回礼。他朝它走过去，它也朝他迎上来，模仿着他的每一步，并在他站住时自个儿也跟着站住。他乐得大喊大叫，跑上前去，伸出一只手，怪物也伸出一只手碰到了他的手，冷得像冰一样。他害怕起来，赶紧把手挪往一旁，怪物的那只手也迅速地跟着挪往一边。他试图往前压上去，可是有什么又平又硬的东西挡住了他。怪物的脸现在都快凑上他自个儿的脸了，似乎充满了恐惧。他拂了拂挡住眼睛的乱发，它跟着模仿他。他向它打去，它也一下对一下地还击。他冲它做出深恶痛绝的表情，它也对他面露极其厌恶的神态。他往后退了回来，它也往后撤了回去。

它是什么呢？小矮人想了一会儿，然后四下张望，看了看房内的其他地方。真是怪了，房内所有东西在这面清水一般的无形墙壁里都有与之一模一样的对应物。没错，一幅画对着殊无二致的一幅画，卧榻对着卧榻。躺在门边壁龛里酣睡的牧神法翁，也有个孪生兄弟在熟睡；立在阳光里的美神维纳斯银像伸出双臂，正朝着另一个和她同样可爱的维纳斯。

是仙女艾柯来了吗？他有一次在山谷里向她大声呼喊，她就一字不落地重复着回应他。她能像模仿嘴巴说出的声音那样，模仿眼睛看见的影像吗？她能创造出一个就像真实世界一样的模仿世界吗？事物的影子能有色彩和生命，能动来动去吗？那会不会是——

小矮人猛一激灵，从胸口掏出那朵美丽的白玫瑰，转身吻了起来。那怪物也掏出一朵白玫瑰，一瓣瓣跟他的一模一样！怪物也吻起了玫瑰，吻得一模一样，然后把它压在心口，姿势令人可怕。

想明白真相时，小矮人绝望地狂叫一声，倒在地上呜咽起来。原来是他，自个儿头大曲腿，弓腰驼背，面目狰狞，奇形怪状。他就是那个怪物，所有孩子嘲笑的也正是他；那位他原以为爱他的小公主——她也只是在嘲笑他的丑态，拿他的弯胳膊曲腿寻开心罢了。他们为什么要把他带出森林呢？林中就没有镜子告诉他，他是多么让人厌恶。为什么他的父亲不杀了他，而是卖了他让他蒙着受辱呢？热泪顺着他的脸颊倾泻而下，他把那朵白玫瑰扯得粉碎。躺倒在地的那个怪物也把花扯碎，把苍白的花瓣胡乱撒向空中。它翻身屈膝趴在地上，他抬头看它时，它也正望着他，满脸的痛苦。他爬起来，生怕再看见它，还用双手捂住了双眼。他爬呀爬，就像一只受了伤的动物，爬到阴暗处，然后就躺在那儿呻吟起来。

就在这时，小公主带着玩伴从开着的落地窗进来了。大伙儿看到那个丑陋的小矮人躺在地上双手握拳捶着地板，样子无比古怪、无比夸张，乐得哈哈大笑起来。他们围着它站成一圈，仔细端详起来。

"他跳的舞有趣儿，"公主说，"可他演的戏更有趣儿。当然喽，没有木偶那么自然，但是说真的，简直就跟木偶一样棒。"她抡起大扇，击掌叫好。

可是小矮人始终没有抬头看，抽泣声越来越小，越来越弱。突然间，他莫名其妙地倒抽了一口气，抱紧了自个儿的身子。随后，他倒了下去，一动不动地躺着。

"太妙了，"公主顿了一下，说道，"可现在你得给我跳舞。"

"没错，"所有的孩子都大声喊起来，"你必须起来跳舞，你聪明得跟巴巴利猴子一样，但比猴子好笑多了。"然而，小矮人没有应声。

小公主跺起脚，大声呼唤她的叔叔。叔叔正带着王宫管家在露台上一边散步，一边看着刚从墨西哥送来的急件，那边最近刚建起了宗教裁判所。"我那有趣的小矮人生闷气啦，"她喊道，"你要把他叫醒，叫他给我跳舞。"

他俩相视一笑，叔叔不紧不慢地走了进来。堂·佩德罗俯下身，用自个儿的刺绣手套掴了他一嘴巴。"你必须跳舞，"他说，"小怪物，你必须得跳舞。西班牙王国和印度群岛的公主需要娱乐啊！"

但是小矮人纹丝不动。

"应该叫掌鞭师傅来，"堂·佩德罗不耐烦地说，然后走回露台。但是王宫管家却神色严峻起来，在小矮人身边跪下，抬手放在他的心窝上。过了一会儿，他耸了耸肩，站起身来，向公主深鞠一躬，说道："我美丽的公主啊，您那有趣的小矮人再也不会跳舞了。真是可惜，他长得那么丑，兴许能博得国王一笑呢。"

"可是为什么他不会再跳舞了呢？"公主一边问，一边大笑起来。

"因为他的心碎了。"王宫管家答道。

公主听完眉头一蹙，再把玫瑰花瓣般娇艳的嘴唇一撇，露出甚是不屑的神情。"从今以后，那些过来陪我玩的人都不能有心。"她嚷了一声，就向外跑到花园里去了。

THE BIRTHDAY OF THE INFANTA

It was the birthday of the Infanta. She was just twelve years of age, and the sun was shining brightly in the gardens of the palace.

Although she was a real Princess and the Infanta of Spain, she had only one birthday every year, just like the children of quite poor people, so it was naturally a matter of great importance to the whole country that she should have a really fine day for the occasion. And a really fine day it certainly was. The tall striped tulips stood straight up upon their stalks, like long rows of soldiers, and looked defiantly across the grass at the roses, and said, "We are quite as splendid as you are now." The purple butterflies fluttered about with gold dust on their wings, visiting each flower in turn; the little lizards crept out of the crevices of the wall, and lay basking in the white glare; and the pomegranates split and cracked with the heat, and showed their bleeding red hearts. Even the pale yellow lemons that hung in such profusion from the mouldering trellis and along the dim arcades seemed to have caught a richer colour from the wonderful sunlight, and the magnolia trees opened their great globe-like blossoms of folded ivory, and filled the air with a sweet heavy perfume.

The little Princess herself walked up and down the terrace with her companions, and played at hide and seek round the stone vases and the old moss-grown statues. On ordinary days she was only allowed to play with children of her own rank, so she had always to play alone, but her birthday was an exception, and the King had given orders that she was to invite any of her young friends whom she liked to come and amuse themselves with her. There was a stately grace about these slim Spanish children as they glided about, the boys with their large-plumed hats and short fluttering cloaks, the girls holding up the trains of their long brocaded gowns, and shielding the sun from their eyes with huge fans of black and silver. But the Infanta was the most graceful of all, and the most tastefully attired, after the somewhat cumbrous fashion of the day. Her robe was of grey satin, the skirt and the wide puffed sleeves heavily embroidered with silver, and the stiff corset studded with rows of fine pearls. Two tiny slippers with big pink rosettes peeped out beneath her dress as she walked. Pink and pearl was her great gauze fan, and in her hair, which like an aureole of faded gold stood out stiffly round her pale little face, she had a beautiful white rose.

From a window in the palace the sad melancholy King watched them. Behind him stood his brother, Don Pedro of Aragon, whom he hated, and his confessor, the Grand Inquisitor of Granada, sat by his side. Sadder even than usual was the King, for as he looked at the Infanta bowing with childish gravity to the assembling counters, or laughing behind her fan at the grim Duchess of Albuquerque who always accompanied her, he thought of the young Queen, her mother, who but a short time before—so it seemed to him—had come from the gay country of France, and had withered away in the sombre splendour of the Spanish court, dying just six months after the birth of her child, and before she had seen the almonds blossom twice in the orchard, or plucked the second year's fruit from the old gnarled fig-tree that stood in the centre of the now grass-grown courtyard. So great had been his love for her that he had not suffered even the grave to hide her from him. She had been embalmed by a Moorish physician, who in return for this service had been granted his life, which for heresy and suspicion of magical practices had been already forfeited, men said, to the Holy Office, and her body was still lying on its tapestried bier in the black marble chapel of the Palace, just as the monks had borne her in on that windy March day nearly twelve years before. Once every month the King, wrapped in a dark cloak and with a muffled lantern in his hand, went in and knelt by her side calling out, "Mi reina! Mi reina!" And sometimes breaking through the formal etiquette that in Spain governs every separate action of life, and sets limits even to the sorrow of a king, he would clutch at the pale jewelled hands in a wild agony of grief, and try to wake by his mad kisses the cold painted face.

Today he seemed to see her again, as he had seen her first at the Castle of Fontainebleau, when he was but fifteen years of age, and she still younger. They had been formally betrothed on that occasion by the Papal Nuncio in the presence of the French King and all the court, and he had returned to the Escurial bearing with him a little ringlet of yellow hair, and the memory of two childish lips bending down to kiss his hand as he stepped into his carriage. Later on had followed the marriage, hastily performed at Burgos, a small town on the frontier between the two countries, and the grand public entry into Madrid with the customary celebration of high mass at the Church of La Atocha, and a more than usually solemn auto-da-fé, in which nearly three hundred heretics, amongst whom were many Englishmen, had been delivered over to the secular arm to be burned.

Certainly he had loved her madly, and to the ruin, many thought, of his country, then at war with England for the possession of the empire of the New World. He had hardly ever permitted her to be out of his sight; for her, he had forgotten, or seemed to have forgotten, all grave affairs of state; and, with that terrible blindness that passion brings upon its servants, he had failed to notice that the elaborate ceremonies by which he sought to please her did but aggravate the strange malady from which she suffered. When she died he was, for a time, like one bereft of reason. Indeed, there is no doubt but that he would have formally abdicated and retired to the great Trappist monastery at Granada, of which he was already titular Prior, had he not been afraid to leave the little Infanta at the mercy of his brother, whose cruelty, even in Spain, was notorious, and who was suspected by many of having caused the Queen's death by means of a pair of poisoned gloves that he had presented to her on the occasion of her visiting his castle in Aragon. Even after the expiration of the three years of public mourning that he had ordained throughout his whole dominions by royal edict, he would never suffer his ministers to speak about any new alliance, and when the Emperor himself sent to him, and offered him the hand of the lovely Archduchess of Bohemia, his niece, in marriage, he bade the ambassadors tell their master that the King of Spain was already wedded to Sorrow, and that though she was but a barren bride he loved her better than Beauty; an answer that cost his crown the rich provinces of the Netherlands, which soon after, at the Emperor's instigation, revolted against him under the leadership of some fanatics of the Reformed Church.

His whole married life, with its fierce, fiery-coloured joys and the terrible agony of its sudden ending, seemed to come back to him today as he watched the Infanta playing on the terrace. She had all the Queen's pretty petulance of manner, the same wilful way of tossing her head, the same proud curved beautiful mouth, the same wonderful smile—vrai sourire de France indeed—as she glanced up now and then at the window, or stretched out her little hand for the stately Spanish gentlemen to kiss. But the shrill laughter of the children grated on his ears, and the bright pitiless sunlight mocked his sorrow, and a dull odour of strange spices, spices such as embalmers use, seemed to taint—or was it fancy—the clear morning air. He buried his face in his hands, and when the Infanta looked up again the curtains had been drawn, and the King had retired.

She made a little moue of disappointment, and shrugged her shoulders. surely he might have stayed with her on her birthday. What did the stupid State affairs matter? Or had he gone to that gloomy chapel, where the candles were always burning, and where she was never allowed to enter? How silly of him, when the sun was shining so brightly, and everybody was so happy! Besides, he would miss the sham bullfight for which the trumpet was already sounding, to say nothing of the puppet show and the other wonderful things. Her uncle and the Grand Inquisitor were much more sensible. They had come out on the terrace, and paid her nice compliments. So she tossed her pretty head, and taking Don Pedro by the hand, she walked slowly down the steps towards a long pavilion of purple silk that had been erected at the end of the garden, the other children following in strict order of precedence, those who had the longest names going first.

A procession of noble boys, fantastically dressed as toreadors, came out to meet her, and the young Count of Tierra-Nueva, a wonderfully handsome lad of about fourteen years of age, uncovering his head with all the grace of a born hidalgo and grandee of Spain, led her solemnly in to a little gilt and ivory chair that was placed on a raised dais above the arena. The children grouped themselves all round, fluttering their big fans and whispering to each other, and Don Pedro and the Grand Inquisitor stood laughing at the entrance. Even the Duchess—the Camerera-Mayor as she was called—a thin, hard-featured woman with a yellow ruff, did not look quite so bad-tempered as usual, and something like a chill smile flitted across her wrinkled face and twitched her thin bloodless lips.

It certainly was a marvellous bullfight, and much nicer, the Infanta thought, than the real bullfight that she had been brought to see at Seville, on the occasion of the visit of the Duke of Parma to her father. Some of the boys pranced about on richly caparisoned hobby horses brandishing long javelins with gay streamers of bright ribands attached to them; others went on foot waving their scarlet cloaks before the bull, and vaulting lightly over the barrier when he charged them; and as for the bull himself, he was just like a live bull, though he was only made of wickerwork and stretched hide, and sometimes insisted on running round the arena on his hind legs, which no live bull ever dreams of doing. He made a splendid fight of it too, and the children got so excited that they stood up upon the benches, and waved their lace handkerchiefs and cried out: Bravo toro! Bravo toro! Just as sensibly as if they had been grownup people. At last, however, after a prolonged combat, during which several of the hobby horses were gored through and through, and, their riders dismounted, the young Count of Tierra-Nueva brought the bull to his knees, and having obtained permission from the Infanta to give the coup de grâce, he plunged his wooden sword into the neck of the animal with such violence that the head came right off, and disclosed the laughing face of little Monsieur de Lorraine, the son of the French Ambassador at Madrid.

The arena was then cleared amidst much applause, and the dead hobby horses dragged solemnly away by two Moorish pages in yellow and black liveries, and after a short interlude, during which a French posture-master performed upon the tightrope, some Italian puppets appeared in the semi-classical tragedy of Sophonisba on the stage of a small theatre that had been built up for the purpose. They acted so well, and their gestures were so extremely natural, that at the close of the play the eyes of the Infanta were quite dim with tears. Indeed some of the children really cried, and had to be comforted with sweetmeats, and the Grand Inquisitor himself was so affected that he could not help saying to Don Pedro that it seemed to him intolerable that things made simply out of wood and coloured wax, and worked mechanically by wires, should be so unhappy and meet with such terrible misfortunes.

An African juggler followed, who brought in a large flat basket covered with a red cloth, and having placed it in the centre of the arena, he took from his turban a curious reed pipe, and blew through it. In a few moments the cloth began to move, and as the pipe grew shriller and shriller two green and gold snakes put out their strange wedge shaped heads and rose slowly up, swaying to and fro with the music as a plant sways in the water. The children, however, were rather frightened at their spotted hoods and quick darting tongues, and were much more pleased when the juggler made a tiny orange tree grow out of the sand and bear pretty white blossoms and clusters of real fruit; and when he took the fan of the little daughter of the Marquess de Las-Torres, and changed it into a blue bird that flew all round the pavilion and sang, their delight and amazement knew no bounds. The solemn minuet, too, performed by the dancing boys from the church of Nuestra Senora Del Pilar, was charming. The Infanta had never before seen this wonderful ceremony which takes place every year at Maytime in front of the high altar of the Virgin, and in her honour; and indeed none of the royal family of Spain had entered the great cathedral of Saragossa since a mad priest, supposed by many to have been in the pay of Elizabeth of England, had tried to administer a poisoned wafer to the Prince of the Asturias. So she had known only by hearsay of "Our Lady's Dance", as it was called, and it certainly was a beautiful sight. The boys wore old-fashioned court dresses of white velvet, and their curious three-cornered hats were fringed with silver and surmounted with huge plumes of ostrich feathers, the dazzling whiteness of their costumes, as they moved about in the sunlight, being still more accentuated by their swarthy faces and long black hair. Everybody was fascinated by the grave dignity with which they moved through the intricate figures of the dance, and by the elaborate grace of their slow gestures, and stately bows, and when they had finished their performance and doffed their great plumed hats to the Infanta, she acknowledged their reverence with much courtesy, and made a vow that she would send a large wax candle to the shrine of Our Lady of Pilar in return for the pleasure that she had given her.

A troop of handsome Egyptians—as the gipsies were termed in those days—then advanced into the arena, and sitting down cross legs, in a circle, began to play softly upon their zithers, moving their bodies to the tune, and humming, almost below their breath, a low dreamy air. When they caught sight of Don Pedro they scowled at him, and some of them looked terrified, for only a few weeks before he had had two of their tribe hanged for sorcery in the marketplace at Seville, but the pretty Infanta charmed them as she leaned back peeping over her fan with her great blue eyes, and they felt sure that one so lovely as she was could never be cruel to anybody. So they played on very gently and just touching the cords of the zithers with their long pointed nails, and their heads began to nod as though they were falling asleep. Suddenly, with a cry so shrill that all the children were startled and Don Pedro's hand clutched at the agate pommel of his dagger, they leapt to their feet and whirled madly round the enclosure beating their tambourines, and chaunting some wild love song in their strange guttural language. Then at another signal they all flung themselves again to the ground and lay there quite still, the dull strumming of the zithers being the only sound that broke the silence. After that they had done this several times, they disappeared for a moment and came back leading a brown shaggy bear by a chain, and carrying on their shoulders some little Barbary apes. The bear stood upon his head with the utmost gravity, and the wizened apes played all kinds of amusing tricks with two gipsy boys who seemed to be their masters, and fought with tiny swords, and fired off guns, and went through a regular soldier's drill just like the King's own bodyguard. In fact the gipsies were a great success.

But the funniest part of the whole morning's entertainment, was undoubtedly the dancing of the little dwarf. When he stumbled into the arena, waddling on his crooked legs and wagging his huge misshapen head from side to side, the children went off into a loud shout of delight, and the Infanta herself laughed so much that the Camerera was obliged to remind her that although there were many precedents in Spain for a King's daughter weeping before her equals, there were none for a Princess of the blood royal making so merry before those who were her inferiors in birth. The dwarf, however, was really quite irresistible, and even at the Spanish court, always noted for its cultivated passion for the horrible, so fantastic a little monster had never been seen. It was his first appearance, too. He had been discovered only the day before, running wild through the forest, by two of the nobles who happened to have been hunting in a remote part of the great cork wood that surrounded the town, and had been carried off by them to the Palace as a surprise for the Infanta; his father, who was a poor charcoal-burner, being but too well pleased to get rid of so ugly and useless a child. Perhaps the most amusing thing about him was his complete unconsciousness of his own grotesque appearance. Indeed he seemed quite happy and full of the highest spirits. When the children laughed, he laughed as freely and as joyously as any of them, and at the close of each dance he made them each the funniest of bows, smiling and nodding at them just as if he was really one of themselves, and not a little misshapen thing that nature, in some humourous mood, had fashioned for others to mock at. As for the Infanta, she absolutely fascinated him. He could not keep his eyes off her, and seemed to dance for her alone, and when at the close of the performance, remembering how she had seen the great ladies of the court throw bouquets to Caffarelli, the famous Italian treble, whom the Pope had sent from his own chapel to Madrid that he might cure the King's melancholy by the sweetness of his voice, she took out of her hair the beautiful white rose, and partly for a jest and partly to tease the Camerera, threw it to him across the arena with her sweetest smile, he took the whole matter quite seriously, and pressing the flower to his rough coarse lips he put his hand upon his heart, and sank on one knee before her, grinning from ear to ear, and with his little bright eyes sparkling with pleasure.

This so upset the gravity of the Infanta that she kept on laughing long after the little dwarf had ran out of the arena, and expressed a desire to her uncle that the dance should be immediately repeated. The Camerera, however, on the plea that the sun was too hot, decided that it would be better that her highness should return without delay to the palace, where a wonderful feast had been already prepared for her, including a real birthday cake with her own initials worked all over it in painted sugar and a lovely silver flag waving from the top. The Infanta accordingly rose up with much dignity, and having given orders that the little dwarf was to dance again for her after the hour of siesta, and conveyed her thanks to the young Count of Tierra-Nueva for his charming reception, she went back to her apartments, the children following in the same order in which they had entered.

Now when the little dwarf heard that he was to dance a second time before the Infanta, and by her own express command, he was so proud that he ran out into the garden, kissing the white rose in an absurd ecstasy of pleasure, and making the most uncouth and clumsy gestures of delight.

The flowers were quite indignant at his daring to intrude into their beautiful home, and when they saw him capering up and down the walks, and waving his arms above his head in such a ridiculous manner, they could not restrain their feelings any longer.

"He is really far too ugly to be allowed to play in any place where we are," cried the tulips.

"He should drink poppy juice, and go to sleep for a thousand years," said the great scarlet lilies, and they grew quite hot and angry.

"He is a perfect horror!" screamed the cactus. "Why, he is twisted and stumpy, and his head is completely out of proportion with his legs. Really he makes me feel prickly all over, and if he comes near me I will sting him with my thorns."

"And he has actually got one of my best blooms," exclaimed the white rose tree. "I gave it to the Infanta this morning myself, as a birthday present, and he has stolen it from her." And she called out: "Thief, thief, thief!" at the top of her voice.

Even the red geraniums, who did not usually give themselves airs, and were known to have a great many poor relations themselves, curled up in disgust when they saw him, and when the violets meekly remarked that though he was certainly extremely plain, still he could not help it, they retorted with a good deal of justice that that was his chief defect, and that there was no reason why one should admire a person because he was incurable; and, indeed, some of the violets themselves felt that the ugliness of the little dwarf was almost ostentatious, and that he would have shown much better taste if he had looked sad, or at least pensive, instead of jumping about merrily, and throwing himself into such grotesque and silly attitudes.

As for the old sundial, who was an extremely remarkable individual, and had once told the time of day to no less a person than the Emperor Charles V. himself, he was so taken aback by the little dwarf's appearance, that he almost forgot to mark two whole minutes with his long shadowy finger, and could not help saying to the great milk white peacock, who was sunning herself on the balustrade, that every one knew that the children of kings were kings, and that the children of charcoal-burners were charcoal-burners, and that it was absurd to pretend that it wasn't so; a statement with which the peacock entirely agreed, and indeed screamed out, "Certainly, certainly," in such a loud, harsh voice, that the goldfish who lived in the basin of the cool splashing fountain put their heads out of the water, and asked the huge stone Tritons what on earth was the matter.

But somehow the birds liked him. They had seen him often in the forest, dancing about like an elf after the eddying leaves, or crouched up in the hollow of some old oak tree, sharing his nuts with the squirrels. They did not mind his being ugly, a bit. Why, even the nightingale herself, who sang so sweetly in the orange groves at night that sometimes the moon leaned down to listen, was not much to look at after all; and, besides, he had been kind to them, and during that terribly bitter winter, when there were no berries on the trees, and the ground was as hard as iron, and the wolves had come down to the very gates of the city to look for food, he had never once forgotten them, but had always given them crumbs out of his little hunch of black bread, and divided with them whatever poor breakfast he had.

So they flew round and round him, just touching his cheek with their wings as they passed, and chattered to each other, and the little dwarf was so pleased that he could not help showing them the beautiful white rose, and telling them that the Infanta herself had given it to him because she loved him.

They did not understand a single word of what he was saying, but that made no matter, for they put their heads on one side, and looked wise, which is quite as good as understanding a thing, and very much easier.

The lizards also took an immense fancy to him, and when he grew tired of running about and flung himself down on the grass to rest, they played and romped all over him, and tried to amuse him in the best way they could. "Every one cannot be as beautiful as a lizard," they cried. "That would be too much to expect. And, though it sounds absurd to say so, he is really not so ugly after all, provided, of course, that one shuts one's eyes, and does not look at him." The lizards were extremely philosophical by nature, and often sat thinking for hours and hours together, when there was nothing else to do, or when the weather was too rainy for them to go out.

The flowers, however, were excessively annoyed at their behaviour, and at the behaviour of the birds. "It only shows," they said. "What a vulgarising effect this incessant rushing and flying about has. Well-bred people always stay exactly in the same place, as we do. No one ever saw us hopping up and down the walks, or galloping madly through the grass after dragonflies. When we do want change of air, we send for the gardener, and he carries us to another bed. This is dignified, and as it should be. But birds and lizards have no sense of repose, and indeed birds have not even a permanent address. They are mere vagrants like the gipsies, and should be treated in exactly the same manner." So they put their noses in the air, and looked very haughty, and were quite delighted when after some time they saw the little dwarf scramble up from the grass, and make his way across the terrace to the palace.

"He should certainly be kept indoors for the rest of his natural life," they said. "Look at his hunched back, and his crooked legs," and they began to titter.

But the little dwarf knew nothing of all this. He liked the birds and the lizards immensely, and thought that the flowers were the most marvellous things in the whole world, except of course the Infanta, but then she had given him the beautiful white rose, and she loved him, and that made a great difference. How he wished that he had gone back with her! She would have put him on her right hand, and smiled at him, and he would have never left her side, but would have made her his playmate, and taught her all kinds of delightful tricks. For though he had never been in a palace before, he knew a great many wonderful things. He could make little cages out of rushes for the grasshoppers to sing in, and fashion the long jointed bamboo into the pipe that Pan loves to hear. He knew the cry of every bird, and could call the starlings from the treetop, or the heron from the mere. He knew the trail of every animal, and could track the hare by its delicate footprints, and the boar by the trampled leaves. All the wild-dances he knew, the mad dance in red raiment with the autumn, the light dance in blue sandals over the corn, the dance with white snow wreaths in winter, and the blossom dance through the orchards in spring. He knew where the wood pigeons built their nests, and once when a fowler had snared the parent birds, he had brought up the young ones himself, and had built a little dovecot for them in the cleft of a pollard elm. They were quite tame, and used to feed out of his hands every morning. She would like them, and the rabbits that scurried about in the long fern, and the jays with their steely feathers and black bills, and the hedgehogs that could curl themselves up into prickly balls, and the great wise tortoises that crawled slowly about, shaking their heads and nibbling at the young leaves. Yes, she must certainly come to the forest and play with him. He would give her his own little bed, and would watch outside the window till dawn, to see that the wild horned cattle did not harm her, nor the gaunt wolves creep too near the hut. And at dawn he would tap at the shutters and wake her, and they would go out and dance together all the day long. It was really not a bit lonely in the forest. Sometimes a Bishop rode through on his white mule, reading out of a painted book. Sometimes in their green velvet caps, and their jerkins of tanned deerskin, the falconers passed by, with hooded hawks on their wrists. At vintage time came the grape treaders, with purple hands and feet, wreathed with glossy ivy and carrying dripping skins of wine; and the charcoal-burners sat round their huge braziers at night, watching the dry logs charring slowly in the fire, and roasting chestnuts in the ashes, and the robbers came out of their caves and made merry with them. Once, too, he had seen a beautiful procession winding up the long dusty road to Toledo. The monks went in front singing sweetly, and carrying bright banners and crosses of gold, and then, in silver armour, with matchlocks and pikes, came the soldiers, and in their midst walked three barefooted men, in strange yellow dresses painted all over with wonderful figures, and carrying lighted candles in their hands. Certainly there was a great deal to look at in the forest, and when she was tired he would find a soft bank of moss for her, or carry her in his arms, for he was very strong, though he knew that he was not tall. He would make her a necklace of red bryony berries, that would be quite as pretty as the white berries that she wore on her dress, and when she was tired of them, she could throw them away, and he would find her others. He would bring her acorn-cups and dew drenched anemones, and tiny glow worms to be stars in the pale gold of her hair.

But where was she? He asked the white rose, and it made him no answer. The whole palace seemed asleep, and even where the shutters had not been closed, heavy curtains had been drawn across the windows to keep out the glare. He wandered all round looking for some place through which he might gain an entrance, and at last he caught sight of a little private door that was lying open. He slipped through, and found himself in a splendid hall, far more splendid, he feared, than the forest, there was so much more gilding everywhere, and even the floor was made of great coloured stones, fitted together into a sort of geometrical pattern. But the little Infanta was not there, only some wonderful white statues that looked down on him from their jasper pedestals, with sad blank eyes and strangely smiling lips.

At the end of the hall hung a richly embroidered curtain of black velvet, powdered with suns and stars, the King's favourite devices, and broidered on the colour he loved best. Perhaps she was hiding behind that? He would try at any rate.

So he stole quietly across, and drew it aside. No, there was only another room, though a prettier room, he thought, than the one he had just left. The walls were hung with a many figured green arras of needle-wrought tapestry representing a hunt, the work of some Flemish artists who had spent more than seven years in its composition. It had once been the chamber of Jean le Fou, as he was called, that mad King who was so enamoured of the chase, that he had often tried in his delirium to mount the huge rearing horses, and to drag down the stag on which the great hounds were leaping, sounding his hunting horn, and stabbing with his dagger at the pale flying deer. It was now used as the council room, and on the centre table were lying the red portfolios of the ministers, stamped with the gold tulips of Spain, and with the arms and emblems of the house of Hapsburg.

The little dwarf looked in wonder all round him, and was half afraid to go on. The strange silent horsemen that galloped so swiftly through the long glades without making any noise, seemed to him like those terrible phantoms of whom he had heard the charcoal-burners speaking—the Comprachos, who hunt only at night, and if they meet a man, turn him into a hind, and chase him. But he thought of the pretty Infanta, and took courage. He wanted to find her alone, and to tell her that he too loved her. Perhaps she was in the room beyond.

He ran across the soft Moorish carpets, and opened the door. No! She was not here either. The room was quite empty.

It was a throne room, used for the reception of foreign ambassadors, when the King, which of late had not been often, consented to give them a personal audience; the same room in which, many years before, envoys had appeared from England to make arrangements for the marriage of their Queen, then one of the Catholic sovereigns of Europe, with the Emperor's eldest son. The hangings were of gilt Cordovan leather, and a heavy gilt chandelier with branches for three hundred wax lights hung down from the black and white ceiling. Underneath a great canopy of gold cloth, on which the lions and towers of Castile were broidered in seed pearls, stood the throne itself, covered with a rich pall of black velvet studded with silver tulips and elaborately fringed with silver and pearls. On the second step of the throne was placed the kneeling-stool of the Infanta, with its cushion of cloth of silver tissue, and below that again, and beyond the limit of the canopy, stood the chair for the Papal Nuncio, who alone had the right to be seated in the King's presence on the occasion of any public ceremonial, and whose Cardinal's hat, with its tangled scarlet tassels, lay on a purple tabouret in front. On the wall, facing the throne, hung a life-sized portrait of Charles V. in hunting dress, with a great mastiff by his side, and a picture of Philip II. receiving the homage of the Netherlands occupied the centre of the other wall. Between the windows stood a black ebony cabinet, inlaid with plates of ivory, on which the figures from Holbein's Dance of Death had been graved—by the hand, some said, of that famous master himself.

But the little dwarf cared nothing for all this magnificence. He would not have given his rose for all the pearls on the canopy, nor one white petal of his rose for the throne itself. What he wanted was to see the Infanta before she went down to the pavilion, and to ask her to come away with him when he had finished his dance. Here, in the palace, the air was close and heavy, but in the forest the wind blew free, and the sunlight with wandering hands of gold moved the tremulous leaves aside. There were flowers, too, in the forest, not so splendid, perhaps, as the flowers in the garden, but more sweetly scented for all that; hyacinths in early spring that flooded with waving purple the cool glens, and grassy knolls; yellow primroses that nestled in little clumps round the gnarled roots of the oak trees; bright celandine, and blue speedwell, and irises lilac and gold. There were grey catkins on the hazels, and the foxgloves drooped with the weight of their dappled bee-haunted cells. The chestnut had its spires of white stars, and the hawthorn its pallid moons of beauty. Yes: surely she would come if he could only find her! She would come with him to the fair forest, and all day long he would dance for her delight. A smile lit up his eyes at the thought, and he passed into the next room.

Of all the rooms this was the brightest and the most beautiful. The walls were covered with a pink flowered Lucca damask, patterned with birds and dotted with dainty blossoms of silver; the furniture was of massive silver, festooned with florid wreaths, and swinging Cupids; in front of the two large fire-places stood great screens broidered with parrots and peacocks, and the floor, which was of sea-green onyx, seemed to stretch far away into the distance. Nor was he alone. Standing under the shadow of the doorway, at the extreme end of the room, he saw a little figure watching him. His heart trembled, a cry of joy broke from his lips, and he moved out into the sunlight.

As he did so, the figure moved out also, and he saw it plainly.

The Infanta! It was a monster, the most grotesque monster he had ever beheld. Not properly shaped, as all other people were, but hunchbacked, and crooked-limbed, with huge lolling head and mane of black hair. The little dwarf frowned, and the monster frowned also. He laughed, and it laughed with him, and held its hands to its sides, just as he himself was doing. He made it a mocking bow, and it returned him a low reverence. He went towards it, and it came to meet him, copying each step that he made, and stopping when he stopped himself. He shouted with amusement, and ran forward, and reached out his hand, and the hand of the monster touched his, and it was as cold as ice. He grew afraid, and moved his hand across, and the monster's hand followed it quickly. He tried to press on, but something smooth and hard stopped him. The face of the monster was now close to his own, and seemed full of terror. He brushed his hair off his eyes. It imitated him. He struck at it, and it returned blow for blow. He loathed it, and it made hideous faces at him. He drew back, and it retreated.

What is it? He thought for a moment, and looked round at the rest of the room. It was strange, but everything seemed to have its double in this invisible wall of clear water. Yes, picture for picture was repeated, and couch for couch. The sleeping Faun that lay in the alcove by the doorway had its twin brother that slumbered, and the silver Venus that stood in the sunlight held out her arms to a Venus as lovely as herself.

Was it Echo? He had called to her once in the valley, and she had answered him word for word. Could she mock the eye, as she mocked the voice? Could she make a mimic world just like the real world? Could the shadows of things have colour and life and movement? Could it be that—

He started, and taking from his breast the beautiful white rose, he turned round, and kissed it. The monster had a rose of its own, petal for petal the same! It kissed it with like kisses, and pressed it to its heart with horrible gestures.

When the truth dawned upon him, he gave a wild cry of despair, and fell sobbing to the ground. So it was he who was misshapen and hunchbacked, foul to look at and grotesque. He himself was the monster, and it was at him that all the children had been laughing, and the little Princess who he had thought loved him—she too had been merely mocking at his ugliness, and making merry over his twisted limbs. Why had they not left him in the forest, where there was no mirror to tell him how loathsome he was? Why had his father not killed him, rather than sell him to his shame? The hot tears poured down his cheeks, and he tore the white rose to pieces. The sprawling monster did the same, and scattered the faint petals in the air. It grovelled on the ground, and, when he looked at it, it watched him with a face drawn with pain. He crept away, lest he should see it, and covered his eyes with his hands. He crawled, like some wounded thing, into the shadow, and lay there moaning.

And at that moment the Infanta herself came in with her companions through the open window, and when they saw the ugly little dwarf lying on the ground and beating the floor with his clenched hands, in the most fantastic and exaggerated manner, they went off into shouts of happy laughter, and stood all round him and watched him.

"His dancing was funny," said the Infanta. "But his acting is funnier still. Indeed he is almost as good as the puppets, only of course not quite so natural." And she fluttered her big fan, and applauded.

But the little dwarf never looked up, and his sobs grew fainter and fainter, and suddenly he gave a curious gasp, and clutched his side. And then he fell back again, and lay quite still.

"That is capital," said the Infanta, after a pause. "But now you must dance for me."

"Yes," cried all the children, "you must get up and dance, for you are as clever as the barbary apes, and much more ridiculous." But the little dwarf made no answer.

And the Infanta stamped her foot, and called out to her uncle, who was walking on the terrace with the Chamberlain, reading some despatches that had just arrived from Mexico, where the Holy Office had recently been established. "My funny little dwarf is sulking," she cried. "You must wake him up, and tell him to dance for me."

They smiled at each other, and sauntered in, and Don Pedro stooped down, and slapped the dwarf on the cheek with his embroidered glove. "You must dance," he said, "petit monsire. You must dance. The Infanta of Spain and the Indies wishes to be amused."

But the little dwarf never moved.

"A whipping master should be sent for," said Don Pedro wearily, and he went back to the terrace. But the Chamberlain looked grave, and he knelt beside the little dwarf, and put his hand upon his heart. And after a few moments he shrugged his shoulders, and rose up, and having made a low bow to the Infanta, he said—

"Mi bella Princesa, your funny little dwarf will never dance again. It is a pity, for he is so ugly that he might have made the King smile."

"But why will he not dance again?" asked the Infanta, laughing.

"Because his heart is broken," answered the Chamberlain.

And the Infanta frowned, and her dainty rose leaf lips curled in pretty disdain. "For the future let those who come to play with me have no hearts," she cried, and she ran out into the garden.

渔夫和他的灵魂

每天傍晚，年轻的渔夫都会出海，把网撒入海中。

风从陆地吹向海洋时，他总是一无所获，有也是寥寥无几。因为那风迅猛，长着黑色的翅膀，就连恶浪也涌起来迎接它。但是当风从海洋吹向岸边时，鱼儿就从深处游来，钻进他的网里，渔夫就把它们捕上来，带到集市上去卖。

每天傍晚，年轻的渔夫都会出海。有一天傍晚收网的时候，渔网沉得几乎拉不上船，他哈哈大笑起来，暗自说道："我肯定逮住了所有在游的鱼，或是网到了什么让人大开眼界的傻海怪，要不就是什么吓人的东西，伟大的女王见了都想要的那种。"他使出浑身力气紧拽着粗绳，手臂上暴起一根根长长的青筋，宛如青铜花瓶上缠绕着的一条条蓝色瓷釉条纹。他再拽起细绳，近了，网口那圈扁扁的软木浮越来越近，网终于浮出了水面。

但是根本没什么鱼在网里，没有任何怪物也没有吓人的东西，只有一条小小的美人鱼，正躺着酣睡呢。

美人鱼的头发宛如湿漉漉的金羊毛，而且每一根发丝单独看上去就像盛在玻璃杯中的一缕金线。她的身体如同象牙一样白，她的尾巴像白银和珍珠，上面缠绕着翠绿的海草；她的耳朵像海贝，她的双唇就像珊瑚。冰冷的海浪冲刷着她的胸脯，海盐结晶在她的眼睑上，闪闪发亮。

美人鱼真是美极了，年轻的渔夫惊叹不已地看着，伸出手把网拉近，俯下身子，紧紧地抱住了她。可他的手刚一碰，她就像受惊的海鸥那样大叫一声，醒了过来。她望着他，紫水晶般的双眼充满了惊恐，还挣扎着试图脱身逃走。可是渔夫紧紧地抱住她，不忍放她走。

等明白自己无法逃走时，美人鱼开始哭泣，说道："求求你放我走吧，我是国王的独生女，我的父亲上了年纪，身边也没有别的亲人。"

但是，年轻的渔夫回答道："我不会放你走的，除非你向我承诺，无论什么时候我呼唤你，你都会前来为我唱歌。因为鱼儿喜欢听海族的歌，这样我每一网都会收获满满。"

"你果真会放我走，要是我答应了你的话？"美人鱼大声问道。

"我真的会放你走。"年轻的渔夫答道。

于是，美人鱼许下渔夫想要的承诺，并以海族的咒语发了誓。渔夫松开了抱着她的双臂，她感到一种莫名的恐惧，浑身颤抖着沉入水中去了。

每天傍晚年轻的渔夫都会出海，呼唤美人鱼后，她就浮上水面为他唱歌。海豚围在她的四周游来游去，桀骜的海鸥在她的头顶上方振翅盘旋。

她唱了一首奇妙的歌。她歌唱海民赶着鱼群挨个岩洞地巡游，肩上还扛着小崽子；歌唱人身鱼尾的海神特里同们蓄着长长的绿胡须，露出毛茸茸的胸脯，国王路过时还要吹响弯弯的海螺；歌唱琥珀王宫，宫中屋顶盖着晶莹的翡翠，路面铺着明亮的珍珠；歌唱海中花园，园内一丛丛珊瑚整日舞动飘摆，犹如一把把巨大的掐丝扇子，鱼儿就像银鸟四处穿梭，秋牡丹紧紧地趴在岩石上，海石竹从棱状黄沙里冒出芽来；她歌唱从北方海域游来的大鲸鱼，鳍上正挂着尖尖的冰凌；歌唱半人半鸟的海妖西壬，尽讲些美妙诱人的事情，让商人们不得不用蜡封堵耳朵，免得受其诱惑而跳海被淹死；歌唱桅杆高高耸立的沉船，冻僵的水手紧抱着帆船的缆索，马鲛鱼通过敞开着的舷窗游进游出；歌唱小小的藤壶，个个都是伟大的旅行家，吸附在船的龙骨上周游世界，逛了一圈又一圈；歌唱住在悬崖峭壁旁边的乌贼，伸出长长的黑色手臂，能够随心所欲地唤来黑夜；她歌唱鹦鹉螺，自己就拥有一艘由蛋白石雕刻而成的小船，挂起一面丝绸帆就可航行；歌唱快乐的雄人鱼，弹起竖琴，能把巨型海怪克拉肯催入梦乡；歌唱孩子们，抓住滑溜溜的江豚，骑在背上欢声大笑；歌唱美人鱼，躺在白色的浪花中，伸出手臂欢迎水手；歌唱鱼尾狮，獠牙弯弯，还有鱼尾马，鬃鬣飘荡。

　　美人鱼唱啊唱啊，所有的金枪鱼都从深海里游过来听，年轻的渔夫撒网捕住它们，还用鱼叉来捉网外的鱼。渔船装满了，美人鱼就会朝他微微一笑，而后沉入大海。

　　然而，美人鱼怎么也不肯游到渔夫能碰到自己的近处。渔夫时常呼唤她，求她，可她就是不肯；他想抓住她时，她就像海豹一样潜入水中，当天他就再也见不着她了。一天天过去，她的歌声渔夫越听越觉得甜美。她的歌声甜美极了，他都忘了要自个儿的渔网，也不管自个儿捕鱼的行当了。金枪鱼举着鲜红色的鱼鳍，鼓着金黄色的眼睛，成群结队地从旁边游过，可他无心理会，鱼叉也闲搁在身旁，一只只柳条筐空空如也。他只是张着嘴，黯然地瞪着写满惊异的双眼，呆呆地坐在船上倾听，直到海雾悄然将他围住，流浪的月儿往他古铜色的四肢照上一层银光。

　　一天傍晚，渔夫唤来美人鱼，对她说："小美人鱼，小美人鱼啊，我爱你！让我当你的新郎吧，因为我爱你。"

　　可是美人鱼摇了摇头。"你有人的灵魂，"她答道，"只有你把灵魂送走，我才能爱上你。"

　　年轻的渔夫自言自语地说："我的灵魂对我有什么用呢？我看不到它，摸不着它，更不认识它。我当然会把它送走，然后幸福就属于我啦。"他兴奋得禁不住大呼一声，从油漆过的小船上站起来，向美人鱼张开双臂。"我要送走灵魂，"他喊道，"你将成为我的新娘，我也将成为你的新郎，我俩将共同生活在大海深处。凡是你唱到的一切，都要带我去看；凡是你渴望的一切，我都要去做，我俩将永不分开。"

小美人鱼开心地笑出声来，用双手捂住了脸。

"可是，我该怎么送走灵魂呢？"年轻的渔夫哭着说，"告诉我该怎么做。瞧，我定会怎么去做！"

"哎呀！我也不知道呢，"小美人鱼回答，"海民是没有灵魂的唉。"她若有所思地望着他，向大海深处沉去。

第二天清晨，没等太阳露出山头一拃高，年轻的渔夫就来到神父家门口，连叩了三下。

见习修士从门洞里往外看，等看清来人是谁才拉开门闩，对他说："进来。"

年轻的渔夫走了进去，跪倒在地板上散发出清香的灯芯草垫上，向正在诵读《圣经》的神父哭诉："神父啊，我爱上了一个海民，可是我的灵魂妨碍我如愿以偿。请告诉我该怎么送走灵魂呢，因为我实在不需要它。我的灵魂对我有什么价值呢？我看不到它，摸不着它，更不认识它。"

神父捶着自个儿的胸脯，答道："哎呀呀，你是疯了，或是吃了什么毒草，要知道灵魂可是人类身上最高贵的部分，是上帝恩赐给我们的，我们就该把它派上高贵的用场。没有什么东西比人的灵魂更加珍贵了，俗世间也没有什么可与之相比。它值天下所有黄金，比国王的红宝石还要珍贵。所以啊，我的孩子，千万不要再想此事了，因为这是一桩不可原宥的大罪。至于海民，他们已经堕落了，愿意与他们交往的人也堕落了。他们犹如荒原野兽，不辨善恶，主也不曾为救赎他们而死。"

年轻的渔夫听完神父这番严厉的忠言，双眼噙满了泪水。他站起身来，对神父说："神父，牧神们住在森林里，活得开开心心，雄人鱼坐在礁石上，弹着赤金竖琴。我恳请您，让我像他们那样吧，因为他们过的是鲜花般的日子。至于我的灵魂，要是它梗在我与我之所爱之间，于我有何裨益？"

"肉身之爱是卑鄙的，"神父紧锁眉头，大声说道，"那些异教生灵也是既卑鄙又邪恶的，虽然上帝悲悯而容忍其在自个儿的世界里流窜。让林间牧神受诅咒吧，让海中歌手受诅咒吧！我曾在夜间听见，他们试图引诱我放下念珠，放弃祷告。他们敲打窗户，放声大笑。他们在我耳边低声说些刺激的段子。他们用种种诱惑来引诱我，当我要祷告时，他们就来做鬼脸揶揄我。他们堕落了，我告诉你，他们堕落了。他们无所谓天堂也无所谓地狱，到哪里都不会赞美上帝的圣名。"

"神父啊，"年轻的渔夫喊道，"您在说什么，恐怕自个儿也不明白。有一次我下网捕到了一位国王的女儿。她比辰星还要娇美，比月亮还要洁白。为其身我愿意交出灵魂，为其爱我愿意放弃天堂。请告诉我我求过您的事吧，好让我安心离去。"

"走吧！走吧！"神父大声喊道，"你的心上人已经堕落了，你会和她一起堕落的。"

神父没有祝福他，反而把他赶出了门。

接下来，年轻的渔夫走进集市，走得很慢，耷拉着脑袋，一副黯然神伤的模样。

商人们见他走来，便开始互相窃窃私语。有一个人迎了上来，喊着他的名字，问道："你有什么要卖的？"

"我要卖我的灵魂，"他答道，"请你买走它，我已烦透了它。我的灵魂对我有什么用呢？我看不到它，摸不着它，更不认识它。"

可是商人们都纷纷拿他开玩笑，说道："一个人的灵魂对我们有什么用呢？连半块破银都不值。将你的身子卖给我们为奴，我们就给你穿上紫色的衣服，再给你戴上戒指，让你成为伟大女王的奴仆。但不要再提什么灵魂不灵魂的，对我们来说啥也不是，对我们的行当也没有任何价值。"

年轻的渔夫自言自语:"这真是件怪事!牧师告诉我灵魂值天下所有黄金,而商人们却说它连半块破银都不值。"他走出集市,来到海边,开始思索自己该怎么做。

中午时分,渔夫想起自个儿有个采集海茴香的同伴,他曾跟自个儿说起过一个年轻的女巫,就住在海湾入口处的一个山洞里,巫术非常了得。于是,他就动身跑起来,实在是急于摆脱自个儿的灵魂。他跑过海滨的沙滩时,身后扬起一团尘云。年轻的女巫手心发痒,知道他要来了,大笑着散下红色的头发。她红发飘飘地站在洞口,手里拿着一束盛开的野蓁芹。

"你缺啥?你缺啥呢?"女巫见他气喘吁吁地冲上陡坡并朝她跪下来时,大声喊道,"莫非在风向不利时要鱼入网吗?我有一支小小的芦管,我一吹鲻鱼就会游进海湾。可这得有个价,小帅哥,这得有个价。你缺啥?你缺啥呢?莫非要一场风暴把船掀翻,再把一箱箱财宝冲上岸吗?我比风神有更多的风暴,因为我侍奉的主比风神强大,用一把筛子和一桶水我就能把大船送入海底。可这得有个价,小帅哥,这得有个价。你缺啥?你缺啥呢?我知道有株花长在山谷里,除了我谁也不知道。它长着紫色的叶子,花心有颗星,花汁白得像牛奶一样。要是你用这花碰一下王后冷漠的嘴唇,她就会跟随你走遍天涯。她就会从国王的床上爬起来,走遍天涯也会跟随你。当然,这得有个价,小帅哥,这得有个价。你缺啥?你缺啥呢?

我能在研钵里把蟾蜍捣碎。你趁自个儿的仇敌入睡时洒在他身上,他就会变成一条黑色的毒蛇,而他的亲娘就会亲手杀了他。用个轮子我就能从天上拽下月亮,用块水晶我就能向你展现死神。你还缺啥?你还缺啥呢?告诉我你的诉求,我就会让你如愿以偿,可你得付我个价,小帅哥,你得付我个价。"

"我求的不过小事一桩,"年轻的渔夫说,"然而神父对我大发雷霆,把我轰了出门。我求的不过小事一桩,然而商人却拿我大开玩笑,拒我于千里之外。所以我来找你,虽然大家说你邪恶,但是无论你要什么价,我都愿意付出。"

"那你求什么呢?"女巫走近他,问道。

"我要把我的灵魂送走。"年轻的渔夫答道。

女巫的脸变得煞白,浑身颤抖,扯起蓝色披风遮住了脸。"小帅哥,小帅哥,"她喃喃地说,"这真是件可怕的事儿。"

渔夫甩了甩棕色的卷发,笑了起来。"我的灵魂对我来说啥也不是,"他答道,"我看不到它,摸不着它,更不认识它。"

"要是我教会你,你会给我什么呢?"女巫问,同时用美丽的眼睛注视着他。

"五块金子,"他说,"外加我的渔网,我住的棚屋,我用的油漆小船。只要教我怎么摆脱灵魂,我会把所有的家当都送给你。"

女巫大笑起来,嘲讽地看着他,并用那支野毒芹打了他一下。"我能把秋天的树叶变成金子,"她答道,"我还能把皎白的月光织成银子,要是我愿意的话。我所侍奉的主比这世界上所有的国王都要富有,并拥有他们的领地。"

"那我该给你什么呢"他大声问道,"要是你不要金又不要银?"

女巫伸出一只苍白纤瘦的手,抚摸着他的头发。"你得同我跳舞,小帅哥。"她喃喃地说道,同时朝他微微一笑。

"就这个?"年轻渔夫惊奇地喊道,站起身来。

"就这个。"女巫回答着,又朝他微微一笑。

"那么日落时就找个秘密的地方,我们一起跳吧,"他说,"跳完舞之后,你要告诉我我想知道的事儿。"

女巫摇了摇头。"待月亮圆了,待月亮圆了。"她喃喃地说着。然后她看了看四周,又侧耳倾听起来。一只蓝色的鸟儿尖叫着从巢中飞起,在沙丘上空盘旋不止;三只长着斑点的鸟儿穿过灰色的荒草丛,发出窸窸窣窣的响声,还不忘互相召唤着。还有海浪哗哗地冲刷着下面的光滑卵石,此外再无别的声音了。于是她伸出一只手把他拉近,干湿的嘴唇凑近他的耳朵。

"今晚你必须到山顶上,"女巫低声说道,"今天是安息日,他会在那儿。"

年轻的渔夫吃惊地看着她,她则露出皓齿大声笑起来。"你说的他是谁呢?"他问道。

"这你就别管了,"女巫答道,"你今晚去就行,站在那棵鹅耳枥的枝丫下,等我来。要是有黑狗向你跑来,就用柳条打它,它就会跑开。要是猫头鹰向你喊话,不要搭理它。待月亮圆了,我就过去找你,我俩就可以在草地上共舞。"

"但你愿不愿向我发誓,你会教我怎么把我的灵魂送走?"渔夫问道。

女巫移到阳光下,风儿微微吹动她的红发。"我以山羊蹄子郑重立誓。"她这么答道。

"女巫中就数你最好了,"年轻的渔夫喊道,"今晚我一定会和你在山顶上跳舞。我的确同意你向我要金要银。可是你既然只要这个,我会让你如愿的,毕竟是小事一桩。"他脱帽致敬,深鞠一躬后,就转身跑回镇上,心里乐开了花。

女巫望着他走远,待他走出视线后方才入洞,从雪松木的雕花匣中取出一面镜子,并把它支在一个架子上。在这面镜子前她用燃着的木炭焚烧马鞭草,并透过缭绕的青烟凝视着镜中的影像。过了一会儿,她气愤地握紧双手。"他本该是我的,"她喃喃自语道,"我和她一样漂亮啊。"

那天晚上,月亮升起时年轻的渔夫爬上了山顶,站在鹅耳枥的枝丫下。环形的大海就像一面锃亮的金属圆盾横卧在他的脚下,一艘艘渔船在小海湾里影影绰绰地来来往往。一只大猫头鹰,双眼黄得像硫磺似的,直唤着他的名字,但他没有搭理。一条黑狗跑过来,朝他汪汪大叫。他挥起柳条就打,狗就呜呜地叫着跑开了。

午夜时分女巫们来了,就像一只只蝙蝠从空中翩翩而至。"唷!"她们刚一落地,就大声喊起来,"这里有个我们不认识的人!"她们四处嗅起来,互相议论着,比划着各种手势。最后到场的是那位年轻的女巫,红发迎风飘扬。她身穿一袭金丝长裙,上面绣着孔雀眼,头上还戴着一顶天鹅绒的小绿帽。

"他在哪儿,他在哪儿呢?"女巫们看到她就纷纷尖叫起来。然而她只是哈哈大笑,跑到鹅耳枥树下,拉起渔夫的一只手,领着他来到月光下,开始跳起舞来。

他们转了一圈又一圈,年轻女巫跳得老高老高,他都能看见她那猩红舞鞋的后跟。然后,穿过跳舞的人群传来了一匹骏马疾驰而过的声响,但不见马的踪影,他感到害怕起来。

"跳快点,"女巫大声喊道,用胳膊搂住他的脖子,呼出的气息热腾腾地扑上了他的脸庞。"快点,再快点!"她大声喊着。渔夫觉得大地似乎都在脚下飞旋起来,脑瓜也晕乎乎的,一阵巨大的恐惧朝他袭来,仿佛有什么邪恶的东西在注视着他。最后他觉察到在一块岩石的阴影处有个人,可先前并没有什么人在那儿。

那是一个男人,身着黑色天鹅绒套装,按着西班牙样式剪裁制成。他的脸出奇得苍白,可嘴唇却像一朵傲然绽放的红花。他看上去疲惫不堪,身体往后靠着,正无精打采地把玩着短剑的剑柄。在他身旁的草地上放着一顶装饰着羽毛的帽子，还有一双骑马手套，上面镶着金边，缝着细珍珠，设计堪称奇妙。他肩上披着一件内衬紫貂皮的短斗篷，纤细白皙的手上戴满了戒指，两只眼皮沉沉地耷拉了下来。

年轻的渔夫注视着他，就像中了邪一样。最终两人目光相遇了，无论渔夫舞到哪儿，他都觉得那人的眼睛在紧盯着自个儿。渔夫听到年轻女巫大声笑起来，赶紧搂住她的腰，带着她疯狂地转了一圈又一圈。

突然树林里传来一阵狗吠，跳舞的人群都停住了，随后成双成对地走上前，跪了下来，亲吻那人的手。他们这样做时，那人骄傲的嘴唇上浮现出一丝笑容，就像鸟儿用翅膀轻点水面荡漾出丝丝笑纹，但是笑容中充满了不屑，他一直盯着年轻的渔夫。

"走吧！让我们过去参拜，"女巫低声说着，就把渔夫领上前。一股对她有求必应的强烈冲动揪住了他，他就跟着她走过去。可是他走近时，却无缘无故地在胸口画了个十字，并念出了上帝的圣名。

渔夫刚做完，女巫们就像老鹰一样地尖叫着飞走了，那张一直注视着他的煞白脸庞，痛苦地抽搐起来。接着那人走到一片小树林前，吹了声口哨，便跑出一匹戴着银鞍银辔的西班牙小马来迎接他。他跳上马鞍，转过身来，悲伤地看了看年轻的渔夫。

红发女巫也想飞走，可是渔夫一把抓住她的手腕，紧紧抓住了她。

"松开我，"女巫大声喊起来，"让我走吧。因为你已经念了不该念的名字，画了不能看的手势。"

"不，"他答道，"我不会放你走，直到你把秘诀告诉我。"

"什么秘诀？"女巫问，像一只野猫似的拼命挣扎，并紧咬着满是泡沫的嘴唇。

"你懂的。"他答道。

女巫那双草绿色的眼睛让泪水模糊了,对渔夫说:"问我什么都行,就这个不行!"

他哈哈大笑起来,把她抓得更紧了。

女巫见自个儿无法挣脱,就低声对他说:"无疑,我和海的女儿一样漂亮,和住在蓝色水波里的人儿一样好看。"她一边向他献媚,一边挪脸凑近他的脸。

但是渔夫皱着眉头把她推了回去,对她说:"要是你不遵守你对我所许的承诺,我就杀了你这个不守信的女巫。"

女巫一听脸色变得像犹大树的花朵一样灰白,浑身颤抖起来。"那就这么办吧,"她喃喃地说,"这是你的灵魂,又不是我的。你想拿它怎样就怎样吧。"她从腰带里取出一把绿色毒蛇皮刀柄的小刀,递给了他。

"这个对我有什么用呢?"渔夫不解地问她。

女巫沉默了片刻,脸上写满了恐惧。然后她把头发从额头往后拂开,奇怪地微笑着对他说:"人们所说身体的影子,并非身体的影子,而是灵魂的身体。你背对着月亮站在海边,沿着你的双脚割开你的影子,那就是你的灵魂。你吩咐你的灵魂离开,它就会依照你的吩咐离开的。"

年轻的渔夫颤抖起来。"这是真的吗?"他喃喃地说。

"是真的,我倒希望我没告诉过你这事儿。"女巫喊道,紧紧地抱着他的膝盖,哭泣起来。

渔夫推开她,留她待在荒草丛中,自个儿走到山边,把刀别在腰带里,开始下山。

他身上的灵魂大声呼喊着,对他说:"瞧!我与你同住了这么多年,而且一直是你的仆人。现在,请不要送我离开你,我对你做过什么坏事吗?"

年轻的渔夫大笑起来。"你没对我做过什么坏事,可是我不需要你呀，"他回答，"天地这么大，有天堂，也有地狱，天堂和地狱之间还有昏暗朦胧的那座房屋。你想去哪儿就去哪儿吧，别给我添麻烦就行，因为我的爱人正在召唤我。"

他的灵魂悲伤地恳求他，但是他没有搭理，只是从一块岩石跳到另一块岩石，脚步稳健，像头野山羊。最后，他终于到了平地，来到了黄沙岸边。

渔夫古铜色的四肢配着结实的身躯，宛如一尊希腊人塑造的雕像，背对着月亮站在沙滩上。浪花伸出一双双白色的手臂，向他招手；波涛中腾起一个个朦胧的人影，向他致敬。面前就躺着他的影子，就是他灵魂的身体，而在他的身后一轮明月悬挂在色如蜂蜜的空中。

他的灵魂对他说："要是你真的一定要把我赶走，那得先给我一颗心才行。这世界冷酷无情，把你的心给我，容我带上。"

渔夫仰头微微一笑，说："要是我把心给你，我该拿什么来爱我的爱人呢？"

"别这样，发发慈悲吧，"他的灵魂说，"把你的心给我吧，因为这世界冷酷无情，真是让我害怕了。"

"我的心属于我的爱人，"他答道，"所以不要耽搁了，你走吧。"

"难道我就不该爱吗？"他的灵魂问道。

"你就走吧，我不需要你了，"年轻的渔夫大声喊道，拿起那把绿色妻蛇皮刀柄的小刀，沿着双脚割开他的影子；影子立起来，站在他面前，看着他，甚至可以说跟他一个模样。

他蹑手蹑脚地后退着，把刀别回腰带，一股敬畏之情袭上身来。"你走吧，"他喃喃地说，"千万不要让我再看到你的脸。"

"不，我俩肯定会再见面。"灵魂说，声音宛如长笛一样低沉，几乎不动嘴皮。

"我们怎么见面呢？"年轻的渔夫喊道，"你不会跟我到大海深处去吧?"

"一年一次,我都会来这儿唤你,"灵魂说,"兴许你会用得着我的。"

"我会用得着你的哪点呢?"年轻的渔夫喊道,"但是随你的便吧。"说完他一头扎进水里,海神特里同们纷纷吹响号角,小美人鱼也浮上来迎接他,搂住他的脖子,亲吻着他。

灵魂孤零零地站立在海滩上,注视着他们。他们沉入大海后,它才哭着穿过沼泽地走了。

一年后灵魂来到海边,呼唤着那个年轻的渔夫。渔夫就从大海深处浮上来,说道:"你为啥唤我?"

灵魂答道:"靠近一点儿,好让我跟你说说话,因为我见到了奇妙的事儿。"

于是渔夫靠近一点儿,躺在浅水里,一只手撑着脑袋,侧耳倾听。

灵魂对他说:"我离开你以后,我转脸向东方旅行。源自东方的一切都是睿智的。我走了整整六天,第七天早晨来到了一座小山,那儿属于鞑靼人的地盘。我坐在一棵柽柳的树荫下,避一避日晒。土地干涸,被烈日烤得烫人。人们在平原上来来往往,仿佛苍蝇在磨光的铜盘上爬来爬去似的。

"到了中午,一团红色沙尘的云雾从地平线上升起。鞑靼人见此就纷纷挽起画弓,跨上小马飞快地迎了上去。妇女们尖叫着逃上马车,躲在毛帘后面。

"暮色降临,鞑靼人回来了,可是人少了五个,而且有不少人负了伤。他们把马套在车上,匆匆赶路。三条豺狼从山洞里跑出来,窥视着他们。然后它们仰头张鼻朝空中嗅了嗅,就向相反的方向跑开了。

"月亮升起时,我看见平原上燃起一堆营火,便走了过去。一群商人正围着营火坐着,身下垫着毯子。他们的骆驼被拴在身后的桩子上，伺候他们的黑人正在沙地上搭建硝皮帐篷，并用霸王树扎起高高的篱墙。

"我走近他们时，商人中的头领起身拔剑，问我是干什么的。

"我说我是我那个国家的王子，刚从鞑靼人那儿逃出来，他们要抓我当奴隶。头领微微一笑，让我看到了系在长竹竿上的五颗人头。

"随后他问我，谁是上帝的先知，我回答说穆罕默德。

"当听到假先知的名字时，他就鞠躬致意，牵起我的手，让我坐在他的身边。一个黑人用木盘给我端上来一些马奶，还有一块烤好的小羊肉。

"天亮时分，我们开始赶路。我骑着一匹红毛骆驼，走在头领的身旁；一个探子手拿长矛，跑在我们的前面。战士们分列两旁，骡子驮着货物跟在后面。商队共有四十头骆驼，骡子的数量则多达两倍。

"我们由鞑靼人的地盘进入了另一个国度，那里的人诅咒月亮。我们看到半狮半鹫的怪兽在白石上看护自个儿的黄金，看到满身鳞甲的恶龙在自个儿的洞穴中酣睡。我们翻越山岭时，大气都不敢出，生怕积雪会塌下来压倒我们，每人眼上都绑了一条纱布。我们穿越山谷时，躲在树洞里的侏儒朝我们射箭，到了夜间我们听到野人敲鼓的声音。来到猴塔时，我们在猴子面前摆些水果，它们就没有伤害我们了。来到蛇塔时，我们用铜碗给蛇送些热牛奶，它们就放我们过去了。一路上我们曾三次来到奥克苏斯河的岸边。我们过河用的是木筏，筏上拴着吹满气的大皮囊。河马冲我们大发雷霆，想要杀了我们。骆驼见此，吓得瑟瑟发抖。

"每个城邦的国王都向我们征收税费，却不许进入城门。他们从城墙上扔给我们面点，用蜂蜜烤制的玉米小糕，还有枣馅的精粉面饼。每扔来一百篮东西，我们就还给他们一颗琥珀珠。

"庄上的居民见我们来了,就往井里投毒,然后逃往深山里去了。一路上我们与之打过仗的有马加达人,他们生下来就很老,然后一年比一年年轻,直到长成小孩时死去;有拉克托伊人,他们自称是老虎的子孙,把自个儿涂成黄黑相间的颜色;有奥兰特人,他们把死人葬在树顶上,活人却住在黑暗的洞穴内,唯恐他们信奉的太阳神杀了自个儿;有克里姆尼人,他们崇拜一条鳄鱼,向它献上绿色的玻璃耳环,喂它吃黄油和新鲜的家禽;有阿加中拜人,长着狗一样的面孔;还有西班牙人,长有马蹄,跑起来比马还要快。我们的商队有三分之一的人死于打仗,还有三分之一死于饥寒。活下来的人嘀嘀咕咕地反对我,说我给他们带来了厄运。于是我从石头下面翻出来一条长了角的蝰蛇,让它咬我。我仍安然无恙,他们见后顿生畏惧。

"第四个月,我们来到伊勒城。当我们到达城墙外的小树林时已是夜间,空气又闷又热,因为月亮正在天蝎宫旅行。我们从树上摘下熟透了的石榴,掰开就喝到了甘甜的果汁。然后我们就躺倒在自个儿的毯子上,等待天明。

"天明时分,我们起身去敲城门。城门由红铜铸成,上面雕着海龙和长有翅膀的飞龙。守城卫士从城垛上望下来,问我们来干什么。商队的通事答道,我们从叙利亚岛来,带着许多货品。他们要了几个人质,并说他们会在正午给我们开城门,还嘱咐我们要等到那个时候。

"等到正午,他们开了城门。我们入城时,人们都从屋内跑出,成群结队地来看我们;一个公告员吹响螺号,呼叫着跑遍全城传递消息。我们站在集市上,黑奴们解开花布包,打开一只只雕花的无花果木箱。他们忙完这些后,商人们便摆出了各自千奇百怪的货品,有埃及来的漫蜡麻布和埃塞俄比亚来的印花麻布,有推罗来的紫色纱布和西顿来的蓝色帷幔,还有冰冷的琥珀杯和精美的玻璃器皿,以及用黏土烧制的珍奇容器。在一家房屋的顶部有群妇女打量着我们，其中一个戴了副烫金的皮面具。

"第一天是教士们来和我们交易，第二天是贵族，第三天是手艺人和奴隶们。他们就按这种惯例与所有商人交易，只要商人们入城留下来。

"我们逗留了一个月。到了月亏时，我有些腻了，就在城中穿街走巷地闲逛起来，逛进了本城神祇的花园。身着黄袍的教士静悄悄地穿过绿树丛，在黑色大理石路面上矗立着一座玫瑰红的神祠，里面供着他们的神。神祠的门涂着金粉，上面铸有发亮的堆金公牛和孔雀。斜坡屋顶铺着海绿色的瓷瓦，突出的屋檐下面挂着一个个小铃铛。当白鸽飞过神祠时，总会用翅膀扑腾着铃铛，弄得叮叮当当地直响。

"神祠前面有一汪清澈的水塘，塘边铺满了有纹理的玛瑙。我躺在水塘边，伸出白皙的手指去触摸那些大树叶。一名教士走上来，站在了我的身后。他脚上穿着凉鞋，一只是用软蛇皮做的，另一只则是用鸟羽编的。他头上戴着黑毡主教帽，别着银月牙儿。他的袍子织有七道黄色，卷曲的头发上抹了些锑粉。

"不一会儿他找我说话，问我意欲何为。

"我告诉他，我想拜见他们的神。

"'神在狩猎。'教士一边说着，一边用他那双小小的斜眼睛奇怪地打量着我。

"'告诉我在哪片林子，我想陪他一起跑马。'我回应道。

"他伸出长长的尖指甲梳理了一下袍子边上软软的穗子。'神在睡觉。'他喃喃地说。

"'告诉我在哪张卧榻，我想去守护他。'我回应道。

"'神在赴宴。'他高声喊道。

"'要是酒甜，我想和他一起喝；要是酒苦，我也想陪他一起喝，'

我回应道。

"他惊诧地低下头,抓住我的一只手,把我拉起来,领着我进了神祠。

"走进第一个房间,我看见一尊神像,端坐在碧玉宝座上,宝座边上镶着一颗颗硕大的东方珍珠。神像由乌木雕刻而成,身材跟真人一般大小。它额头上有一颗红宝石,头发上滴下的浓油落到大腿上。它双脚猩红,沾满了一头新宰小羊羔的鲜血,腰间束着一条铜腰带,上面镶有七颗绿宝石。

"我问教士:'这就是神吗?'他答道:'这就是神。'

"'领我见神去,'我大喊道,'否则我一定会杀了你。'然后我拉了拉他的手,那手就瘪了下去。

"教士苦苦哀求,对我说:'我的主啊,请治好奴才,奴才这就领他去见神。'

"于是我往他的那只手上吹了口气,那手即刻复原如初,他颤抖起来,把我领进了第二个房间。我看见一尊神像,站立在一朵玉石莲花上,莲花上缀着一块块硕大的翡翠。神像由象牙雕刻而成,身材有真人两倍大小。它额头上有一颗橄榄石,胸脯上抹着没药和肉桂。它一只手拿着一根弯弯的玉石权杖,另一只手握着一块圆圆的水晶。它双脚穿着铜靴,粗颈上套着个透明的石膏圈。

"我问教士:'这就是神吗?'

"他答道:'这就是神。'

"'领我见神去,'我大喊道,'否则我一定会杀了你。'然后我摸了摸他的眼,他就失明了。

"教士苦苦哀求,对我说:'我的主啊,请治好奴才,奴才这就领他去见神。'

"于是我往他的那双眼里吹了口气,那眼即刻重见光明,他再次颤抖起来,把我领进了第三个房间。瞧!里面没有神像,也没有其他雕像，只有一面金属圆镜，架在一个石砌圣坛上。

"我问教士：'神在哪儿？'

"教士答道：'没有神，只有你眼前的这面镜子，因为这是智慧之镜。这镜子照得见天地万物，却唯独照不见照镜人的脸。照不见自个儿的脸，所以照镜人就会变得睿智。天地间还有其他不计其数的镜子，但都是意见之镜。唯有这面镜子才是智慧之镜。拥有这面镜子的人知道一切，无所不知。没有它的人，就没有智慧。因此它就是神，我们就崇拜它。'于是我往镜子中看去，镜子果真如他所言。

"我还干了件怪事，可我干了啥已无关紧要，因为我把智慧之镜藏进了山谷，离这儿只有一天的路程。只求你让我再进入你的身体，再当你的仆人，你就会比所有的智者更加睿智，智慧就会属于你。只要让我再次进入你的身体，天下便再也没有人比你更睿智了。"

但是年轻的渔夫大笑了起来。"爱比智慧更好，"他大声喊道，"还有小美人鱼爱我着呢。"

"不，没有什么比智慧更好的了。"灵魂说。

"爱就更好。"年轻的渔夫答完，一头扎进深水里；灵魂又哭着穿过沼泽地走了。

第二年过后灵魂又来到海边，呼唤着那个年轻的渔夫。渔夫就从大海深处浮上来，说："你为啥唤我？"

灵魂答道："靠近一点儿，好让我跟你说说话，因为我见到了奇妙的事儿。"

于是渔夫靠近一点儿，躺在浅水里，一只手撑着脑袋，侧耳倾听。

灵魂对他说："我离开你以后，我转脸向南方旅行。源自南方的一切都是珍贵的。我沿着通往阿什忒城的公路走了整整六天，就是那些朝圣者经常走的尘土飞扬的红色公路；第七天早晨我抬眼一看，瞧！阿什忒城就横卧在我的脚下，因为它坐落在山谷里。

"阿什忒城有九座城门，门前各自立着一匹铜马，马会在阿拉伯贝都因人冲下山时引颈长嘶。城墙的外面用铜皮包着，墙头瞭望塔的屋顶用黄铜铺成。每座瞭望塔上都站着一名弓箭手，手里拿着一把弓。他日出时用箭敲锣，日落时则吹响号角。

"我想进城，但守城卫士拦住我，问我是什么人。我答道我是个伊斯兰教苦行僧，正往麦加去，麦加有一幅绿色的帐幕，幕上有银字的《古兰经》，经文由天使们亲手绣上。卫士听完惊叹不已，恳请我入城来。

"城里简直就是一个大集市。说真的，你真该跟我一起去。窄窄的街道上挂满了华丽的纸灯笼，犹如一只只大蝴蝶在空中飘舞。风吹过屋顶的时候，它们又如五彩的肥皂泡一样起起落落。商人们则在自个儿货摊前坐在丝织的毯子上。他们蓄着直挺挺的黑胡须，缠着缀满了金色亮片的头巾，冰凉的手指滑动着一长串一长串的琥珀和雕花桃核。他们中有的人卖白松香和甘松香，卖印度洋岛屿的奇特香料，卖浓浓的红玫瑰油，还卖没药和小钉子状的丁香。当有人停住跟他们说话时，他们就会拈几撮乳香撒入炭火盆中，让空气弥漫着甜香味。我见到一个叙利亚人，双手拿着一根像芦苇般的细棒子。棒子里冒出一缕缕灰色烟雾，那烧着的香味仿佛春天开放的粉色扁桃花似的。其他商人卖银手镯，上面饰满了乳酪蓝的绿松石，卖镶着小珍珠的铜脚镯，卖镶着黄金托子的虎爪，卖那种镀金大猫爪，也就是豹爪，同样镶着黄金托子，还卖穿孔翡翠耳环和空心玉指环。茶馆里传出来吉他的弹奏声，抽鸦片的烟客朝外望着行人，惨白的脸上露出微笑。

"说实话,你真该跟我一起去。那些卖酒的人肩上扛着大大的黑色皮酒囊,推推搡搡地挤过人群。他们大多兜卖设拉子葡萄酒,甜得像蜂蜜一样。他们将酒盛在小金属杯里,继而在上面撒些玫瑰花瓣。集市上还站着一些卖水果的,兜售各种各样的水果:有熟透的无花果,紫色的果肉带有擦伤的痕迹,有黄如黄玉的甜瓜,散发出浓郁的麝香味,有香橼、番石榴和成串的白葡萄,还有浑圆的金红色橘子和椭圆的金绿色柠檬。有一次,我看到一头大象走过,鼻子上抹着朱砂和姜黄,耳朵上盖着张深红色的丝网。大象在一个摊位前停下来,吃起摊位上的橘子,那人见此一笑了之。你真想象不出,他们这个民族的人是多么古怪。他们高兴时就来到卖鸟的那儿,买上一只被关在笼中的鸟儿,然后再把它放走,好让快乐翻倍;他们伤心时就用荆棘鞭打自个儿,免得悲伤消减。

"一天傍晚,我遇到一些黑人穿过集市,抬着一顶沉甸甸的轿子。轿子由镀金竹板做成,轿杆漆成了朱红色,上面镶着黄铜孔雀。轿窗上垂着薄薄的纱帘,上面绣着甲虫的翅膀和细小的珍珠。从我身边经过时,有个脸色苍白的切尔卡西亚人从轿里望出来,对我微微一笑。我尾随其后,黑人便加快脚步,还对我横眉竖目。但我才不管呢,心里充满了好奇。

"最后,他们停在了一座方形的白屋前。屋子没有窗户,只有一扇像墓门一样的小门。他们放下轿子,用铜锤敲了三下门。一个身着绿长袍的亚美尼亚人从门洞里往外看,看清是他们来了才开门,在地上铺开地毯,那个女人才走了出来。她进去时,转过身又对我微微一笑。我还从未见过这么白的人。

"月亮升起时，我回到原地去找那座房屋，可它已经不在那儿了。见此情形，我明白了那个女人是谁，为什么对我微笑了。

"当然了，你真该跟我一起去。新月节来临时，年轻的皇帝会出宫，走入清真寺做礼拜。他的头发和胡须都用玫瑰花瓣染红了，两颊抹了层细细的金粉，脚掌和手掌都用藏红花染成了黄色。

"日出之际皇帝身着银袍从宫中走出，日落时分他又身着金袍返回宫中。人们纷纷跪拜在地，遮住脸庞，可我却不愿这样做。我站在一个卖枣的摊位旁边，等待着。皇帝见我，便扬起他那画过的双眉，停了下来。我站着一动不动，没有向他行礼。众人见我如此大胆，都很惊讶，纷纷劝我逃出城去。我没有搭理，而是走过去和那些出售各种千奇百怪神像的贩子坐在一块儿。他们遭人憎恨，原因是自个儿行当所在。我跟他们说起我的所作所为时，他们每人送我一尊神像，并恳请我离开他们。

"当天晚上，我正躺在石榴大街那家茶馆的垫子上，皇帝的卫士进来，把我带到了皇宫。我进宫时，每入一道门，他们就在我身后立刻关上那道门，并穿上链子拴住。里面有一个大大的庭院，四周环绕着拱廊。墙壁是用白色雪花石膏砌的，这儿那儿地镶着一块块蓝色和绿色的瓷砖。柱子是用绿色大理石做的，路面则铺着一种桃红色大理石。我真是见所未见啊！

"我穿过庭院时，有两个戴着面纱的女人从阳台上望下来，还骂了我一句。卫士们急匆匆地往前走，长矛的矛柄戳得光亮的地板咚咚直响。他们打开了一道精致的象牙门，我发现自个儿来到了一座七层的水景花园。园里种着郁金香、月光花，还有银斑点点的芦荟。一股喷泉在昏暗的夜空中倾泻而下，宛如一根纤细的水晶芦苇。一棵棵柏树就像是一支支燃尽的火把。其中一棵柏树上有只夜莺正唱得欢。

"在花园尽头有一座小小的亭子。我们靠近的时候，有两个太监出来迎接。太监身材肥胖，走起路来摇摇摆摆，还用眼皮发黄的眼睛好奇地打量着我。其中一个太监把卫队长拉到旁边，低声说着什么。另一个太监拿着一只椭圆形的紫色珐琅盒子，从中不停地拿出香锭来咀嚼，取锭的手势十分夸张。

"过了片刻，卫士长就解散了卫队。卫士们就回宫去了，太监则慢腾腾地跟在后面，边走边从树上摘些甜甜的桑果。太监中年长的那位曾转过身来，不怀好意地冲我微笑。

"然后卫士长用手示意我往亭子的入口处走。我就毫不胆怯地走上前，拉开那幅沉重的帘子，迈了进去。

"年轻的皇帝正躺在一张染了色的狮皮卧榻上，手腕上栖着一只矛隼。皇帝身后站着一个缠着黄铜包头巾的努比亚人，上身赤裸，两只穿孔的耳朵上挂着沉甸甸的耳环。榻边的桌子上放着一把威风凛凛的钢制弯刀。

"皇帝见到我，就皱起眉头问：'你姓甚名谁？难道你不知道我就是这座城的皇帝吗？'但我没有回答他。

"皇帝用手指着那把弯刀，努比亚人就一把抓起刀，冲上来，狠命地砍我。刀锋呼啸着划过我的身体，却丝毫没伤着我。那人却一个趔趄扑倒在地上，待爬起来时吓得牙齿打颤，躲到卧榻后面去了。

"皇帝一跃而起，从兵器架上抄起一根长矛，向我投来。我一把接住，折成两段。他又向我射箭，但我双手一举，那箭便停在半空中了。这之后，他从白皮腰带上拔出一把短剑，一下子刺入努比亚人的喉咙,生怕这个奴仆说出自个儿不光彩的事儿。努比亚人像一条被践踏的蛇,扭动翻滚起来,嘴唇里涌出了鲜红的血沫。

"人一死,皇帝就朝我转过身来,拿着一块镶了花边的紫色丝绸小手绢,拭去眉心亮晶晶的汗珠,对我说道:'你是我不能伤害的先知,还是我不能伤害的先知之子?我祈求你今晚就离开我这座城,因为有你在城中,我就不再是一城之主了。'

"于是我回应他说:'你分给我一半财宝我就走。把你的财宝给我一半,我就走开。'

"皇帝拉起我的一只手,领我出来,走入花园。卫士长见了我,一脸愕然。太监见了我,膝盖一抖,吓得纷纷跪倒在地上。

"宫中有间密室,密室的八面墙壁都由红斑岩砌成,天花板上包着铜皮,挂了几盏灯。皇帝伸手碰了碰其中的一面墙,墙壁豁然打开,我俩便沿着一条通道走了进去,通道里燃着一把把火炬。通道两边都是壁龛,龛里摆着大酒缸,缸里装满了银圆。我们来到通道正中间的时候,皇帝念出了那句平时不可说的话,一道装有暗弹簧的花岗岩门一下子就往后弹开了。他用双手捂着脸,生怕会亮晕他的双眼。

"你都无法相信,那是一个多么神奇的地方。那儿有许多巨大的玳瑁壳,壳里装满了珍珠,还有许多硕大的月亮石,空心处堆满了红宝石。金子储存在橡皮箱内,金粉则保存在皮制瓶里。还有蛋白石和蓝宝石,前者盛在水晶杯里,后者盛在翡翠杯里。圆圆的祖母绿整整齐齐地摆放在薄薄的象牙板上。一处角落里就堆满了圆鼓鼓的丝绸袋,有的袋子装满了绿松石,其余的则装满了绿宝石。那儿有一个个象牙号角,里面堆满了紫水晶,还有一个个黄铜号角,里面积满了玉髓和红玉髓。那儿的柱子由杉木做成,上面挂着一串串黄色的猞猁石。那儿还有一块块扁平的椭圆形盾牌,上面放着石榴石,酒红色和草绿色的都有。然而,我说了这么多珍宝,也不过是那儿的一个零头罢了。

"皇帝放开捂着脸的手，对我说。'这就是我的藏宝室，里面的一半珍宝归你，就如我承诺给你的那样。而且，我还会给你配一些骆驼和赶骆驼的人，他们会听你调遣。拿上你的那份财宝，去世界上任何一个你想去的地方。此事得连夜办妥，因为太阳是我的父亲，我可不想让他老人家看到，在我的城中竟有一个我不能杀的人。'

"我却回答他说：'这儿的金子归你，银子也归你，还有贵重珠宝和有价之物统统归你。至于我嘛，我不需要这些东西。我什么都不要，只要你戴在手指上的那枚小小的指环。'

"皇帝皱起了眉头。'这不过是个铅指环罢了，'他喊道，'一点儿价值也没有。既然如此，还是拿上一半财宝，离开我的这座城吧。'

"'不，'我答道，'我什么都不拿，只要那枚铅指环，因为我知道那里面写着什么，有什么用处。'

"皇帝颤抖起来，央求我说：'那就把所有财宝都拿上，赶紧离开我这座城。我的那一半也归你啦。'

"我还干了件怪事，可我干了啥已无关紧要，因为我把财富之环藏进了山洞，离这儿只有一天的路程。离这儿只有一天的路程，它正等着你去呢。谁拥有了这枚指环，就会比这世界上所有的国王都要富有。所以，你来吧，取了它，这世界上所有的财富就统统归你了。"

但是年轻的渔夫大笑了起来。"爱比财富更好，"他大声喊道，"还有小美人鱼爱着我呢。"

"不，没有什么比财富更好的了。"灵魂说。

"爱就更好。"年轻的渔夫答完，一头扎进深水里；灵魂又哭着穿过沼泽地走了。

第三年过后灵魂又来到海边，呼唤着那个年轻的渔夫。他就从大海深处浮上来，说："你为啥唤我？"

灵魂答道:"靠近一点儿,好让我跟你说说话,因为我见到了奇妙的事儿。"

于是渔夫靠近一点儿,躺在浅水里,一只手撑着脑袋,侧耳倾听。

灵魂对他说:"在我所知道的一座城里有一家客栈,就开在一条河边上。我和水手们坐在那儿,他们喝着颜色不同的两种酒,吃着大麦做的面包,还有和着醋、用月桂叶包着的小咸鱼。我们正坐着逗乐时,走进来一个老头,拿着一条皮毡和一把鲁特琴,琴上装有两个琥珀做的尖角。老头把皮毡铺在地上,再用羽毛管弹响了他那把鲁特琴的金属琴弦,

正值此时一个蒙着面纱的姑娘跑了进来,开始在我们面前跳舞。姑娘的脸上蒙着薄纱,可是双脚赤裸着;她在皮毡上翩翩舞动,宛如一对小小的白鸽。我真是见所未见,况且她跳舞的那座城离这儿只有一天的路程。

此刻年轻的渔夫听了他的灵魂的这番话,突然想起小美人鱼没有脚就跳不了舞。一股强烈的愿望油然而生,他暗自想道:"只有一天的路程,去了我也能返回爱人的身边。"于是他哈哈大笑,从浅水中站起,大踏步走向岸边。

渔夫走到岸边踏上干地后,又哈哈大笑起来,向他的灵魂伸出双臂。他的灵魂欣喜若狂地大叫一声,跑上去迎接他,进入了他的身体,年轻的渔夫方才看到面前沙地上伸展出的那道身体的影子,也就是灵魂的身体。

他的灵魂对他说:"咱们不要耽搁了,要马上离开这儿,因为海

里的神祇会嫉妒的，而且还有听其差遣的怪物。"

于是他们匆忙上路，在月光下走了一整夜，又顶着日头走了一整天，当日傍晚时分他们来到了一座城。

年轻的渔夫问他的灵魂："这就是你对我说的那座她跳舞的城吗？"

他的灵魂答道："不是这座城，而是另外一座。不过，咱们还是进去吧。"于是他们就进去，穿过了一条又一条街道。在经过珠宝商大街的时候，年轻的渔夫看见一只漂亮的银杯摆放在货摊上，他的灵魂见此对他说："拿走那只银杯，藏起来。"

渔夫就拿起银杯，藏在自个儿短袍的衣褶里，而后他们就匆匆地出了城。

他们出城刚走了三英里左右，年轻渔夫就皱起眉头，猛地扔开杯子，问他的灵魂："你干吗叫我拿走杯子藏起来，这是干坏事吧？"

但是他的灵魂答道："息怒，息怒。"

第二天傍晚，他们来到了下一座城，年轻的渔夫对他的灵魂说："这就是你对我说的那座她跳舞的城吗？"

他的灵魂答道："不是这座城，而是另外一座。不过，咱们还是进去吧。"于是，他们就进去，穿过了一条又一条街道。在经过草鞋贩子街的时候，年轻的渔夫看见一个小孩站在水缸边。他的灵魂见此对他说："去揍那个小孩。"于是他动手揍了孩子，直到把小孩揍哭，而后他们就匆匆地出了城。

他们出城刚走了三英里左右，年轻的渔夫就愤怒起来，问他的灵魂："你干吗叫我揍小孩，这是干坏事吧？"

但是他的灵魂答道："息怒，息怒。"

第三天傍晚，他们来到了下一座城，年轻的渔夫对他的灵魂说："这就是你对我说的那座她跳舞的城吗？"

他的灵魂答道："兴许就是这座城，那么咱们进去吧。"

于是，他们就进去，穿过了一条又一条街道，但是年轻的渔夫始终无法找到那条河，也找不到河边的那个客栈。城里的人好奇地打量着他，他就害怕起来，对他的灵魂说："咱们走吧，那个双脚白皙的跳舞姑娘并不在这儿。"

但是他的灵魂回应："不，咱们还是歇一歇吧，夜已经黑了，路上会有强盗的。"

于是，渔夫自个儿在集市上坐下来歇息。不一会儿，走过来一个头戴兜帽的商人，身披一件鞑靼人的布织斗篷，手提一盏牛角穿洞做成的灯笼，灯笼杆子是根有节的芦苇。商人问他："你为啥坐在集市上，没看见货摊都关门了，货物也都打包了吗？"

年轻的渔夫答道："我在这城里找不到客栈，又没什么亲人可留我过夜。"

"咱们不都是亲人吗？"商人说，"不都是同一个上帝创造的吗？那就跟我走吧，我家正好有间客房。"

于是，年轻的渔夫站起来，跟着商人去了他家。待他穿过一片石榴园进了家，商人便用一个铜盘端来玫瑰水让他洗手，又给他端来熟透的甜瓜让他解渴，又将一碗米饭和一块烤羔羊肉端到他的面前。

渔夫吃完后，商人便领他去客房，安排他睡觉歇息。年轻的渔夫谢过他，吻了戴在自个儿手上的指环，然后就一头躺在了染过色的山羊毛毯上。他将一床山羊毛织成的黑色被单盖上了身，就呼呼地入睡了。

拂晓前三小时，黑夜仍未消逝，他的灵魂就叫醒了他，对他说："快起来，去商人的房间，就是摸到他睡觉的房间，杀了他，拿走他的金子，我们用得着。"

于是，年轻渔夫起身，悄悄地潜入商人的房间。商人的脚上横放着一把弯刀，身旁的托盘上堆放着九包金子。渔夫伸出一只手摸到那把刀，碰到刀的刹那间商人猛然惊醒，起身一把抄起刀，对年轻的渔夫大叫道："莫非你要以恶报善，用流血来回报我对你的恩情吗？"

他的灵魂对他说："揍他。"渔夫就揍起商人，揍得他晕倒过去，然后一把夺过九包金子，仓促地越过石榴园逃了出去，一路都是朝着启明星的方向。

他们出城刚走了三英里左右，年轻的渔夫就捶胸顿足起来，对他的灵魂说："你干吗叫我杀了商人又拿走金子？无疑，你就是个恶棍。"

但是他的灵魂回应道："息怒，息怒。"

"不，"年轻的渔夫大声叫道，"我息怒不了。你叫我做的所有事情，我都恨，连你，我也恨。我要你说明白，你为什么要这么坑我？"

他的灵魂回答他说："当初你把我赶到这个世界上的时候，就没有把心交给我，所以我就学会了所有这些事情，而且乐此不疲。"

"此话怎讲？"年轻的渔夫喃喃地说。

"你知道的，"他的灵魂答道，"你知道得清清楚楚。莫非忘了你没有把心给我？我不信你忘了。所以呢，你不要自寻烦恼，也不要跟我过不去，而应息怒为上，毕竟这世上没有什么痛苦抛不开，也没有什么开心寻不来。"

年轻的渔夫听了这番话，浑身颤抖起来，对他的灵魂说："不，你就是恶棍，使我忘了我的爱人，并用种种诱惑来诱我上当，让我踏上了罪孽之路。"

他的灵魂回答："你到底没有忘记，当初你把我赶到这个世界上的时候，就没有把心交给我。来吧，让咱们到另一座城里，好好乐乐，咱们有九包金子呢。"

然而，年轻的渔夫拿起那九包金子，狠狠地摔到地下，用脚猛踩起来。

"不,"渔夫高声嚷起来,"我不会再跟你有任何瓜葛,也不会再跟你去任何地方。以前我怎么送走你的,现在我照样送走你,因为你对我没有一点好处。"他背对着月亮,用那把绿色蟒蛇皮刀柄的小刀,沿着双脚奋力割开那道影子,也就是灵魂的身体。

然而他的灵魂没有从他身上移开,也没有搭理他的命令,反而对他说:"那女巫告诉你的魔法不管用了,因为我不能离开你,你也无法赶走我。人这一辈子可以送走灵魂一次,可要是又收回了灵魂,那他就必须与它相伴终生了。这是对他的惩罚,也是对他的回报。"

年轻的渔夫脸色煞白,紧握双手,大叫起来:"她就是个女巫骗子,没有告诉过我这个。"

"不对,"他的灵魂回应,"她可是忠于自个儿所崇拜的神,她会永远做他的仆人。"

意识到自个儿再也无法摆脱自个儿的灵魂,况且是个邪恶的灵魂,还要与其终生相伴,年轻的渔夫一头栽倒在地,痛哭了起来。

天亮了,年轻的渔夫爬起来,对他的灵魂说:"我要绑住自个儿的手,免得听你使唤;要闭住自个儿的嘴,免得替你说话。我还要回到我爱人安住的地方。我要回到大海里,回到她经常唱歌的那个小海湾,我要呼唤她,告诉她我做过的坏事,还有你对我做过的坏事。"

他的灵魂又引诱他,说道:"谁是你的爱人,你非得要回到她身边去吗?世界上比她漂亮的人多的是。有萨玛利斯的舞女,她们能模仿各种鸟兽翩翩起舞。她们用指甲花把双脚染成红色,手里舞着小小的铜铃。她们边舞边笑,笑声宛如流水潺潺一般清澈。跟我走吧,我引你去见见她们。你对那些罪恶的事情耿耿于怀,到底是为啥呢?世上好吃的东西,难道不是为好吃的人做的吗?好喝的东西,难不成有毒吗?不要自寻烦恼了,跟我到别的城逛逛吧。旁边就有座小城,城里有个种满了郁金香的花园。园子赏心悦目,还养着一些白孔雀和蓝胸孔雀。它们向着太阳开屏时,尾巴光彩夺目,或如象牙盘,又如镀金盘。喂养孔雀的姑娘为了逗它们开心,有时手舞,有时足蹈。姑娘双眼染上了锑色,鼻孔形如燕子的双翅。其中的一侧鼻孔还穿了个钩子,钩上挂着一朵珍珠雕成的花。她边笑边舞,脚踝上的一对银镯宛如银铃似的叮叮当当作响。所以不要再自寻烦恼了,就跟我去这座城吧。"

可是年轻的渔夫没有回应他的灵魂,而是用缄默的封印封住自个儿的嘴巴,再用绳索紧紧地绑住自个儿的双手,然后掉头向他出发的地方走去,一直走到他的爱人曾经经常唱歌的那个小海湾。他的灵魂一路上继续引诱他,他就是不搭理;它设法叫他做些坏事,他就是不去做。他内心的爱啊,竟有如此强大的力量!

渔夫到了海边,便解开手上的绳索,揭走嘴上的封印,开始呼唤小美人鱼。尽管他喊了一整天,向她百般央求,但是美人鱼没有应声前来。

他的灵魂就嘲笑他,说道:"没错,你没有从你的爱人那儿得到多少快乐。你呀,就像个大旱天里还拼命往破罐里倒水的人。你倾其所有,却不曾得到丝毫回报。最好还是跟我走吧,我知道欢乐谷在哪儿,那儿又有些什么花样。"

可是年轻的渔夫没有回应他的灵魂,而是在岩石的裂缝处,用树枝给自个儿搭了个棚屋,一住就是一年。天天早上他都呼唤美人鱼,中午再呼唤一遍,夜里还叨念着她的名字。然而,她从未浮出大海来见他,他也未在大海的任何一处见着她,尽管渔夫寻遍了洞穴和碧水浅滩,也找遍了潮汐留下的水池和海底深处的井坑。

他的灵魂不停地用邪恶引诱他,在他耳边低声说些恐怖的事儿。然而他始终不为所动,他的爱啊,竟有如此强大的力量!

一年过后,灵魂暗自思量:"我曾用邪恶引诱我的主人,但他的爱比我还强大。现在我要改用善良来引诱他,兴许他就会跟我走。"

于是，灵魂对年轻的渔夫说："我已告诉你世间的快乐了，可你却对我充耳不闻。现在让我再告诉你世间的痛苦，或许你会听得进去。说实话，痛苦才是这个世界的主，没有一个人能逃出它的罗网。有人缺衣，有人少食。同是守寡妇人，有的身穿紫袍，有的衣不遮体。沼泽中，麻风病人来来往往，却彼此相残。大路上，乞丐们来回奔波，却行囊空空。各座城中的大街小巷里饥荒横冲直撞，家家户户的大门口瘟疫稳坐如山。来吧，让我们前去，去拯救这一切，让其不再发生。你为啥停在这儿呼唤你的爱人，没看到她不会应声前来吗？再说，什么是爱，你非得要如此看重吗？"

但是年轻的渔夫没有回答，他的爱啊，竟有如此强大的力量。天天早上他都呼唤美人鱼，中午再呼唤一遍，夜里还叨念着她的名字。然而，她从未浮出大海来见他，他也未在大海的任何一处见着她，尽管渔夫寻遍了海中的沟壑和浪底的幽谷，也找遍了夜色下深紫和晨曦中灰白的各片海域。

第二年过后，灵魂趁夜间对独坐棚屋的年轻的渔夫说："真想不到！我曾用邪恶引诱你，也曾用善良引诱你，可是你的爱比我还强大。算了吧，我不再引诱你了，可是得求你让我进入你的心，我就会同你融为一体，就像从前一样。"

"你当然可以进来，"年轻的渔夫说道，"往日没有心的陪伴就独自流浪世界，你一定受了很多的苦。"

"哎呀！"他的灵魂大声叫起来，"我找不到入口呢，你这颗心啊，竟被爱裹得这么严实。"

"可我倒希望自个儿能帮帮你。"年轻的渔夫回答。

他正说着，海里传来了一声巨大的哀嚎，就像海族有谁死了时人们听到的哀嚎声一模一样。年轻的渔夫猛地跃起，离开棚屋，跑向海边。只见黑色的浪涛急匆匆地向海岸边赶来，扛着一副比白银还白的担子。这担就像浪头一样白，仿佛一朵鲜花般地在浪涛中上下飘飘荡荡。浪头把它从浪涛上接过来，浪花又把它从浪头上接过来，最终是海岸接纳了它。年轻的渔夫方才看清楚，在自个儿脚边躺着小美人鱼。她死了，就躺在他的脚边。

渔夫哭起来，就像个因痛苦而伤心欲绝的人，一头扑倒在她的身旁，亲吻着那冰凉的红色嘴唇，抚摸着那湿漉漉的琥珀色头发。他哭起来，就像个因喜悦而浑身颤抖的人，伸出古铜色的双臂把她抱在胸前。两唇冰冷，他却亲吻着；蜜色头发咸湿有加，他却痛苦并欣喜地吮了又吮。他吻着那紧闭的眼，眼角上挂着的狂野浪花还没有他的泪花咸呢。

渔夫对着逝者忏悔。他把自个儿经历的苦难当作苦酒，灌进她那犹如贝壳一般的耳朵。他用手指轻抚着那细如苇秆的喉管，同时拉着那双小手挽在自个儿的脖子上。他的欣喜变得越来越苦，痛苦中又充满着奇异的愉悦。

黑色的海水越逼越近，白色的浪花声声哀嚎，就像个麻风病人。浪花伸出白色的爪子抓着海岸。从海王的宫殿里又传出来哀嚎声，远处的大海那边特里同海神们则吹出了嘶哑的号角声。

"逃吧，"他的灵魂劝说，"海水逼上来了，你要是逗留不逃，会淹死的。逃吧，我怕了，你的爱如此强大，一直对我紧闭心扉呢。快逃到一个安全的地方去。你该不会，让我在另一个世界没有心的陪伴吧？"

然而，年轻的渔夫没有听从他的灵魂，而是呼唤着小美人鱼，说："爱比智慧要好，比财富要贵，比人间女子的双脚还要美。烈火烧不毁它，大水浇不灭它。黎明时我呼唤你，可你就是不回应我。月亮都听到了我唤你的名字，可你仍然不理我。只怪我一时鬼迷心窍地离你而去，这一走真是自作自受。但是，你的爱与我同在，无比强大，不可匹敌。我见识过恶，也见识过善。既然你都死了，我肯定也要随你一块儿去死。"

他的灵魂恳求他离开，但他就是不愿走，因为他的爱啊，是如此强大。海水越逼越近，腾起浪涛要淹没他。他知道自个儿死期已近，就疯狂地亲吻着美人鱼那冰凉的嘴唇，自个儿的心从里面破碎了！当他的心被满满的爱撑破时，灵魂就找到了一个入口，钻了进去，同他融为一体，就像从前一样。海水终于用浪涛淹没了这位年轻的渔夫。

清晨时分，神父前去为大海祈福，因为它一直骚动不安。与神父一同前往的有僧侣和乐师，有手捧蜡烛的，有摇香炉的，还有好大一群人。

神父到达海边时，看到淹死的年轻渔夫漂在浪头上，双臂紧抱着小美人鱼的尸首。他皱起眉头往后退，画了个十字，大声喊起来："我不会为大海祈福，也不会为海中任何生灵祈福。愿诅咒归于海民，愿诅咒归于一切与海民交往的人。至于他，竟然为了爱而离弃上帝，所以才横尸于此，就把他的尸首和他爱人的尸首捞起来，埋在漂洗场的角落里吧，上面不插任何标志，也不做任何记号，这样就没有人知道他们安息在什么地方了。因为他们生前该受诅咒，死后仍要受诅咒。"

人们就遵照神父的吩咐而行，来到寸草不生的漂洗场的角落里，挖出一个深坑，将两具尸首埋了进去。

第三年的一个神圣节日，神父去那个小礼拜堂，准备向人们展示主为大众在十字架上所受的创伤，并向他们宣讲上帝的愤怒。

他披上法袍，走了进来，朝着圣坛俯首行礼，只见圣坛上面摆满了从未见过的奇花。奇怪的是花儿的模样，有着一种莫名其妙的美，搅得他心神不宁；花儿的气味香甜浓郁，直扑鼻孔，弄得他万分欣喜，却又不知道自个儿为何欣喜。

神父打开圣龛给龛里的圣体匣上香，向人们展示洁净的圣饼后又把它退回重重纱幕后藏好，接下来开始对人们宣讲，原本想对他们宣讲上帝的愤怒。但是洁白的花儿美啊，搅得他心神不宁，芬芳的花香直扑鼻孔，于是话到嘴边又变了。他没有宣讲上帝的愤怒，倒是宣讲起其名为爱的那位上帝。至于为什么，他也不明白。

神父宣讲完毕后人们都哭了起来，他则走回圣器收藏室，双眼噙满了泪水。教堂执事跟了进来，开始帮他脱去法袍，褪下白麻布圣衣，并解下腰带、佩在左臂上的饰带和披在双肩上的圣带。而他站立着，恍如做梦似的。

执事脱去他的法袍后，他就反看着他们说："圣坛上摆着的是什么花儿，哪儿来的？"

执事答道："是什么花儿，我们也说不清，不过都是从漂洗场的角落里移来的。"神父一听就全身颤抖起来，回到自己的屋子，开始祈祷。

清晨时分，仍在曙光里，神父就带领僧侣和乐师、捧蜡烛的和摇香炉的、还有好大一群人浩浩荡荡地出发，来到海边，为大海祈福，为海中所有生灵祈福。他为之祈福的还有林中牧神法翁们，林间舞来舞去的小精灵们，以及叶间探头探脑且两眼贼亮的那些家伙们。上帝创造的世界上所有生灵他都为之祈福，人们的心中就充满了欢喜和惊叹。漂洗场的角落里再也没有长出任何种类的花儿，那地方还是像以前一样荒芜。海民再也没有像往常一样光顾这个海湾，而是去了大海的其他地方。

THE FISHERMAN AND HIS SOUL

Every evening the young fisherman went out upon the sea, and threw his nets into the water.

When the wind blew from the land he caught nothing, or but little at best, for it was a bitter and black-winged wind, and rough waves rose up to meet it. But when the wind blew to the shore, the fish came in from the deep, and swam into the meshes of his nets, and he took them to the marketplace and sold them.

Every evening he went out upon the sea, and one evening the net was so heavy that hardly could he draw it into the boat. And he laughed, and said to himself, "Surely I have caught all the fish that swim, or snared some dull monster that will be a marvel to men, or some thing of horror that the great Queen will desire," and putting forth all his strength, he tugged at the coarse ropes till, like lines of blue enamel round a vase of bronze, the long veins rose up on his arms. He tugged at the thin ropes, and nearer and nearer came the circle of flat corks, and the net rose at last to the top of the water.

But no fish at all was in it, nor any monster or thing of horror, but only a little mermaid lying fast asleep.

Her hair was as a wet fleece of gold, and each separate hair as a thread of fine gold in a cup of glass. Her body was as white ivory, and her tail was of silver and pearl. Silver and pearl was her tail, and the green weeds of the sea coiled round it; and like seashells were her ears, and her lips were like sea coral. The cold waves dashed over her cold breasts, and the salt glistened upon her eyelids.

So beautiful was she that when the young fisherman saw her he was filled with wonder, and he put out his hand and drew the net close to him, and leaning over the side he clasped her in his arms. And when he touched her, she gave a cry like a startled sea gull, and woke, and looked at him in terror with her mauve-amethyst eyes, and struggled that she might escape. But he held her tightly to him, and would not suffer her to depart.

And when she saw that she could in no way escape from him, she began to weep, and said, "I pray you let me go, for I am the only daughter of a king, and my father is aged and alone."

But the young fisherman answered, "I will not let you go save you make me a promise that whenever I call you, you will come and sing to me, for the fish delight to listen to the song of the seafolk, and so shall my nets be full."

"Will you in very truth let me go, if I promise you this?" cried the mermaid.

"In very truth I will let you go," said the young fisherman.

So she made him the promise he desired, and sware it by the oath of the seafolk. And he loosened his arms from about her, and she sank down into the water, trembling with a strange fear.

Every evening the young fisherman went out upon the sea, and called to the mermaid, and she rose out of the water and sang to him. Round and round her swam the dolphins, and the wild gulls wheeled above her head.

And she sang a marvellous song. For she sang of the seafolk who drive their flocks from cave to cave, and carry the little calves on their shoulders; of the Tritons who have long green beards, and hairy breasts, and blow through twisted conchs when the King passes by; of the palace of the King which is all of amber, with a roof of clear emerald, and a pavement of bright pearl; and of the gardens of the sea where the great filigrane fans of coral wave all day long, and the fish dart about like silver birds, and the anemones cling to the rocks, and the pinks bourgeon in the ribbed yellow sand. She sang of the big whales that come down from the north seas and have sharp icicles hanging to their fins; of the Sirens who tell of such wonderful things that the merchants have to stop their ears with wax lest they should hear them, and leap into the water and be drowned; of the sunken galleys with their tall masts, and the frozen sailors clinging to the rigging, and the mackerel swimming in and out of the open portholes; of the little barnacles who are great travellers, and cling to the keels of the ships and go round and round the world; and of the cuttlefish who live in the sides of the cliffs and stretch out their long black arms, and can make night come when they will it. She sang of the nautilus who has a boat of her own that is carved out of an opal and steered with a silken sail; of the happy Mermen who play upon harps and can charm the great Kraken to sleep; of the little children who catch hold of the slippery porpoises and ride laughing upon their backs; of the mermaids who lie in the white foam and hold out their arms to the mariners; and of the sea lions with their curved tusks, and the sea horses with their floating manes.

And as she sang, all the tunny-fish came in from the deep to listen to her, and the young fisherman threw his nets round them and caught them, and others he took with a spear. And when his boat was well-laden, the mermaid would sink down into the sea, smiling at him.

Yet would she never come near him that he might touch her. Oftentimes he called to her and prayed of her, but she would not; and when he sought to seize her she dived into the water as a seal might dive, nor did he see her again that day. And each day the sound of her voice became sweeter to his ears. So sweet was her voice that he forgot his nets and his cunning, and had no care of his craft. Vermilion-finned and with eyes of bossy gold, the tunnies went by in shoals, but he didn't heed them. His spear lay by his side unused, and his baskets of plaited osier were empty. With lips parted, and eyes dim with wonder, he sat idle in his boat and listened, listening till the sea mists crept round him, and the wandering moon stained his brown limbs with silver.

And one evening he called to her, and said, "Little mermaid, little mermaid, I love you. Take me for your bridegroom, for I love you."

But the mermaid shook her head. "You have a human soul," she answered. "If only you would send away your soul, then could I love you."

And the young fisherman said to himself, "Of what use is my soul to me? I cannot see it. I may not touch it. I do not know it. Surely I will send it away from me, and much gladness shall be mine." And a cry of joy broke from his lips, and standing up in the painted boat, he held out his arms to the mermaid. "I will send my soul away," he cried, "and you shall be my bride, and I will be your bridegroom, and in the depth of the sea we will dwell together, and all that you have sung of you shall show me, and all that you desire I will do, nor shall our lives be divided."

And the little mermaid laughed for pleasure and hid her face in her hands.

"But how shall I send my soul from me?" cried the young fisherman. "Tell me how I may do it, and lo! It shall be done."

"Alas! I don't know," said the little mermaid. "The seafolk have no souls." And she sank down into the deep, looking wistfully at him.

Now early on the next morning, before the sun was the span of a man's hand above the hill, the young fisherman went to the house of the priest and knocked three times at the door.

The novice looked out through the wicket, and when he saw who it was, he drew back the latch and said to him, "Enter."

And the young fisherman passed in, and knelt down on the sweet-smelling rushes of the floor, and cried to the priest who was reading out of the Holy Book and said to him, "Father, I am in love with one of the seafolk, and my soul hinder me from having my desire. Tell me how I can send my soul away from me, for in truth I have no need of it. Of what value is my soul to me? I cannot see it. I may not touch it. I do not know it."

And the priest beat his breast, and answered, "Alack, alack, you are mad, or have eaten of some poisonous herb, for the soul is the noblest part of man, and was given to us by God that we should nobly use it. There is no thing more precious than a human soul, nor any earthly thing that can be weighed with it. It is worth all the gold that is in the world, and is more precious than the rubies of the kings. Therefore, my son, do not think any more of this matter, for it is a sin that may not be forgiven. And as for the seafolk, they are lost, and they who would traffic with them are lost also. They are as the beasts of the field that don't know good from evil, and for them the Lord has not died."

The young fisherman's eyes filled with tears when he heard the bitter words of the priest, and he rose up from his knees and said to him, "Father, the Fauns live in the forest and are glad, and on the rocks sit the Mermen with their harps of red gold. Let me be as they are, I beg you, for their days are as the days of flowers. And as for my soul, what does my soul profit me, if it stands between me and the thing that I love?"

"The love of the body is vile," cried the Priest, knitting his brows, "and vile and evil are the pagan things God suffers to wander through his world. Accursed be the Fauns of the woodland, and accursed be the singers of the sea! I have heard them at night-time, and they have sought to lure me from my beads. They tap at the window, and laugh. They whisper into my ears the tale of their perilous joys. They tempt me with temptations, and when I would pray they make mouths at me. They are lost, I tell you, they are lost. For them there is no heaven nor hell, and in neither shall they praise God's name."

"Father," cried the young fisherman, "you don't know what you say. Once in my net I snared the daughter of a king. She is fairer than the morning star, and whiter than the moon. For her body I would give my soul, and for her love I would surrender heaven. Tell me what I ask of you, and let me go in peace."

"Away! Away!" cried the priest, "your leman is lost, and you shall be lost with her."

And he gave him no blessing, but drove him from his door.

And the young fisherman went down into the market place, and he walked slowly, and with bowed head, as one who is in sorrow.

And when the merchants saw him coming, they began to whisper to each other, and one of them came forth to meet him, and called him by name, and said to him, "What do you have to sell?"

"I will sell you my soul," he answered. "I pray you buy it of me, for I am weary of it. Of what use is my soul to me? I cannot see it. I may not touch it. I do not know it."

But the merchants mocked at him, and said, "Of what use is a man's soul to us? It is not worth a clipped piece of silver. Sell us your body for a slave, and we will clothe you in sea-purple, and put a ring upon your finger, and make you the minion of the great Queen. But talk not of the soul, for us it is nothing, nor has it any value for our service."

And the young fisherman said to himself, "How strange a thing this is! The priest tells me that the soul is worth all the gold in the world, and the merchants say that it is not worth a clipped piece of silver." And he passed out of the marketplace, and went down to the shore of the sea, and began to ponder on what he should do.

And at noon he remembered how one of his companions, who was a gatherer of samphire, had told him of a certain young witch who dwelt in a cave at the head of the bay and was very cunning in her witcheries. And he set to and ran, so eager was he to get rid of his soul, and a cloud of dust followed him as he sped round the sand of the shore. By the itching of her palm the young witch knew his coming, and she laughed and let down her red hair. With her red hair falling around her, she stood at the opening of the cave, and in her hand she had a spray of wild hemlock that was blossoming.

"What do you lack? What do you lack?" she cried, as he came panting up the steep, and bent down before her. "Fish for your net, when the wind is foul? I have a little reed pipe, and when I blow on it the mullet come sailing into the bay. But it has a price, pretty boy, it has a price. What do you lack? What do you lack? A storm to wreck the ships, and wash the chests of rich treasure ashore? I have more storms than the wind has, for I serve one who is stronger than the wind, and with a sieve and a pail of water I can send the great galleys to the bottom of the sea. But I have a price, pretty boy, I have a price. What do you lack? What do you lack? I know a flower that grows in the valley, none knows it but I. It has purple leaves, and a star in its heart, and its juice is as white as milk.

Should you touch with this flower the hard lips of the Queen, she would follow you all over the world. Out of the bed of the King she would rise, and over the whole world she would follow you. And it has a price, pretty boy, it has a price. What do you lack? What do you lack? I can pound a toad in a mortar, and make broth of it, and stir the broth with a dead man's hand. Sprinkle it on yours enemy while he sleeps, and he will turn into a black viper, and his own mother will slay him. With a wheel I can draw the moon from heaven, and in a crystal I can show you death. What do you lack? What do you lack? Tell me your desire, and I will give it to you, and you shall pay me a price, pretty boy, you shall pay me a price."

"My desire is but for a little thing," said the young fisherman, "yet has the priest been wroth with me, and driven me forth. It is but for a little thing, and the merchants have mocked at me, and denied me. Therefore am I come to you, though men call you evil, and whatever be your price I shall pay it."

"What would you do?" asked the witch, coming near to him.

"I would send my soul away from me," answered the young fisherman.

The witch grew pale, and shuddered, and hid her face in her blue mantle. "Pretty boy, pretty boy," she muttered, "that is a terrible thing to do."

He tossed his brown curls and laughed. "My soul is nothing to me," he answered. "I cannot see it. I may not touch it. I do not know it."

"What will you give me if I tell you?" asked the witch, looking down at him with her beautiful eyes.

"Five pieces of gold," he said, "and my nets, and the wattled house where I live, and the painted boat in which I sail. Only tell me how to get rid of my soul, and I will give you all that I possess."

She laughed mockingly at him, and struck him with the spray of hemlock. "I can turn the autumn leaves into gold," she answered, "and I can weave the pale moonbeams into silver if I will it. He whom I serve is richer than all the kings of this world, and has their dominions."

"What then shall I give you," he cried, "if your price be neither gold nor silver?"

The witch stroked his hair with her thin white hand. "You must dance with me, pretty boy," she murmured, and she smiled at him as she spoke.

"Nothing but that?" cried the young fisherman in wonder and he rose to his feet.

"Nothing but that," she answered, and she smiled at him again.

"Then at sunset in some secret place we shall dance together," he said. "And after that we have danced you shall tell me the thing which I desire to know."

She shook her head. "When the moon is full, when the moon is full," she muttered. Then she peered all round, and listened. A blue bird rose screaming from its nest and circled over the dunes, and three spotted birds rustled through the coarse grey grass and whistled to each other. There was no other sound save the sound of a wave fretting the smooth pebbles below. So she reached out her hand, and drew him near to her and put her dry lips close to his ear.

"Tonight you must come to the top of the mountain," she whispered. "It is a Sabbath, and he will be there."

The young fisherman started and looked at her, and she showed her white teeth and laughed. "Who is he, of whom you speak?" he asked.

"It doesn't matter." she answered. "Go there tonight, and stand under the branches of the hornbeam, and wait for my coming. If a black dog run towards you, strike it with a rod of willow, and it will go away. If an owl speak to you, make it no answer. When the moon is full I shall be with you, and we will dance together on the grass."

"But will you swear to me to tell me how I may send my soul from me?" he made question.

She moved out into the sunlight, and through her red hair rippled the wind. "By the hoofs of the goat I swear it," she made answer.

"You are the best of the witches," cried the young fisherman, "And I will surely dance with you tonight on the top of the mountain. I would indeed that you had asked of me either gold or silver. But such as your price is you shall have it, for it is but a little thing." And he doffed his cap to her, and bent his head low, and ran back to the town filled with a great joy.

And the witch watched him as he went, and when he had passed from her sight she entered her cave, and having taken a mirror from a box of carved cedarwood, she set it up on a frame, and burned vervain on lighted charcoal before it, and peered through the coils of the smoke. And after a time she clenched her hands in anger. "He should have been mine," she muttered, "I am as fair as she is."

And that evening, when the moon had risen, the young fisherman climbed up to the top of the mountain, and stood under the branches of the hornbeam. Like a targe of polished metal the round sea lay at his feet, and the shadows of the fishing boats moved in the little bay. A great owl, with yellow sulphurous eyes, called to him by his name, but he made it no answer. A black dog ran towards him and snarled. He struck it with a rod of willow, and it went away whining.

At midnight the witches came flying through the air like bats. "Phew!" they cried, as they lit upon the ground, "There is some one here we don't know!" and they sniffed about, and chattered to each other, and made signs. Last of all came the young witch, with her red hair streaming in the wind. She wore a dress of gold tissue embroidered with peacocks' eyes, and a little cap of green velvet was on her head.

"Where is he, where is he?" shrieked the witches when they saw her, but she only laughed, and ran to the hornbeam, and taking the fisherman by the hand she led him out into the moonlight and began to dance.

Round and round they whirled, and the young witch jumped so high that he could see the scarlet heels of her shoes. Then right across the dancers came the sound of the galloping of a horse, but no horse was to be seen, and he felt afraid.

"Faster," cried the witch, and she threw her arms about his neck, and her breath was hot upon his face. "Faster, faster!" she cried, and the earth seemed to spin beneath his feet, and his brain grew troubled, and a great terror fell on him, as of some evil thing that was watching him, and at last he became aware that under the shadow of a rock there was a figure that had not been there before.

It was a man dressed in a suit of black velvet, cut in the Spanish fashion. His face was strangely pale, but his lips were like a proud red flower. He seemed weary, and was leaning back toying in a listless manner with the pommel of his dagger. On the grass beside him lay a plumed hat, and a pair of riding-gloves gauntleted with gilt lace, and sewn with seed pearls wrought into a curious device. A short cloak lined with sables hang from his shoulder, and his delicate white hands were gemmed with rings. Heavy eyelids drooped over his eyes.

The young fisherman watched him, as one snared in a spell. At last their eyes met, and wherever he danced it seemed to him that the eyes of the man were upon him. He heard the witch laugh, and caught her by the waist, and whirled her madly round and round.

Suddenly a dog bayed in the wood, and the dancers stopped, and going up two by two, knelt down, and kissed the man's hands. As they did so, a little smile touched his proud lips, as a bird's wing touches the water and makes it laugh. But there was disdain in it. He kept looking at the young fisherman.

"Come! Let us worship," whispered the witch, and she led him up, and a great desire to do as she besought him seized on him, and he followed her. But when he came close, and without knowing why he did it, he made on his breast the sign of the cross, and called upon the holy name.

No sooner had he done so than the witches screamed like hawks and flew away, and the pallid face that had been watching him twitched with a spasm of pain. The man went over to a little wood, and whistled. A jennet with silver trappings came running to meet him. As he leapt upon the saddle he turned round, and looked at the young fisherman sadly.

And the witch with the red hair tried to fly away also, but the fisherman caught her by her wrists, and held her fast.

"Loose me," she cried, "and let me go. For you have named what should not be named, and shown the sign that may not be looked at."

"No," he answered, "but I will not let you go till you have told me the secret."

"What secret?" said the witch, wrestling with him like a wild cat, and biting her foam-flecked lips.

"You know," he made answer.

Her grass-green eyes grew dim with tears, and she said to the fisherman, "Ask me anything but that!"

He laughed, and held her all the more tightly.

And when she saw that she could not free herself, she whispered to him, "Surely I am as fair as the daughters of the sea, and as comely as those that dwell in the blue waters," and she fawned on him and put her face close to his.

But he thrust her back frowning, and said to her, "If you don't keep the promise that you made to me I will slay you for a false witch."

She grew grey as a blossom of the Judas tree, and shuddered. "Be it so," she muttered. "It is your soul and not mine. Do with it as you will." And she took from her girdle a little knife that had a handle of green viper's skin, and gave it to him.

"What shall this serve me?" he asked of her, wondering.

She was silent for a few moments, and a look of terror came over her face. Then she brushed her hair back from her forehead, and smiling strangely she said to him, "What men call the shadow of the body is not the shadow of the body, but is the body of the soul. Stand on the sea shore with your back to the moon, and cut away from around your feet your shadow, which is your soul's body, and bid your soul leave you, and it will do so."

The young fisherman trembled. "Is this true?" he murmured.

"It is true, and I would that I had not told you of it," she cried, and she clung to his knees weeping.

He put her from him and left her in the rank grass, and going to the edge of the mountain he placed the knife in his belt and began to climb down.

And his soul that was within him called out to him and said, "Lo! I have dwelt with you for all these years, and have been your servant. Send me not away from you now, for what evil have I done you?"

And the young fisherman laughed. "You have done me no evil, but I have no need of you," he answered. "The world is wide, and there is Heaven also, and Hell, and that dim twilight house that lies between. Go wherever you will, but don't trouble me, for my love is calling to me."

And his soul besought him piteously, but he didn't heed it, but leapt from crag to crag, being sure-footed as a wild goat, and at last he reached the level ground and the yellow shore of the sea.

Bronze-limbed and well-knit, like a statue wrought by a Grecian, he stood on the sand with his back to the moon, and out of the foam came white arms that beckoned to him, and out of the waves rose dim forms that did him homage. Before him lay his shadow, which was the body of his soul, and behind him hung the moon in the honey-coloured air.

And his soul said to him, "If indeed you must drive me from you, don't send me forth without a heart. The world is cruel; give me your heart to take with me."

He tossed his head and smiled. "With what should I love my love if I gave you my heart?" he cried.

"No, but be merciful," said his soul, "give me your heart, for the world is very cruel, and I am afraid."

"My heart is my love's," he answered, "therefore do not tarry, but get you gone."

"Shouldn't I love also?" asked his soul.

"Get you gone, for I have no need of you," cried the young fisherman, and he took the little knife with its handle of green viper's skin, and cut away his shadow from around his feet, and it rose up and stood before him, and looked at him, and it was even as himself.

He crept back, and thrust the knife into his belt, and a feeling of awe came over him. "Get you gone," he murmured, "and do not let me see your face any more."

"No, but we must meet again," said the soul. Its voice was low and flute-like, and its lips hardly moved while it spoke.

"How shall we meet?" cried the young fisherman. "You will not follow me into the depths of the sea?"

"Once every year I will come to this place, and call to you," said the soul. 'It may be that you will have need of me."

"What need should I have of you?" cried the young fisherman, "But be it as you will," and he plunged into the waters and the Tritons blew their horns and the little mermaid rose up to meet him, and put her arms around his neck and kissed him on the mouth.

And the soul stood on the lonely beach and watched them. And when they had sunk down into the sea, it went weeping away over the marshes.

And after a year was over the soul came down to the shore of the sea and called to the young fisherman, and he rose out of the deep, and said, "Why do you call to me?"

And the soul answered, "Come nearer that I may speak with you, for I have seen marvellous things."

So he came nearer, and couched in the shallow water, and leaned his head upon his hand and listened.

And the soul said to him, "When I left you I turned my face to the east and journeyed. From the east comes everything that is wise. Six days I journeyed, and on the morning of the seventh day I came to a hill that is in the country of the Tartars. I sat down under the shade of a tamarisk tree to shelter myself from the sun. The land was dry and burnt up with the heat. The people went to and fro over the plain like flies crawling upon a disk of polished copper.

"When it was noon a cloud of red dust rose up from the flat rim of the land. When the Tartars saw it, they strung their painted bows, and having leapt upon their little horses they galloped to meet it. The women fled screaming to the waggons, and hid themselves behind the felt curtains.

"At twilight the Tartars returned, but five of them were missing, and of those that didn't come back a few had been wounded. They harnessed their horses to the waggons and drove hastily away. Three jackals came out of a cave and peered after them. Then they sniffed up the air with their nostrils, and trotted off in the opposite direction.

"When the moon rose I saw a camp-fire burning on the plain, and went towards it. A company of merchants were seated round it on carpets. Their camels were picketed behind them, and the negroes who were their servants were pitching tents of tanned skin upon the sand, and making a high wall of the prickly pear.

"As I came near them, the chief of the merchants rose up and drew his sword, and asked me my business.

"I answered that I was a prince in my own land, and that I had escaped from the Tartars, who had sought to make me their slave. The chief smiled, and showed me five heads fixed upon long reeds of bamboo.

"Then he asked me who was the prophet of God, and I answered him Mohammed.

"When he heard the name of the false prophet, he bowed and took me by the hand, and placed me by his side. A Negro brought me some mare's milk in a wooden dish, and a piece of lamb's flesh roasted.

"At daybreak we started on our journey. I rode on a red-haired camel by the side of the chief, and a runner ran before us carrying a spear. The men of war were on either hand, and the mules followed with the merchandise. There were forty camels in the caravan, and the mules were twice forty in number.

"We went from the country of the Tartars into the country of those who curse the moon. We saw the Gryphons guarding their gold on the white rocks, and the scaled dragons sleeping in their caves. As we passed over the mountains we held our breath lest the snows might fall on us, and each man tied a veil of gauze before his eyes. As we passed through the valleys the Pygmies shot arrows at us from the hollows of the trees, and at night-time we heard the wild men beating on their drums. When we came to the Tower of Apes we set fruits before them, and they did not harm us. When we came to the Tower of Serpents we gave them warm milk in howls of brass, and they let us go by. Three times in our journey we came to the banks of the Oxus. We crossed it on rafts of wood with great bladders of blown hide. The river-horses raged against us and sought to slay us. When the camels saw them they trembled.

"The kings of each city levied tolls on us, but would not suffer us to enter their gates. They threw us bread over the walls, little maize-cakes baked in honey and cakes of fine flour filled with dates. For every hundred baskets we gave them a bead of amber.

"When the dwellers in the villages saw us coming, they poisoned the wells and fled to the hill-summits. We fought with the Magadae who are born old, and grow younger and younger every year, and die when they are little children; and with the Laktroi who say that they are the sons of tigers, and paint themselves yellow and black; and with the Aurantes who bury their dead on the tops of trees, and themselves live in dark caverns lest the sun, who is their god, should slay them; and with the Krimnians who worship a crocodile, and give it earrings of green glass, and feed it with butter and fresh fowls; and with the Agazonbae, who are dog-faced; and with the Sibans, who have horses' feet, and run more swiftly than horses. A third of our company died in battle, and a third died of want. The rest murmured against me, and said that I had brought them an evil fortune. I took a horned adder from beneath a stone and let it sting me. When they saw that I did not sicken they grew afraid.

"In the fourth month we reached the city of Illel. It was night-time when we came to the grove that is outside the walls, and the air was sultry, for the moon was travelling in Scorpion. We took the ripe pomegranates from the trees, and brake them, and drank their sweet juices. Then we lay down on our carpets, and waited for the dawn.

"And at dawn we rose and knocked at the gate of the city. It was wrought out of red bronze, and carved with sea-dragons and dragons that have wings. The guards looked down from the battlements and asked us our business. The interpreter of the caravan answered that we had come from the island of Syria with much merchandise. They took hostages, and told us that they would open the gate to us at noon, and bade us tarry till then.

"When it was noon they opened the gate, and as we entered in the people came crowding out of the houses to look at us, and a crier went round the city crying through a shell. We stood in the marketplace, and the Negroes uncorded the bales of figured cloths and opened the carved chests of sycamore. And when they had ended their task, the merchants set forth their strange wares, the waxed linen from Egypt and the painted linen from the country of the Ethiops, the purple sponges from Tyre and the blue hangings from Sidon, the cups of cold amber and the fine vessels of glass and the curious vessels of burnt clay. From the roof of a house a company of women watched us. One of them wore a mask of gilded leather.

"And on the first day the priests came and bartered with us, and on the second day came the nobles, and on the third day came the craftsmen and the slaves. And this is their custom with all merchants as long as they tarry in the city.

"And we tarried for a moon, and when the moon was waning, I wearied and wandered away through the streets of the city and came to the garden of its god. The priests in their yellow robes moved silently through the green trees, and on a pavement of black marble stood the rose-red house in which the god had his dwelling. Its doors were of powdered lacquer, and bulls and peacocks were wrought on them in raised and polished gold. The tilted roof was of sea-green porcelain, and the jutting eaves were festooned with little bells. When the white doves flew past, they struck the bells with their wings and made them tinkle.

"In front of the temple was a pool of clear water paved with veined onyx. I lay down beside it, and with my pale fingers I touched the broad leaves. One of the priests came towards me and stood behind me. He had sandals on his feet, one of soft serpent-skin and the other of birds' plumage. On his head was a mitre of black felt decorated with silver crescents. Seven yellows were woven into his robe, and his frizzed hair was stained with antimony.

"After a little while he spoke to me, and asked me my desire.

"I told him that my desire was to see the god.

"'The god is hunting,' said the priest, looking strangely at me with his small slanting eyes.

"'Tell me in what forest, and I will ride with him,' I answered.

"He combed out the soft fringes of his tunic with his long pointed nails. 'The god is asleep,' he murmured.

"'Tell me on what couch, and I will watch by him,' I answered.

"'The god is at the feast,' he cried.

"'If the wine be sweet I will drink it with him, and if it be bitter I will drink it with him also,' was my answer.

"He bowed his head in wonder, and, taking me by the hand, he raised me up, and led me into the temple.

"And in the first chamber I saw an idol seated on a throne of jasper bordered with great orient pearls. It was carved out of ebony, and in stature was of the stature of a man. On its forehead was a ruby, and thick oil dripped from its hair on to its thighs. Its feet were red with the blood of a newly-slain kid, and its loins girt with a copper belt that was studded with seven beryls.

"And I said to the priest, 'Is this the god?' And he answered me, 'This is the god.'

"'Show me the god,' I cried, 'or I will surely slay you.' And I touched his hand, and it became withered.

"And the priest besought me, saying, 'Let my lord heal his servant, and I will show him the god.'

"So I breathed with my breath upon his hand, and it became whole again, and he trembled and led me into the second chamber, and I saw an idol standing on a lotus of jade hung with great emeralds. It was carved out of ivory, and in stature was twice the stature of a man. On its forehead was a chrysolite, and its breasts were smeared with myrrh and cinnamon. In one hand it held a crooked sceptre of jade, and in the other a round crystal. It ware buskins of brass, and its thick neck was circled with a circle of selenites.

"And I said to the priest, 'Is this the god?'

"And he answered me, 'This is the god.'

"'Show me the god,' I cried, 'or I will surely slay you.' And I touched his eyes, and they became blind.

"And the priest besought me, saying, 'Let my lord heal his servant, and I will show him the god.'

"So I breathed with my breath upon his eyes, and the sight came back to them, and he trembled again, and led me into the third chamber, and lo! there was no idol in it, nor image of any kind, but only a mirror of round metal set on an altar of stone.

"And I said to the priest, 'Where is the god?'

"And he answered me, 'There is no god but this mirror that you see, for this is the Mirror of Wisdom. And it reflects all things that are in heaven and on earth, save only the face of him who looks into it. This it reflecteth not, so that he who looks into it may be wise. Many other mirrors are there, but they are mirrors of Opinion. This only is the Mirror of Wisdom. And they who possess this mirror know everything, nor is there anything hidden from them. And they who possess it not have not Wisdom. Therefore is it the god, and we worship it.' And I looked into the mirror, and it was even as he had said to me.

"And I did a strange thing, but what I did does not matter, for in a valley that is but a day's journey from this place have I hidden the Mirror of Wisdom. Do but suffer me to enter into you again and be your servant, and you shall be wiser than all the wise men, and wisdom shall be yours. Suffer me to enter into you, and none will be as wise as you."

But the young fisherman laughed. "Love is better than wisdom," he cried, "and the little mermaid loves me."

"No, but there is nothing better than wisdom," said the soul.

"Love is better," answered the young fisherman, and he plunged into the deep, and the soul went weeping away over the marshes.

And after the second year was over, the soul came down to the shore of the sea, and called to the young fisherman, and he rose out of the deep and said, "Why do you call to me?"

And the soul answered, "Come nearer, that I may speak with you, for I have seen marvellous things."

So he came nearer, and couched in the shallow water, and leaned his head upon his hand and listened.

And the soul said to him, "When I left you, I turned my face to the south and journeyed. From the south comes everything that is precious. Six days I journeyed along the highways that lead to the city of Ashter, along the dusty red-dyed highways by which the pilgrims are wont to go did I journey, and on the morning of the seventh day I lifted up my eyes, and lo! The city lay at my feet, for it is in a valley.

"There are nine gates to this city, and in front of each gate stands a bronze horse that neighs when the Bedouins come down from the mountains. The walls are cased with copper, and the watch-towers on the walls are roofed with brass. In every tower stands an archer with a bow in his hand. At sunrise he strikes with an arrow on a gong, and at sunset he blows through a horn of horn.

"When I sought to enter, the guards stopped me and asked of me who I was. I made answer that I was a Dervish and on my way to the city of Mecca, where there was a green veil on which the Koran was embroidered in silver letters by the hands of the angels. They were filled with wonder, and entreated me to pass in.

"Inside it is even as a bazaar. Surely you should have been with me. Across the narrow streets the gay lanterns of paper flutter like large butterflies. When the wind blows over the roofs they rise and fall as painted bubbles do. In front of their booths sit the merchants on silken carpets. They have straight black beards, and their turbans are covered with golden sequins, and long strings of amber and carved peach stones glide through their cool fingers. Some of them sell galbanum and nard, and curious perfumes from the islands of the Indian Sea, and the thick oil of red roses, and myrrh and little nail-shaped cloves. When one stops to speak to them, they throw pinches of frankincense upon a charcoal brazier and make the air sweet. I saw a Syrian who held in his hands a thin rod like a reed. Grey threads of smoke came from it, and its odour as it burned was as the odour of the pink almond in spring. Others sell silver bracelets embossed all over with creamy blue turquoise stones, and anklets of brass wire fringed with little pearls, and tigers' claws set in gold, and the claws of that gilt cat, the leopard, set in gold also, and earrings of pierced emerald, and finger-rings of hollowed jade. From the tea-houses comes the sound of the guitar, and the opium-smokers with their white smiling faces look out at the passers-by.

"Of a truth you should have been with me. The wine sellers elbow their way through the crowd with great black skins on their shoulders. Most of them sell the wine of Schiraz, which is as sweet as honey. They serve it in little metal cups and strew rose leaves upon it. In the market-place stand the fruitsellers, who sell all kinds of fruit: ripe figs, with their bruised purple flesh, melons, smelling of musk and yellow as topazes, citrons and rose-apples and clusters of white grapes, round red-gold oranges, and oval lemons of green gold. Once I saw an elephant go by. Its trunk was painted with vermilion and turmeric, and over its ears it had a net of crimson silk cord. It stopped opposite one of the booths and began eating the oranges, and the man only laughed. You can not think how strange a people they are. When they are glad they go to the bird sellers and buy of them a caged bird, and set it free that their joy may be greater, and when they are sad they scourge themselves with thorns that their sorrow may not grow less.

"One evening I met some Negroes carrying a heavy palanquin through the bazaar. It was made of gilded bamboo, and the poles were of vermilion lacquer studded with brass peacocks. Across the windows hung thin curtains of muslin embroidered with beetles' wings and with tiny seed pearls, and as it passed by a pale-faced Circassian looked out and smiled at me. I followed behind, and the Negroes hurried their steps and scowled. But I did not care. I felt a great curiosity come over me.

"At last they stopped at a square white house. There were no windows to it, only a little door like the door of a tomb. They set down the palanquin and knocked three times with a copper hammer. An Armenian in a caftan of green leather peered through the wicket, and when he saw them he opened, and spread a carpet on the ground, and the woman stepped out. As she went in, she turned round and smiled at me again. I had never seen any one so pale.

"When the moon rose I returned to the same place and sought for the house, but it was no longer there. When I saw that, I knew who the woman was, and wherefore she had smiled at me.

"Certainly you should have been with me. On the feast of the New Moon the young Emperor came forth from his palace and went into the mosque to pray. His hair and beard were dyed with rose-leaves, and his cheeks were powdered with a fine gold dust. The palms of his feet and hands were yellow with saffron.

"At sunrise he went forth from his palace in a robe of silver, and at sunset he returned to it again in a robe of gold. The people flung themselves on the ground and hid their faces, but I would not do so. I stood by the stall of a seller of dates and waited. When the Emperor saw me, he raised his painted eyebrows and stopped. I stood quite still, and made him no obeisance. The people marvelled at my boldness, and counselled me to flee from the city. I paid no heed to them, but went and sat with the sellers of strange gods, who by reason of their craft are abominated. When I told them what I had done, each of them gave me a god and prayed me to leave them.

"That night, as I lay on a cushion in the teahouse that is in the Street of Pomegranates, the guards of the Emperor entered and led me to the palace. As I went in they closed each door behind me, and put a chain across it. Inside was a great court with an arcade running all round. The walls were of white alabaster, set here and there with blue and green tiles. The pillars were of green marble, and the pavement of a kind of peach-blossom marble. I had never seen anything like it before.

"As I passed across the courts, two veiled women looked down from a balcony and cursed me. The guards hastened on, and the butts of the lances rang upon the polished floor. They opened a gate of wrought ivory, and I found myself in a watered garden of seven terraces. It was planted with tulip-cups and moonflowers, and silver-studded aloes. Like a slim reed of crystal a fountain hung in the dusky air. The cypress trees were like burnt-out torches. From one of them a nightingale was singing.

"At the end of the garden stood a little pavilion. As we approached it two eunuchs came out to meet us. Their fat bodies swayed as they walked, and they glanced curiously at me with their yellow-lidded eyes. One of them drew aside the captain of the guard, and in a low voice whispered to him. The other kept munching scented pastilles, which he took with an affected gesture out of an oval box of lilac enamel.

"After a few moments the captain of the guard dismissed the soldiers. They went back to the palace, the eunuchs following slowly behind and plucking the sweet mulberries from the trees as they passed. Once the elder of the two turned round, and smiled at me with an evil smile.

"Then the captain of the guard motioned me towards the entrance of the pavilion. I walked on without trembling, and drawing the heavy curtain aside I entered in.

"The young Emperor was stretched on a couch of dyed lion skins, and a gerfalcon perched upon his wrist. Behind him stood a brass-turbaned Nubian, naked down to the waist, and with heavy earrings in his split ears. On a table by the side of the couch lay a mighty scimitar of steel.

"When the Emperor saw me he frowned, and said to me, 'What is your name? Don't you know that I am Emperor of this city?' But I made him no answer.

"He pointed with his finger at the scimitar, and the Nubian seized it, and rushing forward struck at me with great violence. The blade whizzed through me, and did me no hurt. The man fell sprawling on the floor, and when he rose up his teeth chattered with terror and he hid himself behind the couch.

"The Emperor leapt to his feet, and taking a lance from a stand of arms, he threw it at me. I caught it in its flight, and brake the shaft into two pieces. He shot at me with an arrow, but I held up my hands and it stopped in mid-air. Then he drew a dagger from a belt of white leather, and stabbed the Nubian in the throat lest the slave should tell of his dishonour. The man writhed like a trampled snake, and a red foam bubbled from his lips.

"As soon as he was dead the Emperor turned to me, and when he had wiped away the bright sweat from his brow with a little napkin of purfled and purple silk, he said to me, 'Are you a prophet, that I may not harm you, or the son of a prophet, that I can do you no hurt? I pray you leave my city tonight, for while you are in it I am no longer its lord.'

"And I answered him, 'I will go for half of your treasure. Give me half of your treasure, and I will go away.'

"He took me by the hand, and led me out into the garden. When the captain of the guard saw me, he wondered. When the eunuchs saw me, their knees shook and they fell upon the ground in fear.

"There is a chamber in the palace that has eight walls of red porphyry, and a brass-sealed ceiling hung with lamps. The Emperor touched one of the walls and it opened, and we passed down a corridor that was lit with many torches. In niches upon each side stood great wine jars filled to the brim with silver pieces. When we reached the centre of the corridor the Emperor spoke the word that may not be spoken, and a granite door swung back on a secret spring, and he put his hands before his face lest his eyes should be dazzled.

"You could not believe how marvellous a place it was. There were huge tortoise-shells full of pearls, and hollowed moonstones of great size piled up with red rubies. The gold was stored in coffers of elephant-hide, and the gold-dust in leather bottles. There were opals and sapphires, the former in cups of crystal, and the latter in cups of jade. Round green emeralds were ranged in order upon thin plates of ivory, and in one corner were silk bags filled, some with turquoise-stones, and others with beryls. The ivory horns were heaped with purple amethysts, and the horns of brass with chalcedonies and sards. The pillars, which were of cedar, were hung with strings of yellow lynx-stones. In the flat oval shields there were carbuncles, both wine-coloured and coloured like grass. And yet I have told you but a tithe of what was there.

"And when the Emperor had taken away his hands from before his face he said to me, 'This is my house of treasure, and half that is in it is yours, even as I promised to you. And I will give you camels and camel drivers, and they shall do your bidding and take your share of the treasure to whatever part of the world you desire to go. And the thing shall be done tonight, for I would not that the Sun, who is my father, should see that there is in my city a man whom I cannot slay.'

"But I answered him, 'The gold that is here is yours, and the silver also is yours, and yours are the precious jewels and the things of price. As for me, I have no need of these. Nor shall I take aught from you but that little ring that you wear on the finger of your hand.'

"And the Emperor frowned. 'It is but a ring of lead,' he cried, 'nor has it any value. Therefore take your half of the treasure and go from my city.'

"'No,' I answered, 'but I will take nought but that leaden ring, for I know what is written within it, and for what purpose.'

"And the Emperor trembled, and besought me and said, 'Take all the treasure and go from my city. The half that is mine shall be yours also.'

"And I did a strange thing, but what I did matters not, for in a cave that is but a day's journey from this place have, I hidden the Ring of Riches. It is but a day's journey from this place, and it waits for your coming. He who has this Ring is richer than all the kings of the world. Come therefore and take it, and the world's riches shall be yours."

But the young fisherman laughed. "Love is better than riches," he cried, "and the little mermaid loves me."

"No, but there is nothing better than riches," said the soul.

"Love is better," answered the young fisherman, and he plunged into the deep, and the soul went weeping away over the marshes.

And after the third year was over, the soul came down to the shore of the sea, and called to the young fisherman, and he rose out of the deep and said, "Why do you call to me?"

And the soul answered, "Come nearer, that I may speak with you, for I have seen marvellous things."

So he came nearer, and couched in the shallow water, and leaned his head upon his hand and listened.

And the soul said to him, "In a city that I know of there is an inn that standeth by a river. I sat there with sailors who drank of two different coloured wines, and ate bread made of barley, and little salt fish served in bay leaves with vinegar. And as we sat and made merry, there entered to us an old man bearing a leathern carpet and a lute that had two horns of amber. And when he had laid out the carpet on the floor, he struck with a quill on the wire strings of his lute, and a girl whose face was veiled ran in and began to dance before us. Her face was veiled with a veil of gauze, but her feet were naked. Naked were her feet, and they moved over the carpet like little white pigeons. Never have I seen anything so marvellous; and the city in which she dances is but a day's journey from this place."

Now when the young fisherman heard the words of his soul, he remembered that the little mermaid had no feet and could not dance. And a great desire came over him, and he said to himself, "It is but a day's journey, and I can return to my love," and he laughed, and stood up in the shallow water, and strode towards the shore.

And when he had reached the dry shore he laughed again, and held out his arms to his soul. And his soul gave a great cry of joy and ran to meet him, and entered into him, and the young fisherman saw stretched before him upon the sand that shadow of the body that is the body of the soul.

And his soul said to him, "Let us not tarry, but get hence at once, for the sea gods are jealous, and have monsters that do their bidding."

So they made haste, and all that night they journeyed beneath the moon, and all the next day they journeyed beneath the sun, and on the evening of the day they came to a city.

And the young fisherman said to his soul, "Is this the city in which she dances of whom you did speak to me?"

And his soul answered him, "It is not this city, but another. Nevertheless let us enter in." So they entered in and passed through the streets, and as they passed through the Street of the Jewellers the young fisherman saw a fair silver cup set forth in a booth. And his soul said to him, "Take that silver cup and hide it."

So he took the cup and hid it in the fold of his tunic, and they went hurriedly out of the city.

And after that they had gone a league from the city, the young fisherman frowned, and flung the cup away, and said to his soul, "Why did you tell me to take this cup and hide it, for it was an evil thing to do?"

But his soul answered him, "Be at peace, be at peace."

And on the evening of the second day they came to a city, and the young fisherman said to his soul, "Is this the city in which she dances of whom you did speak to me?"

And his soul answered him, "It is not this city, but another. Nevertheless let us enter in." So they entered in and passed through the streets, and as they passed through the street of the Sellers of Sandals, the young fisherman saw a child standing by a jar of water. And his soul said to him, "Smite that child." So he smote the child till it wept, and when he had done this they went hurriedly out of the city.

And after that they had gone a league from the city the young fisherman grew wroth, and said to his soul, "Why did you tell me to smite the child, for it was an evil thing to do?"

But his soul answered him, "Be at peace, be at peace."

And on the evening of the third day they came to a city, and the young fisherman said to his soul, "Is this the city in which she dances of whom you did speak to me?"

And his soul answered him, "It may be that it is in this city, therefore let us enter in."

So they entered in and passed through the streets, but nowhere could the young fisherman find the river or the inn that stood by its side. And the people of the city looked curiously at him, and he grew afraid and said to his soul, "Let us go hence, for she who dances with white feet is not here."

But his soul answered, "No, but let us tarry, for the night is dark and there will be robbers on the way."

So he sat him down in the marketplace and rested, and after a time there went by a hooded merchant who had a cloak of cloth of Tartary, and bare a lantern of pierced horn at the end of a jointed reed. And the merchant said to him, "Why do you sit in the marketplace, seeing that the booths are closed and the bales corded?"

And the young fisherman answered him, "I can find no inn in this city, nor have I any kinsman who might give me shelter."

"Are we not all kinsmen?" said the merchant. "And did not one God make us? Therefore come with me, for I have a guest-chamber."

So the young fisherman rose up and followed the merchant to his house.

And when he had passed through a garden of pomegranates and entered into the house, the merchant brought him rosewater in a copper dish that he might wash his hands, and ripe melons that he might quench his thirst, and set a bowl of rice and a piece of roasted kid before him.

And after that he had finished, the merchant led him to the guest-chamber, and bade him sleep and be at rest. And the young fisherman gave him thanks, and kissed the ring that was on his hand, and flung himself down on the carpets of dyed goat's hair. And when he had covered himself with a covering of black lamb's wool he fell asleep.

And three hours before dawn, and while it was still night, his soul waked him and said to him, "Rise up and go to the room of the merchant, even to the room in which he sleeps, and slay him, and take from him his gold, for we have need of it."

And the young fisherman rose up and crept towards the room of the merchant, and over the feet of the merchant there was lying a curved sword, and the tray by the side of the merchant held nine purses of gold. And he reached out his hand and touched the sword, and when he touched it the merchant started and awoke, and leaping up seized himself the sword and cried to the young fisherman, "Do you return evil for good, and pay with the shedding of blood for the kindness that I have shown you?"

And his soul said to the young fisherman, "Strike him," and he struck him so that he swooned and he seized then the nine purses of gold, and fled hastily through the garden of pomegranates, and set his face to the star that is the star of morning.

And when they had gone a league from the city, the young fisherman beat his breast, and said to his soul, "Why did you bid me slay the merchant and take his gold? Surely you are evil."

But his soul answered him, "Be at peace, be at peace."

"No," cried the young fisherman, "I may not be at peace, for all that you have made me to do I hate. You also I hate, and I bid you tell me wherefore you have wrought with me in this wise."

And his soul answered him, "When you did send me forth into the world you didnot give me heart, so I learned to do all these things and love them."

"What do you say?" murmured the young fisherman.

"You know," answered his soul, "you know it well. Have you forgotten that you did not give me heart? I don't believe. And so trouble not yourself nor me, but be at peace, for there is no pain that you shall not give away, nor any pleasure that you shall not receive."

And when the young fisherman heard these words he trembled and said to his soul, "No, but you are evil, and have made me forget my love, and have tempted me with temptations, and have set my feet in the ways of sin."

And his soul answered him, "You have not forgotten that when you did send me forth into the world you gave me no heart. Come, let us go to another city, and make merry, for we have nine purses of gold."

But the young fisherman took the nine purses of gold, and flung them down, and trampled on them.

"No," he cried, "but I will have nothing to do with you, nor will I journey with you anywhere, but even as I sent you away before, so will I send you away now, for you have wrought me no good." And he turned his back to the moon, and with the little knife that had the handle of green viper's skin he strove to cut from his feet that shadow of the body which is the body of the soul.

Yet his soul stirred not from him, nor paid heed to his command, but said to him, "The spell that the witch told you avails you no more, for I may not leave you, nor may you drive me forth. Once in his life may a man send his soul away, but he who receives back his soul must keep it with him for ever, and this is his punishment and his reward."

And the young fisherman grew pale and clenched his hands and cried, "She was a false witch in that she told me not that."

"No," answered his soul, "but she was true to Him she worships, and whose servant she will be ever."

And when the young fisherman knew that he could no longer get rid of his soul, and that it was an evil soul and would abide with him always, he fell upon the ground weeping bitterly.

And when it was day the young fisherman rose up and said to his soul, "I will bind my hands that I may not do your bidding, and close my lips that I may not speak your words, and I will return to the place where she whom I love has her dwelling. Even to the sea will I return, and to the little bay where she is wont to sing, and I will call to her and tell her the evil I have done and the evil you have wrought on me."

And his soul tempted him and said, "Who is your love, that you should return to her? The world has many fairer than she is. There are the dancing-girls of Samaris who dance in the manner of all kinds of birds and beasts. Their feet are painted with henna, and in their hands they have little copper bells. They laugh while they dance, and their laughter is as clear as the laughter of water. Come with me and I will show them to you. For what is this trouble of yours about the things of sin? Is that which is pleasant to eat not made for the eater? Is there poison in that which is sweet to drink? Trouble not yourself, but come with me to another city. There is a little city hard by in which there is a garden of tulip-trees. And there dwell in this comely garden white peacocks and peacocks that have blue breasts. Their tails when they spread them to the sun are like disks of ivory and like gilt disks. And she who feeds them dances for their pleasure, and sometimes she dances on her hands and at other times she dances with her feet. Her eyes are coloured with stibium, and her nostrils are shaped like the wings of a swallow. From a hook in one of her nostrils hangs a flower that is carved out of a pearl. She laughs while she dances, and the silver rings that are about her ankles tinkle like bells of silver. And so trouble not yourself any more, but come with me to this city."

But the young fisherman did not answer his soul, but closed his lips with the seal of silence and with a tight cord bound his hands, and journeyed back to the place from which he had come, even to the little bay where his love had been used to sing. And ever did his soul tempt him by the way, but he made it no answer, nor would he do any of the wickedness that it sought to make him to do, so great was the power of the love that was within him.

And when he had reached the shore of the sea, he loosed the cord from his hands, and took the seal of silence from his lips, and called to the little mermaid. But she came not to his call, though he called to her all day long and besought her.

And his soul mocked him and said, "Surely you have but little joy out of your love. You are as one who in time of death pours water into a broken vessel. You give away what you have, and is not given to you in return. It were better for you to come with me, for I know where the Valley of Pleasure lies, and what things are wrought there."

But the young fisherman did not answer his soul, but in a cleft of the rock he built himself a house of wattles, and abode there for the space of a year. And every morning he called to the mermaid, and every noon he called to her again, and at night time he spoke her name. Yet never did she rise out of the sea to meet him, nor in any place of the sea could he find her though he sought for her in the caves and in the green water, in the pools of the tide and in the wells that are at the bottom of the deep.

And ever did his soul tempt him with evil, and whisper of terrible things. Yet did it not prevail against him, so great was the power of his love.

And after the year was over, the soul thought within himself, "I have tempted my master with evil, and his love is stronger than I am. I will tempt him now with good, and it may be that he will come with me."

So he spoke to the young fisherman and said, "I have told you of the joy of the world, and you have turned a deaf ear to me. Suffer me now to tell you of the world's pain, and it may be that you will hearken. For of a truth pain is the Lord of this world, nor is there any one who escapes from its net. There be some who lack raiment, and others who lack bread. There be widows who sit in purple, and widows who sit in rags. To and fro over the fens go the lepers, and they are cruel to each other. The beggars go up and down on the highways, and their wallets are empty. Through the streets of the cities walks Famine, and the Plague sits at their gates. Come, let us go forth and mend these things, and make them not to be. Wherefore should you tarry here calling to your love, seeing she not come to your call? And what is love, that you should set this high store upon it?"

But the young fisherman did not answer it, so great was the power of his love. And every morning he called to the mermaid, and every noon he called to her again, and at night time he spoke her name. Yet never did she rise out of the sea to meet him, nor in any place of the sea could he find her, though he sought for her in the rivers of the sea, and in the valleys that are under the waves, in the sea that the night makes purple, and in the sea that the dawn leaves grey.

And after the second year was over, the soul said to the young fisherman at night-time, and as he sat in the wattled house alone, "Lo! Now I have tempted you with evil, and I have tempted you with good, and your love is stronger than I am. Wherefore will I tempt you no longer, but I pray you to suffer me to enter your heart, that I may be one with you even as before."

"Surely you may enter," said the young fisherman, "for in the days when with no heart you did go through the world you must have much suffered."

"Alas!" cried his soul, "I can find no place of entrance, so compassed about with love is this heart of yours."

"Yet I would that I could help you," said the young fisherman.

And as he spoke there came a great cry of mourning from the sea, even the cry that men hear when one of the seafolk is dead. And the young fisherman leapt up, and left his wattled house, and ran down to the shore. And the black waves came hurrying to the shore, bearing with them a burden that was whiter than silver. White as the surf it was, and like a flower it tossed on the waves. And the surf took it from the waves, and the foam took it from the surf, and the shore received it, and lying at his feet the young fisherman saw the body of the little mermaid. Dead at his feet it was lying.

Weeping as one smitten with pain he flung himself down beside it, and he kissed the cold red of the mouth, and toyed with the wet amber of the hair. He flung himself down beside it on the sand, weeping as one trembling with joy, and in his brown arms he held it to his breast. Cold were the lips, yet he kissed them. Salt was the honey of the hair, yet he tasted it with a bitter joy. He kissed the closed eyelids, and the wild spray that lay upon their cups was less salt than his tears.

And to the dead thing he made confession. Into the shells of its ears he poured the harsh wine of his tale. He put the little hands round his neck, and with his fingers he touched the thin reed of the throat. Bitter, bitter was his joy, and full of strange gladness was his pain.

The black sea came nearer, and the white foam moaned like a leper. With white claws of foam the sea grabbled at the shore. From the palace of the sea king came the cry of mourning again, and far out upon the sea the great Tritons blew hoarsely upon their horns.

"Flee away," said his soul, "for ever does the sea come nigher, and if you tarry it will slay you. Flee away, for I am afraid, seeing that your heart is closed against me by reason of the greatness of your love. Flee away to a place of safety. Surely you will not send me without a heart into another world?"

But the young fisherman did not listen to his soul, but called on the little mermaid and said, "Love is better than wisdom, and more precious than riches, and fairer than the feet of the daughters of men. The fires cannot destroy it, nor can the waters quench it. I called on you at dawn, and you did not come to my call. The moon heard your name, yet had you no heed of me. For evilly had I left you, and to my own hurt had I wandered away. Yet ever did your love abide with me, and ever was it strong, nor did anything prevail against it, though I have looked upon evil and looked upon good. And now that you are dead, surely I will die with you also."

And his soul besought him to depart, but he would not, so great was his love. And the sea came nearer, and sought to cover him with its waves, and when he knew that the end was at hand he kissed with mad lips the cold lips of the mermaid, and the heart that was within him brake. And as through the fulness of his love his heart did break, the soul found an entrance and entered in, and was one with him even as before. And the sea covered the young fisherman with its waves.

And in the morning the priest went forth to bless the sea, for it had been troubled. And with him went the monks and the musicians, and the candle-bearers, and the swingers of censers, and a great company.

And when the priest reached the shore he saw the young fisherman lying drowned in the surf, and clasped in his arms was the body of the little mermaid. And he drew back frowning, and having made the sign of the cross, he cried aloud and said, "I will not bless the sea nor anything that is in it. Accursed be the seafolk, and accursed be all they who traffic with them. And as for him who for love's sake forsook God, and so lies here with his leman slain by God's judgment, take up his body and the body of his leman, and bury them in the corner of the Field of the Fullers, and set no mark above them, nor sign of any kind, that none may know the place of their resting. For accursed were they in their lives, and accursed shall they be in their deaths also."

And the people did as he commanded them, and in the corner of the Field of the Fullers, where no sweet herbs grew, they dug a deep pit, and laid the dead things within it.

And when the third year was over, and on a day that was a holy day, the priest went up to the chapel, that he might show to the people the wounds of the Lord, and speak to them about the wrath of God.

And when he had robed himself with his robes, and entered in and bowed himself before the altar, he saw that the altar was covered with strange flowers that never had been seen before. Strange were they to look at, and of curious beauty, and their beauty troubled him, and their odour was sweet in his nostrils. And he felt glad, and understood not why he was glad.

And after that he had opened the tabernacle, and incensed the monstrance that was in it, and shown the fair wafer to the people, and hid it again behind the veil of veils, he began to speak to the people, desiring to speak to them of the wrath of God. But the beauty of the white flowers troubled him, and their odour was sweet in his nostrils, and there came another word into his lips, and he spoke not of the wrath of God, but of the God whose name is love. And why he so spoke, he knew not.

And when he had finished his word the people wept, and the priest went back to the sacristy, and his eyes were full of tears. And the deacons came in and began to unrobe him, and took from him the alb and the girdle, the maniple and the stole. And he stood as one in a dream.

And after that they had unrobed him, he looked at them and said, "What are the flowers that stand on the altar, and whence do they come?"

And they answered him, "What flowers they are we cannot tell, but they come from the corner of the Fullers' Field" And the priest trembled, and returned to his own house and prayed.

And in the morning, while it was still dawn, he went forth with the monks and the musicians, and the candle-bearers and the swingers of censers, and a great company, and came to the shore of the sea, and blessed the sea, and all the wild things that are in it. The Fauns also he blessed, and the little things that dance in the woodland, and the bright-eyed things that peer through the leaves. All the things in God's world he blessed, and the people were filled with joy and wonder. Yet never again in the corner of the Fullers' Field grew flowers of any kind, but the field remained barren even as before. Nor came the seafolk into the bay as they had been wont to do, for they went to another part of the sea.

星孩儿

　　很久以前,有两个穷苦的樵夫正穿过一片广袤的松树林往家赶。那是一个寒冬的夜晚,地上覆盖着厚厚的积雪,树枝也裹上了银装,在他们经过时,冰霜时而压断两旁的小树枝。当他们来到山谷时,一条瀑布如同白练一动不动地悬在空中,因为她刚被冰王吻过了。

　　实在太冷了,连鸟兽都不知道该如何是好。

　　"嗷~"豺狼夹着尾巴,一瘸一拐地穿过灌木丛,怒号起来,"这天气真是让人害怕。政府怎么就不管呢?"

　　"唧!唧!唧!"绿色的朱顶雀喳喳地叫着,"苍老的大地已经死啦,所以他们才给她穿上白色的寿衣。

　　"是大地要出嫁,这是新娘的婚纱呢,"斑鸠们互相低声耳语。他们的粉红小脚冻得够呛,可是他们仍然觉得,自个儿有责任用乐观浪漫的态度来看待眼前的局面。

　　"胡说八道!"豺狼吼起来,"我告诉你们吧,这都是政府的过错。要是你们不信我的话,我就把你们吃掉。"豺狼有一颗十分务实的头脑,从来不会因为争吵激烈而乱了阵脚。

　　"呃,就我来说,"天生就是哲学家的啄木鸟说道,"解释这解释那的,我半点儿兴趣都没有。要是一件事儿是这样,那它就是这样,眼下就是天冷得受不了了。"

　　确实冷得受不了了。住在高高杉树上的小松鼠,不停地互相摩擦着鼻子,好让他们自个儿暖和起来;兔子蜷缩成一团躲在洞里,不敢往外看。唯一似乎喜欢这天气的只有大猫头鹰了。他们的羽毛让霜冻得硬邦邦的，可他们毫不在意；他们骨碌碌地转着黄色的大眼睛，相互隔着林子呼喊着："图—威！图—武！图—威！图—武！天气真让我们爽啊！"

两个樵夫继续赶路，使劲地朝手指上哈着热气，迈着钉过铁掌的大靴，重重地踏过冻成块的积雪。有一次，他们陷进了一个深坑，待爬出来时浑身雪白，就像正在磨面的磨坊师傅一样；有一次，他们在沼泽泥水冻成的又硬又滑的冰面上摔倒了，柴禾散了捆，只好重新捡起，再捆在一块儿；还有一次，他们以为自己迷路了，吓得要死，因为他俩知道谁要敢倒在雪姑娘的怀抱里睡觉，雪姑娘就不会手下留情了。然而，他们相信圣·马丁是个心地善良的旅行之神，会看护好所有游子。于是，他俩先原路返回，再小心前行，终于来到了林子的边缘，远远地看见了村子里的灯火。

他们因脱离险境而欣喜若狂，哈哈大笑起来，在他俩眼里大地成了一朵银花，月亮则成了一朵金花。

然而，大笑过后他俩禁不住伤心起来，因为想起自家都一贫如洗。其中的一个樵夫对另一个说："我们开心什么呢，没看见日子偏向富人，不是偏向咱们这样的穷人吗？还不如就在林里子冻死，或遇着猛兽扑上来咬死咱俩算了。"

"真是这样，"他的同伴答道，"一些人拥有得多，其他人拥有得少。不公已经瓜分了这个世界，没有任何东西分得公平，除了悲伤。"

正当他俩互相哀叹自个儿的痛苦时，怪事发生了。从天上落下一颗非常明亮而又美丽的星星。它从天际滑落下来，掠过其他星星的身旁。他俩惊讶地望着，它似乎就坠落在一丛柳树的后面，树丛旁边有一个小羊圈，羊圈也不远，用块石头就能扔得到。

"哇塞！谁找到了，准有坛金子。"他俩齐声喊着，就动身跑了过去，实在是太想要金子了。

其中一人比他的同伴跑得快，超了过去，再奋力挤过那丛柳树，来到了树丛的背面。瞧！果真有件金灿灿的东西躺在白皑皑的雪地上。于是，他急忙冲上去，弯下腰，伸出双手一把抓住了那件东西。那是一件用金丝织成的斗篷，上面精心地绣着众多星星，裹了一层又一层。他向他的同伴大声呼喊，说找到了从天而降的宝物。同伴一赶上来，他们就在雪地里坐下来，解开那一层层裹着的斗篷，好分享里面的金块。没承想，哎！没有黄金，没有白银，里面啥宝物也没有，只有一个呼呼大睡的小小孩童。

他俩中一个对另一个说道："咱们的妄想痛苦地收场了，更谈不上什么好运，毕竟一个小孩能给大人带来什么好处呢？咱俩就把小孩丢在这儿吧，赶紧赶路，要知道咱俩都是穷人，又有自个儿的孩子，没法子掰出面包来多喂一张嘴。"

可是他的同伴回答："不行，把孩子丢在雪地里，让他饿死，这是在作孽啊！我和你一样穷，也有许多张嘴要养，锅里也没什么吃的，可我还是想带他回家，我的妻子会照顾他的。"

于是，他轻手轻脚地抱起孩子，再用斗篷缠紧以防他冻着。然后，他下山往村庄走去。见他这么傻，心肠却这么软，他的同伴都惊呆了。

赶到村庄时，同伴对他说："你得了这个孩子，该把斗篷分给我了，上山打猎见者有份嘛。"

但他回答："不行，因为斗篷不是我的，也不是你的，而是这个孩子的。"说完他便与同伴告别，来到自家门前，伸手敲了起来。

他的妻子打开门，见丈夫平安归来，就伸开双臂搂住他的脖子亲着，然后卸下他背上的柴禾，掸掉他靴上的积雪，再叫他进屋来。

可是他对妻子说："咱在林子里捡到一样东西，带了回来，要交给你好好照顾呢。"他立在门槛上，不再往里走了。

"什么东西？"妻子大声喊道，"快给我看看，家里边空荡荡的，咱们缺很多东西呢。"他把斗篷往后拉开来，给妻子看那个熟睡的孩子。

"哎呀呀，当家的！"妻子喃喃地说，"咱们自个儿的孩子还不够多，要让你弄个人家都不要的小孩来炉边添堵吗？谁晓得他会不会给咱们带来什么厄运呢？还有，咱们又能拿出什么养他呢？"妻子冲他大发雷霆。

"不不，他可是个星孩儿。"他答道，还把发现星孩儿的奇怪经过告诉了妻子。

可妻子仍不肯消气，反而一个劲儿地数落他，怒气冲冲地嚷道："咱们自家孩子都缺吃少穿的，还要去养别人家的吗？谁来照顾咱们这一家子？谁来给咱们吃的穿的呢？"

"不要这样嘛，上帝连鸟雀也要关心，也要养活呢。"他答道。

"没看到鸟雀会在冬天饿死吗？"妻子问道，"现在不正是冬天吗？"

他答不上来，只是立在门槛上，不肯往里走。

一阵冷风从林子里刮了过来，吹进开着的门，使妻子浑身颤抖，哆嗦起来，对他说道："你还不关上门？冷风进屋，我冷死啦。"

"一户人家，心肠冷漠，吹进来的风能不冷吗？"他反问道。那妇人没有回答他，而是静静地往火炉边靠近。

不一会儿，妻子转过身来看着他，双眼噙满了泪水。他迅速走了进来，把孩子放进她的怀里。她亲了孩子，然后把他放到一张小床上，上面正躺着他们最小的孩子。第二天，樵夫拿起那件奇特的金斗篷，放进了一个大箱子；他妻子取下孩子颈上的那条琥珀链子，也一同放了进去。

就这么着，星孩儿和樵夫的孩子们一同长大，跟他们一起吃饭，跟他们一同玩耍。一年一年过去，星孩儿长得愈加漂亮，让住在这个村庄的所有人都惊讶不已，因为大伙儿都是黑皮肤、黑眼睛，可是他宛如刚剖开的象牙一样白净、娇嫩，满头鬈发仿佛一圈圈黄水仙。还有，他的嘴唇犹如红色的花瓣儿，眼睛如同一汪清水边上的紫罗兰，身体犹如原野之上没人割过的一丛水仙花。

然而，他的美貌却让他变坏了，他渐渐地骄傲起来，变得又残酷又自私。樵夫的孩子和村中的其他孩子，他统统看不起，说他们出身卑贱，唯独自个儿高贵，出自一颗星星，他凌驾于他们之上，把他们唤作奴仆。他毫不怜悯穷人，也不怜悯那些眼盲的、身残的或其他遭受疾病痛苦的人，反而扔石子赶他们上大路，好让他们到别处去讨吃的。所以，除歹徒惯犯外没有谁会再次到那个村庄乞讨了。没错，他已经被美迷住了心窍，总是嘲笑那些瘦小或丑陋的人，拿他们开涮；而对自个儿钟爱有加，夏天无风时他会躺在牧师果园的水井旁边，低头欣赏自个儿的脸蛋，看到自个儿的白皙美貌，禁不住高兴得哈哈大笑起来。

时常，樵夫和妻子会斥责一番，对他说："我们先前对你，可不像你现在对那些落难无助的人那样啊！为什么你要对那些可怜的人那么残酷呢？"

时常，年长的神父会派人把他找去，想方设法地教他要爱天下生灵，对他说："飞蝇是你的兄弟，不可伤它。林间漫游的野鸟有自个儿的自由，不可捉来取乐。蛇蜥和鼹鼠也都是上帝造出的，各有其位。你又是谁，竟要给上帝的世界带来痛苦？就连野外的牛都赞美他呢。"

然而，星孩儿并不听他们的话，反而会皱着眉头撇起嘴巴，扭头就回去找他的伙伴们，然后领着他们胡闹去。星孩儿长得帅，跑得快，会跳舞，会吹笛，还会音乐，所以伙伴们都争相模仿。星孩儿到哪儿，他们就到哪儿；星孩儿吩咐做啥，他们就做啥。当星孩儿用芦苇尖去刺鼹鼠迟钝的双眼时，他们就哈哈大笑；当星孩儿拿石子去砸麻风病人时，他们也是哈哈大笑。于是，在所有方面星孩儿都支配并影响着他们，他们也就变得像他一样铁石心肠。

一天，村庄上来了一个可怜的女乞丐。她穿着破破烂烂的衣服，沿着粗粝不平的道路一路走来，双脚被磨得鲜血直流，整个情形惨不忍睹。又累又乏，她只得坐在一棵栗树下面歇息。

星孩儿看见她，就对伙伴们说："看哪！竟来了个臭叫花子，还敢坐在那棵好看的栗树下面。快来，轰走她。她长得丑，太烦人了。"

于是星孩儿大步走近，向她扔石子，还嘲笑她。她看着他，眼里充满了恐惧，但目光始终盯在他的身上。正在旁边的草料场里劈柴的樵夫看见了，就跑上来阻止星孩儿，并呵斥道："你确实有副硬心肠，没有同情心，这个可怜的妇人哪里得罪了你，你竟然这么对待她？"

星孩儿气得面红耳赤，跺着脚说道："你是谁啊，有什么资格对我说三道四？我又不是你的儿子，不用听你吩咐。"

"你说得没错，"樵夫回答，"可是我先前在林子里找到你的时候，却是动了怜悯之心的。"

妇人听到这番话后大叫一声，昏倒了过去。樵夫赶紧把她抱回家里，由妻子照料着。等她从昏迷中醒来时，夫妻俩给她端来肉和喝的，并嘱咐她宽心些。

然而妇人不吃也不喝，却问樵夫："难道说，那个孩子是你从林子里找回的？莫非发生在十年前的今天？"

樵夫答道："是的，我确实是在林子里找回他的，正是十年前的今天。"

"那当时你在他身上可见着什么信物了？"她大声问道，"他脖子上莫非挂着条琥珀链子？他身上莫非还裹着件金丝斗篷，上面绣着星星？"

"没错，"樵夫答道，"正像你说的那样。"于是他把斗篷和琥珀链子从先前存放的箱子里取出来，展示给她看。

妇人见了，喜极而泣，说道："他就是我的小儿子呀，是我在林子里把他弄丢了。我请你们快快把他唤来，为了找他，我几乎走遍了整个世界。"

于是，樵夫和他的妻子走出屋去，唤来星孩儿，对他说："进屋去吧，在里面你会见着自个儿的妈妈，她正等着你呢。"

于是，星孩儿就跑了进去，内心充满了惊讶和欢欣。然而，一见到正在屋内等他的妇人，他就轻蔑地大笑起来，说道："怎么了，哪儿有我的妈妈？我眼前啥人也没有，只有这个臭要饭的。"

妇人回答他说："我就是你的妈妈呀。"

"你疯了，敢这样说！"星孩儿愤怒地大声叫道，"我才不是你的儿子呢。你只是个要饭的，长得丑，还穿得破。所以，你还是滚开，别再让我见到你这张丑脸。"

"不，你的确是我的小儿子，是我在林子里生下的孩儿。"妇人哭着说，一下子跪了下来，向他伸出双臂。"强盗把你从我身边偷走，丢在那儿等死，"她喃喃地说，"但是我一见到你时就认出了你，我也认出了那些信物，就是这件金丝斗篷和这条琥珀链子。所以啊，我求你跟我走吧,我走遍了全世界就是为了找你。跟我走吧,因为我需要你的爱啊。"

但是星孩儿一动不动地待在原地,一点儿也不为她心动。屋内除了那位妇人的痛哭声,听不到一点点声音。

星孩儿终于开口对她说话了,话音硬邦邦、冷冰冰的。"要是你真的是我妈,"他说,"你最好还是走得远远的,不要来这里让我丢脸,要知道我一直以为自个儿是星星的孩子,而不是叫花子的孩子,可你却偏偏来告诉我,我就是。所以啊,你还是离开这儿,别再让我见到你。"

"唉呀呀!我的儿啊,"妇人哭着说,"我走前,你就不想亲亲我?妈妈找你找得好苦哇!"

"不行,"星孩儿说道,"看着你都嫌脏。亲你,我还不如去亲妻蛇,亲癞蛤蟆呢。"

那位妇人站起身来,向林子里走去,一路上哭得撕心裂肺。星孩儿见她走了,一下子高兴起来,急忙跑回去找他的玩伴,还想接着和他们一块儿玩呢。

然而,大伙见星孩儿来了,都嘲笑他,说道:"哈哈,你就像癞蛤蟆一样脏,像妻蝰蛇一样可恶。滚开去,咱们可不能忍受跟你一块儿玩。"说着他们就把他赶出了花园。

星孩儿皱起眉头,自言自语地说道:"他们这是对我说什么呢?我要到水井边照一照,水井会告诉我自个儿有多么美。"

于是,他走到水井边,照了一照。瞧!他那张脸就像蛤蟆的脸,身上还长了鳞片,就像只蛤蟆。他一下子扑倒在草地上,哭了起来,自言自语道:"这肯定是恶有恶报呀。我不认自个儿的妈妈,把她赶走,而且对她又傲慢又残酷。我要去找她,哪怕走遍整个世界。我不找到她,就决不罢休。"

这时来了樵夫的小女儿,她把一只手搭在星孩儿的肩上,说道:

"你失去美貌又有什么要紧呢?留下来和我们在一起吧,我不会笑你的。"

星孩儿对她说:"不行,我对妈妈那么坏,作为惩罚让我有了这报应。所以我得走,哪怕走遍这世界,也要找到妈妈,得到她的宽恕。"

于是,星孩儿跑进了林子,呼唤母亲回到自个儿身边,可是没有人回应。整整一天他都在呼唤她,直到日落之后他才躺了下来,身下积着片片树叶像极了一张床。鸟儿和其他动物还记得他以往的残酷,都纷纷逃走了。他就孤零零地躺着,只有蛤蟆在盯着他,还有毒蛇慢慢地从身边爬过。

到了清晨,星孩儿起身,从树上摘一些苦浆果当早餐,接着又动身行走在广袤的树林里,痛心地哭着。一路上无论遇上谁,他都要上前询问对方是否见过他的母亲。

星孩儿问鼹鼠:"你有本事钻到地下。请你告诉我,我妈妈可在那儿?"

鼹鼠答道:"你弄瞎了我的双眼。我怎么会知道呢?"

星孩儿问朱顶雀:"你有本事飞过高高的树顶,放眼整个世界。告诉我,你可见到我的妈妈了?"

朱顶雀答道:"你为寻开心,剪断了我的双翅。我怎么飞得起来呢?"

对着那只孤零零地住在杉树上的小松鼠,星孩儿问道:"我的妈妈在哪儿呢?"

松鼠答道:"你已杀了我的妈妈。莫非你还想杀了自个儿的妈妈吗?"

星孩儿哭着垂下了头,祈求上帝所造万物的宽恕,继续在树林里穿行,想找到那个乞讨的妇人。第三天,他穿过树林的尽头,来到了平原上。

星孩儿路过一个又一个村庄时,孩子们总是嘲笑他,还扔石子砸他；乡里人甚至不容他睡在牛棚里，因为他看上去是那么脏，生怕他会把棚里储存的谷物给弄霉了；雇工把他赶走了，没有一个人同情他。他也没在那儿打听到关于那个乞讨的妇人，也就是他母亲的消息。尽管三年来他一直在满世界地奔波，经常会恍恍惚惚地看见妈妈仿佛就在他前方的路上，他呼喊着追上去，直到双脚被尖硬的石块磨蹭得鲜血淋漓。然而，他总是追赶不上，路边的居民也总说自个儿没见过她，也没见过任何长得像她的妇人，而且还总拿他的悲痛来寻开心。

三年来，他一直在满世界地奔波，这个世界没有给他爱，没有给他关怀，也没有给他宽容，可是这个世界正是他从前不可一世时给自个儿造下的啊！

一天傍晚，星孩儿来到一座城门前。这座城沿河而建，四周围着坚固的城墙。他疲惫不堪，双脚酸痛，但还是打起精神想进城。然而，站岗把守城门的卫士们把手中的长戟一横，粗暴地问他："你到城里去干什么？"

"我正在找我的妈妈，"星孩儿答道，"求你们放我进去吧，说不定，她就在这座城里呢。"

卫士们却嘲弄他，其中一人竟摆弄着自个儿的黑胡子，放下手中的盾牌，高声嚷起来："说实话，你的妈妈见到你也不会高兴的，瞧你那丑模样，比烂泥里跳的蛤蟆、爬的蝰蛇还要难看。快滚开，快滚开，你的妈妈不住在这城里。"

又有一个卫士，一手拿着黄旗，盘问他说："谁是你的妈妈，你为什么要找她呢？"

星孩儿答道："我的妈妈跟我一样是个要饭的，先前我对她很坏；求你们放我进去吧，要是她住在这城里的话，说不定她就原谅我了。"然而他们就是不同意，还用长矛刺他。

星孩儿哭着转过身时，走过来一个人，身上的铠甲镶着朵朵金花，头盔顶上铸着一尊长有双翅的雄狮，向卫士们打听是谁想要进城。他们答道："是个要饭的，他母亲也个要饭的，我们把他赶走了。"

"不，"他大笑着喊道，"我们可以把这个臭家伙卖为奴隶，他可以换一碗甜酒。"

有位老者路过，面带凶相，叫喊起来："我就出这个价买下他了。"他付完钱，就拉着星孩儿的一只手，领着他进城了。

接下来，他俩穿过一条又一条街道，来到了一扇小门前，门就开在石榴树阴下的一堵墙上。老者用一枚雕刻着花纹的碧玉戒指碰了碰门，门就打开了。他俩走下五级黄铜台阶，进入了一座花园，园里种满了黑色的罂粟花，还堆积着许多用黏土烧制的绿瓦罐。然后，老者就从自个儿的头巾上抽出一条印花丝巾，用来蒙住星孩儿的双眼，并推着他走在自个儿的前面。等丝巾从眼上解下来时，星孩儿发现自己走进了一间地牢，牢里点着一盏牛角灯。

老者用木盘盛了些发霉的面包，放到星孩儿面前，说了声"吃吧"；然后，往杯子里倒了些有咸味的水，说了声"喝吧"。当星孩儿吃饱喝足时，老者就走了出去，把身后的牢门锁上，并用铁链拴紧。

翌日，老者又来见星孩儿。老者实是利比亚最高明的魔法师，学艺于一位隐居尼罗河边墓群中的大师。老者见到星孩儿就皱起眉头，说道："离这座异教徒之城的城门不远处有一片树林，林中藏有三块金子。一块是白金，另一块是黄金，第三块是赤金。今天你得把那块白金拿给我，要是拿不来，我就得抽你一百鞭子。赶快动身去找吧，太阳下山时我会在花园门口等着你。你一定要把那块白金拿来，不然就有你好看的，因为你是我的奴隶，是我用一碗甜酒的价钱买下了你。"老者用那条印花丝巾蒙住星孩儿的双眼，领着他走出房屋，穿过罂粟园，迈上五级黄铜台阶。然后，老者再用戒指打开那扇小门，把他放回大街。

于是，星孩儿走出城门，来到魔法师告诉他的那片树林。

眼下这片树林看上去真是非常地美丽，似乎到处都是鸟语花香。于是，星孩儿高高兴兴地走了进去。可是林子的美丽几乎于他无益，因为无论他走到哪里，尖刺和荆棘都会蹿出地面，阻挡他的去路，荨麻恶狠狠地刺他，刺蓟举着匕首扎他，搞得他苦不堪言。他到哪里都找不到魔法师所说的那块白金，尽管他从早上找到正午，又从正午找到太阳下山。日落时分，他掉头往回走，禁不住痛哭起来，因为他知道等待他的是什么命运。

然而，星孩儿刚到树林的边缘时，听到灌木丛中传来一声叫唤，像是有谁在哀叫。他忘记自个儿的忧伤了，赶紧跑回叫声传来的地方，只见一只小小的野兔在夹子上动弹不得，是哪位猎人布设的。

星孩儿顿生怜悯之情，就把野兔放了，并对它说："我自个儿不过是个奴隶罢了，倒是可以给你自由。"

野兔回答他："你真是给了我自由，那我该怎么回报你呢？"

星孩儿对它说："我正在找一块白金，可是到处都没找着。要是我不把它拿给我的主人，他就会打我。"

"你跟我走吧，"野兔说，"我带你去找它，因为我知道它藏在哪儿，藏在那儿有什么目的。"

于是，星孩儿就跟着野兔走去。瞧！在一棵大橡树的树缝里，他看到了自个儿要找的那块白金。他万分高兴，抓起白金，对野兔说："我帮你的一点儿小忙，你已经成倍地偿还我了；我对你的一点儿善心，你已经百倍地报答我了。"

"哪里话，"野兔答道，"不过是你如何对我，我便怎样待你罢了。"说完它就飞快地跑开了，星孩儿则向城里赶去。

眼下的城门口坐着一个人，原来是麻风病人，脸上套着一个灰色的麻布头罩，双眼透过麻布的眼洞闪闪发光，像是烧红的煤球。他见星孩儿走上前来，就敲着木碗，摇着铃铛，开口说道："给点儿钱吧，要不我得饿死。他们把我赶出了城，没有一个人可怜我呐。"

"唉呀！"星孩儿喊道："我钱包里也只有块金子，要是我不拿回去，主人就会打我，因为我是他的奴隶。"

然而麻风病人苦苦哀求，百般祈求，直到星孩儿心生怜悯，把那块白金送给了他。

星孩儿回到魔法师的房子跟前时，魔法师打开门，把他带了进去，开口便问："你拿来了那块白金吗？"星孩儿回答道："没有。"魔法师随即猛扑过来，打了他一顿，并在他面前放了一个空木盘，说了声"吃吧"，又放了一个空杯子，说了声"喝吧"，之后再次把他投入了地牢。

翌日，魔法师来见他，说道："要是今天你不把那块黄金拿给我，我定要继续押你为奴，还要抽你三百鞭子。"

于是，星孩儿走向那片树林，整整一天都在寻找那块黄金。可是，他到哪里都找不着。日落时分，他自个儿坐了下来，暗自流泪；他哭得正伤心时，先前从夹子上救下的那只小野兔来到了自个儿的身边。

野兔问他："你为什么哭呢？又在林子里找什么呢？"

星孩儿答道："我正在找一块藏在这儿的黄金，要是找不着，主人就会打我，并继续押我为奴。"

"跟我来吧。"野兔喊着，跑过树林，最终来到一个水塘边。塘底就躺着要找的那块黄金。

"我该怎么谢你呢?"星孩儿说,"瞧!这已是你第二次帮我了。"

"哪里话,是你先可怜我的。"野兔说完,就飞快地跑开了。

星孩儿抄起那块黄金,放进钱包,就急急忙忙地往城里赶去。然而那个麻风病人见他来了,赶忙跑着迎了上去,接着跪下来哭道:"给点儿钱吧,要不我得饿死。"

星孩儿对他说:"我钱包里也只有块黄金,如果我不把它带给我的主人,他就会打我,继续押我为奴。"

但是麻风病人苦苦哀求,星孩儿又生怜悯,就把那块黄金给了他。

星孩儿回到魔法师的房子跟前时,魔法师打开门,把他带了进去,开口便问:"你拿来了那块黄金吗?"星孩儿回答道:"没有。"魔法师随即猛扑过来,打了他一顿,并给他上了锁链,又一次把他投入了地牢。

翌日,魔法师来见他,说道:"要是今天你把那块赤金拿给我,我就会放了你;但要是拿不来,我定会杀了你。"

于是,星孩儿走向那片树林,整整一天都在寻找那块赤金。可是,他到哪里都找不着。黄昏时分,他自个儿坐了下来,暗自流泪;他哭得正伤心时,那只小野兔又来到了自个儿的身边。

野兔告诉他:"你要找的那块赤金就藏在你身后的山洞里呢。不哭不哭,高兴起来才对。"

"我该怎样谢你呢?"星孩儿说,"瞧!这都是你第三次帮助我了。"

"哪里话,是你先可怜我的,"野兔说完,就飞快地跑开了。

星孩儿进入山洞,在最远的角落里找到了那块赤金。于是,他把赤金放进钱包,急急忙忙地往城里赶去。那个麻风病人见他来了,就站到路的中央,大声哭着,对他说道:"把那块赤金给我吧,要不我一定会饿死的。"星孩儿再次心生怜悯,把那块赤金给了他,并说道："你比我更需要钱。"然而，他心情沉重起来，因为他知道等着他的是什么厄运。

但是，星孩儿穿过城门时，卫士们向他鞠躬行礼，齐声赞叹："多么美啊，我们的君主！"一群市民跟在他后面高声欢呼："确实美啊，天下无人可以媲美！"星孩儿听后痛哭起来，心中暗想："他们都在嘲笑我，拿我的不幸寻开心。"人们越聚越多，星孩儿就迷失了方向，最后糊里糊涂地来到了一个大型广场，场上建有一座国王的宫殿。

宫殿的大门开了，本城的僧侣和显贵们都跑出来迎候，向星孩儿致敬，开口齐呼："您就是吾等期待已久的君主，就是吾王之子。"

星孩儿回应他们说："我不是什么国王的儿子，只是一个可怜的要饭妇人的孩子。还有啊，我知道自个儿有多难看，你们怎么还硬说我美呢？"

这时，那个铠甲上镶着朵朵金花、头盔上铸有双翅雄狮的人举起一面盾牌，高声喊道："吾主怎么硬说自个儿不美呢？"

星孩儿定睛一看盾牌，啊！他的脸蛋恢复如初，曾经的美貌又回到了他的身上，他还看到自个儿的双眼闪耀着以前未曾见过的神采。

僧侣和显贵们都跪了下来，对他说道："古有预言，今降贵主，统领吾等。所以，还请戴上这顶王冠，接受这根权杖，以公正和仁慈做我们的君主吧。"

然而，星孩儿他对他们说："我不配，因为我连生我的母亲也不认，在我找到母亲并得到她的宽恕之前，我无法安心。所以，让我走吧，即使你们给我王冠和权杖，我也不能逗留在这儿，必须走遍世界。"他一边说着话，一边把脸从他们身上转向通往城门的那条大街。瞧！在士兵周围拥挤的人群中，他看见了那个要饭的妇人，那可是他的母亲，母亲的身旁站着那个先前坐在路边的麻风病人。

一声欢呼脱口而出，他跑了过去，跪下来，亲吻起母亲脚上的伤口，并用自个儿的眼泪清洗着。他俯伏在地，哭得肝肠寸断，开口对母亲说："妈妈，孩儿过去骄狂嚣瑟，拒不认您；如今潦倒卑微，求您认下孩儿吧。妈妈呀，孩儿过去恩将仇报；时至今日，求您爱爱孩儿吧。妈妈呀，孩儿过去拒您于千里之外；今日今时，求您收下孩儿吧。"可是那个要饭的妇人一言不答。

然后，星孩儿伸出双手，紧握那个麻风病人的苍白双脚，对他说："我过去同情你三次。请让妈妈开口跟我说一次话。"可是那个麻风病人也一言不答。

星孩儿又一次痛哭流涕，说道："妈妈呀，孩儿所受苦难深重，快受不了了。求您宽恕孩儿，让我安安心心地回树林去吧。"那要饭的妇人听完伸出一只手放在他的头顶，对他说了声"起来吧"；麻风病人也伸出手放在他的头顶，对他说了声"起来吧"。

星孩儿站起身来，看着他们。啊，他们原来一个是国王，一个是王后！

王后对他说："这是你的父亲，你曾出手援助他。"

而后国王说："这是你的母亲，你曾用泪水清洗她的双脚。"他们俯身搂着星孩儿的脖子亲吻着，然后领他入宫，给他穿上华美的衣袍，继而把王冠戴在他的头上，把权杖交到他的手中。这座沿河而建的城邑便由他来治理，他也就成了这儿的君主。他以莫大的公正和仁慈对待所有人，将邪恶的魔法师驱逐出境，给樵夫两口子送去许多贵重的礼物，还给他们的孩子册封了一些高贵的头衔。他也不容任何人虐待飞鸟走兽，总是教人关爱、仁慈和乐善好施，向穷困潦倒之人发放面包，向衣不蔽体之人发放衣物。举国上下，一片祥和富足。

然而，星孩儿的统治年限不长，他所受的苦难过于深重，考验他的烈火又过于凶猛，三年之后他就去世了。之后是位邪恶的君主继位。

THE STAR-CHILD

Once upon a time two poor woodcutters were making their way home through a great pine forest. It was winter, and a night of bitter cold. The snow lay thick upon the ground, and upon the branches of the trees: the frost kept snapping the little twigs on either side of them, as they passed: and when they came to the Mountain-Torrent she was hanging motionless in air, for the Ice-king had kissed her.

So cold was it that even the animals and the birds did not know what to make of it.

"Ugh!" snarled the wolf, as he limped through the brushwood with his tail between his legs, "This is perfectly monstrous weather. Why doesn't the government look to it?"

"Weet! Weet! Weet!" twittered the green linnets. "The old earth is dead and they have laid her out in her white shroud."

"The earth is going to be married, and this is her bridal dress," whispered the turtledoves to each other. Their little pink feet were quite frost-bitten, but they felt that it was their duty to take a romantic view of the situation.

"Nonsense!" growled the wolf. "I tell you that it is all the fault of the government, and if you don't believe me I shall eat you." The wolf had a thoroughly practical mind, and was never at a loss for a good argument.

"Well, for my own part," said the woodpecker, who was a born philosopher, "I don't care an atomic theory for explanations. If a thing is so, it is so, and at present it is terribly cold."

Terribly cold it certainly was. The little squirrels, who lived inside the tall firtree, kept rubbing each other's noses to keep themselves warm, and the

Rabbits curled themselves up in their holes, and did not venture even to look out of doors. The only people who seemed to enjoy it were the great horned owls. Their feathers were quite stiff with rime, but they did not mind, and they rolled their large yellow eyes, and called out to each other across the forest, "Tu-whit! Tu-whoo! Tu-whit! Tu-whoo! What delightful weather we are having!"

On and on went the two woodcutters, blowing lustily upon their fingers, and stamping with their huge iron-shod boots upon the caked snow. Once they sank into a deep drift, and came out as white as millers are, when the stones are grinding; and once they slipped on the hard smooth ice where the marsh water was frozen, and their faggots fell out of their bundles, and they had to pick them up and bind them together again; and once they thought that they had lost their way, and a great terror seized on them, for they knew that the snow is cruel to those who sleep in her arms. But they put their trust in the good Saint Martin, who watches over all travellers, and retraced their steps, and went warily, and at last they reached the outskirts of the forest, and saw, far down in the valley beneath them, the lights of the village in which they dwelt.

So overjoyed were they at their deliverance that they laughed aloud, and the earth seemed to them like a flower of silver, and the moon like a flower of gold.

Yet, after that they had laughed they became sad, for they remembered their poverty, and one of them said to the other, "Why did we make merry, seeing that life is for the rich, and not for such as we are? Better that we had died of cold in the forest, or that some wild beast had fallen upon us and slain us."

"Truly," answered his companion, "much is given to some, and little is given to others. Injustice has not parcelled out the world, nor is there equal division of aught save of sorrow."

But as they were bewailing their misery to each other, this strange thing happened. There fell from heaven a very bright and beautiful star. It slipped down the side of the sky, passing by the other stars in its course, and, as they watched it wondering, it seemed to them to sink behind a clump of willow trees that stood hard by a little sheepfold no more than a stone's-throw away.

"Why! There is a crook of gold for whoever finds it," they cried, and they set to and ran, so eager were they for the gold.

And one of them ran faster than his mate, and outstripped him, and forced his way through the willows, and came out on the other side, and lo! There was indeed a thing of gold lying on the white snow. So he hastened towards it, and stooping down placed his hands upon it, and it was a cloak of golden tissue, curiously wrought with stars, and wrapped in many folds. And he cried out to his comrade that he had found the treasure that had fallen from the sky, and when his comrade had come up, they sat them down in the snow, and loosened the folds of the cloak that they might divide the pieces of gold. But, alas! No gold was in it, nor silver, nor, indeed, treasure of any kind, but only a little child who was asleep.

And one of them said to the other, "This is a bitter ending to our hope, nor have we any good fortune, for what does a child profit to a man? Let us leave it here, and go our way, seeing that we are poor men, and have children of our own whose bread we may not give to another."

But his companion answered him, "No, but it were an evil thing to leave the child to perish here in the snow, and though I am as poor as you are, and have many mouths to feed, and but little in the pot, yet will I bring it home with me, and my wife shall have care of it."

So very tenderly he took up the child, and wrapped the cloak around it to shield it from the harsh cold, and made his way down the hill to the village, his comrade marvelling much at his foolishness and softness of heart.

And when they came to the village, his comrade said to him, "You have the child, therefore give me the cloak, for it is meet that we should share."

But he answered him, "No, for the cloak is neither mine nor yours, but the child's only," and he bade him godspeed, and went to his own house and knocked.

And when his wife opened the door and saw that her husband had returned safe to her, she put her arms round his neck and kissed him, and took from his back the bundle of faggots, and brushed the snow off his boots, and bade him come in.

But he said to her, "I have found something in the forest, and I have brought it to you to have care of it," and he did not stir from the threshold.

"What is it?" she cried. "Show it to me, for the house is bare, and we have need of many things." And he drew the cloak back, and showed her the sleeping child.

"Alack, goodman!" she murmured, "Don't we have children of our own, that you must bring a changeling to sit by the hearth? And who knows if it will not bring us bad fortune? And how shall we tend it?" And she was wroth against him.

"No, but it is a Star-Child," he answered. And he told her the strange manner of the finding of it.

But she would not be appeased, but mocked at him, and spoke angrily, and cried, "Our children lack bread, and shall we feed the child of another? Who is there, who cares for us? And who gives us food?"

"No, but God cares for the sparrows even, and feedes them," he answered.

"Do not the sparrows die of hunger in the winter?" she asked. "And is it not winter now?"

And the man answered nothing, but did not stir from the threshold.

And a bitter wind from the forest came in through the open door, and made her tremble, and she shivered, and said to him, "Will you not close the door? There comes a bitter wind into the house, and I am cold."

"Into a house where a heart is hard comes there not always a bitter wind?" he asked. And the woman answered him nothing, but crept closer to the fire.

And after a time she turned round and looked at him, and her eyes were full of tears. And he came in swiftly, and placed the child in her arms, and she kissed it, and laid it in a little bed where the youngest of their own children was lying. And on the morrow the woodcutter took the curious cloak of gold and placed it in a great chest, and a chain of amber that was round the child's neck his wife took and set it in the chest also.

So the Star-Child was brought up with the children of the woodcutter, and sat at the same board with them, and was their playmate. And every year he became more beautiful to look at, so that all those who dwelt in the village were filled with wonder, for, while they were swarthy and black haired, he was white and delicate as sawn ivory, and his curls were like the rings of the daffodil. His lips, also, were like the petals of a red flower, and his eyes were like violets by a river of pure water, and his body like the narcissus of a field where the mower comes not.

Yet did his beauty work him evil. For he grew proud, and cruel, and selfish. The children of the woodcutter, and the other children of the village, he despised, saying that they were of mean parentage, while he was noble, being sprang from a star, and he made himself master over them, and called them his servants. No pity had he for the poor, or for those who were blind or maimed or in any way afflicted, but would cast stones at them and drive them forth on to the highway, and bid them beg their bread elsewhere, so that none save the outlaws came twice to that village to ask for alms. Indeed, he was as one enamoured of beauty, and would mock at the weakly and ill-favoured, and make jest of them; and himself he loved, and in summer, when the winds were still, he would lie by the well in the priest's orchard and look down at the marvel of his own face, and laugh for the pleasure he had in his fairness.

Often did the woodcutter and his wife chide him, and say, "We did not deal with you as you deal with those who are left desolate, and have none to succour them. Wherefore are you so cruel to all who need pity?"

Often did the old priest send for him, and seek to teach him the love of living things, saying to him, "The fly is your brother. Do no harm it. The wild birds that roam through the forest have their freedom. Snare them not for your pleasure. God made the blindworm and the mole, and each has its place. Who are you to bring pain into God's world? Even the cattle of the field praise Him."

But the Star-Child did not heed their words, but would frown and flout, and go back to his companions, and lead them. And his companions followed him, for he was fair, and fleet of foot, and could dance, and pipe, and make music. And wherever the Star-Child led them they followed, and whatever the Star-Child bade them do, that did they. And when he pierced with a sharp reed the dim eyes of the mole, they laughed, and when he cast stones at the leper they laughed also. And in all things he ruled them, and they became hard of heart even as he was.

Now there passed one day through the village a poor beggar woman. Her garments were torn and ragged, and her feet were bleeding from the rough road on which she had travelled, and she was in very evil plight. And being weary she sat her down under a chestnut tree to rest.

But when the Star-Child saw her, he said to his companions, "See! There sits a foul beggar woman under that fair and green-leaved tree. Come, let us drive her hence, for she is ugly and ill-favoured."

So he came near and threw stones at her, and mocked her, and she looked at him with terror in her eyes, nor did she move her gaze from him. And when the woodcutter, who was cleaving logs in a haggard hard by, saw what the Star-Child was doing, he ran up and rebuked him, and said to him, "Surely you are hard of heart and do not know mercy, for what evil has this poor woman done to you that you should treat her in this wise?"

And the Star-Child grew red with anger, and stamped his foot upon the ground, and said, "Who are you to question me what I do? I am not son of you to do your bidding."

"You speak truly," answered the woodcutter, "yet did I show you pity when I found you in the forest."

And when the woman heard these words she gave a loud cry, and fell into a swoon. And the woodcutter carried her to his own house, and his wife had care of her, and when she rose up from the swoon into which she had fallen, they set meat and drink before her, and bade her have comfort.

But she would neither eat nor drink, but said to the woodcutter, "Didn't you say that the child was found in the forest? And wasn't it ten years from this day?"

And the woodcutter answered, "Yea, it was in the forest that I found him, and it is ten years from this day."

"And what signs did you find with him?" she cried. "Did he wear upon his neck a chain of amber? Was not round him a cloak of gold tissue broidered with stars?"

"Truly," answered the woodcutter, "it was even as you say." And he took the cloak and the amber chain from the chest where they lay, and showed them to her.

And when she saw them she wept for joy, and said, "He is my little son whom I lost in the forest. I pray you send for him quickly, for in search of him have I wandered over the whole world."

So the woodcutter and his wife went out and called to the Star-Child, and said to him, "Go into the house, and there shall you find your mother, who is waiting for you."

So he ran in, filled with wonder and great gladness. But when he saw her who was waiting there, he laughed scornfully and said, "Why, where is my mother? For I see none here but this vile beggar woman."

And the woman answered him, "I am your mother."

"You are mad to say so," cried the Star-Child angrily. "I am not son of you, for you are a beggar, and ugly, and in rags. Therefore get you hence, and let me see your foul face no more."

"No, but you are indeed my little son, whom I bare in the forest," she cried, and she fell on her knees, and held out her arms to him. "The robbers stole you from me, and left you to die," she murmured, "but I recognised you when I saw you, and the signs also have I recognised, the cloak of golden tissue and the amber chain. Therefore I pray you come with me, for over the whole world have I wandered in search of you. Come with me, my son, for I have need of your love."

But the Star-Child did not stir from his place, but shut the doors of his heart against her, nor was there any sound heard save the sound of the woman weeping for pain.

And at last he spoke to her, and his voice was hard and bitter. "If in very truth you are my mother," he said, "it had been better had you stayed away, and not come here to bring me to shame, seeing that I thought I was the child of some star, and not a beggar's child, as you tell me that I am. Therefore get you hence, and let me see you no more."

"Alas! my son," she cried, "will you not kiss me before I go? For I have suffered much to find you."

"No," said the Star-Child, "but you are too foul to look at, and rather would I kiss the adder or the toad than you."

So the woman rose up, and went away into the forest weeping bitterly, and when the Star-Child saw that she had gone, he was glad, and ran back to his playmates that he might play with them.

But when they beheld him coming, they mocked him and said, "Why, you are as foul as the toad, and as loathsome as the adder. Get you hence, for we will not suffer you to play with us," and they drave him out of the garden.

And the Star-Child frowned and said to himself, "What is this that they say to me? I will go to the well of water and look into it, and it shall tell me of my beauty."

So he went to the well of water and looked into it, and lo! His face was as the face of a toad, and his body was sealed like an adder. And he flung himself down on the grass and wept, and said to himself, "Surely this has come upon me by reason of my sin. For I have denied my mother, and driven her away, and been proud, and cruel to her. Wherefore I will go and seek her through the whole world, nor will I rest till I have found her."

And there came to him the little daughter of the woodcutter, and she put her hand upon his shoulder and said, "What does it matter if you have lost your comeliness? Stay with us, and I will not mock at you."

And he said to her, "No, but I have been cruel to my mother, and as a punishment has this evil been sent to me. Wherefore I must go hence, and wander through the world till I find her, and she give me her forgiveness."

So he ran away into the forest and called out to his mother to come to him, but there was no answer. All day long he called to her, and, when the sun set he lay down to sleep on a bed of leaves, and the birds and the animals fled from him, for they remembered his cruelty, and he was alone save for the toad that watched him, and the slow adder that crawled past.

And in the morning he rose up, and plucked some bitter berries from the trees and ate them, and took his way through the great wood, weeping sorely. And of everything that he met he made inquiry if perchance they had seen his mother.

He said to the mole, "You can go beneath the earth. Tell me, is my mother there?"

And the mole answered, "You have blinded mine eyes. How should I know?"

He said to the Linnet, "You can fly over the tops of the tall trees, and can see the whole world. Tell me, can you see my mother?"

And the linnet answered, "You have clipt my wings for your pleasure. How should I fly?"

And to the little squirrel who lived in the firtree, and was lonely, he said, "Where is my mother?"

And the squirrel answered, "You have slain mine. Do you seek to slay yours also?"

And the Star-Child wept and bowed his head, and prayed forgiveness of God's things, and went on through the forest, seeking for the beggar woman. And on the third day he came to the other side of the forest and went down into the plain.

And when he passed through the villages the children mocked him, and threw stones at him, and the carlots would not suffer him even to sleep in the byres lest he might bring mildew on the stored corn, so foul was he to look at, and their hired men drave him away, and there was none who had pity on him. Nor could he hear anywhere of the beggar woman who was his mother, though for the space of three years he wandered over the world, and often seemed to see her on the road in front of him, and would call to her, and run after her till the sharp flints made his feet to bleed. But overtake her he could not, and those who dwelt by the way did ever deny that they had seen her, or any like to her, and they made sport of his sorrow.

For the space of three years he wandered over the world, and in the world there was neither love nor loving kindness nor charity for him, but it was even such a world as he had made for himself in the days of his great pride.

And one evening he came to the gate of a strong-walled city that stood by a river, and, weary and footsore though he was, he made to enter in. But the soldiers who stood on guard dropped their halberts across the entrance, and said roughly to him, "What is your business in the city?"

"I am seeking for my mother," he answered, "and I pray you to suffer me to pass, for it may be that she is in this city."

But they mocked at him, and one of them wagged a black beard, and set down his shield and cried, "Of a truth, your mother will not be merry when she sees you, for you are more ill-favoured than the toad of the marsh, or the adder that crawls in the fen. Get you gone. Get you gone. Your mother dwells not in this city."

And another, who held a yellow banner in his hand, said to him, "Who is Your mother, and wherefore are you seeking for her?"

And he answered, "My mother is a beggar even as I am, and I have treated her evilly, and I pray ye to suffer me to pass that she may give me her forgiveness, if it be that she tarries in this city." But they would not, and pricked him with their spears.

And, as he turned away weeping, one whose armour was inlaid with gilt flowers, and on whose helmet couched a lion that had wings, came up and made inquiry of the soldiers who it was who had sought entrance. And they said to him, "It is a beggar and the child of a beggar, and we have driven him away."

"No," he cried, laughing, "but we will sell the foul thing for a slave, and his price shall be the price of a bowl of sweet wine."

And an old and evil-visaged man who was passing by called out, and said, "I will buy him for that price," and, when he had paid the price, he took the Star-Child by the hand and led him into the city.

And after that they had gone through many streets they came to a little door that was set in a wall that was covered with a pomegranate tree. And the old man touched the door with a ring of graved jasper and it opened, and they went down five steps of brass into a garden filled with black poppies and green jars of burnt clay. And the old man took then from his turban a scarf of figured silk, and bound with it the eyes of the Star-Child, and drave him in front of him. And when the scarf was taken off his eyes, the Star-Child found himself in a dungeon, that was lit by a lantern of horn.

And the old man set before him some mouldy bread on a trencher and said, "Eat," and some brackish water in a cup and said, "Drink," and when he had eaten and drunk, the old man went out, locking the door behind him and fastening it with an iron chain.

And on the morrow the old man, who was indeed the subtlest of the magicians of Libya and had learned his art from one who dwelt in the tombs of the Nile, came in to him and frowned at him, and said, "In a wood that is nigh to the gate of this city of Giaours there are three pieces of gold. One is of white gold, and another is of yellow gold, and the gold of the third one is red. Today you shall bring me the piece of white gold, and if you don't bring it back, I will beat you with a hundred stripes. Get you away quickly, and at sunset I will be waiting for you at the door of the garden. See that you bring the white gold, or it shall go ill with you, for you are my slave, and I have bought you for the price of a bowl of sweet wine." And he bound the eyes of the Star-Child with the scarf of figured silk, and led him through the house, and through the garden of poppies, and up the five steps of brass. And having opened the little door with his ring he set him in the street.

And the Star-Child went out of the gate of the city, and came to the wood of which the magician had spoken to him.

Now this wood was very fair to look at from without, and seemed full of singing birds and of sweet-scented flowers, and the Star-Child entered it gladly. Yet did its beauty profit him little, for wherever he went harsh briars and thorns shot up from the ground and encompassed him, and evil nettles stung him, and the thistle pierced him with her daggers, so that he was in sore distress. Nor could he anywhere find the piece of white gold of which the magician had spoken, though he sought for it from morn to noon, and from noon to sunset. And at sunset he set his face towards home, weeping bitterly, for he knew what fate was in store for him.

But when he had reached the outskirts of the wood, he heard from a thicket a cry as of some one in pain. And forgetting his own sorrow he ran back to the place, and saw there a little hare caught in a trap that some hunter had set for it.

And the Star-Child had pity on it, and released it, and said to it, "I am myself but a slave, yet may I give you your freedom."

And the hare answered him, and said, "Surely you have given me freedom, and what shall I give you in return?"

And the Star-Child said to it, "I am seeking for a piece of white gold, nor can I anywhere find it, and if I do not bring it to my master he will beat me."

"Come with me," said the hare, "and I will lead you to it, for I know where it is hidden, and for what purpose."

So the Star-Child went with the hare, and lo! In the cleft of a great oak tree he saw the piece of white gold that he was seeking. And he was filled with joy, and seized it, and said to the hare, "The service that I did to you you have rendered back again many times over, and the kindness that I showed you you have repaid a hundredfold."

"No," answered the hare, "but as you dealt with me, so I did deal with you," and it ran away swiftly, and the Star-Child went towards the city.

Now at the gate of the city there was seated one who was a leper. Over his face hung a cowl of grey linen, and through the eyelets his eyes gleamed like red coals. And when he saw the Star-Child coming, he struck upon a wooden bowl, and clattered his bell, and called out to him, and said, "Give me a piece of money, or I must die of hunger. For they have thrust me out of the city, and there is no one who has pity on me."

"Alas!" cried the Star-Child, "I have but one piece of money in my wallet, and if I don't bring it to my master he will beat me, for I am his slave."

But the leper entreated him, and prayed of him, till the Star-Child had pity, and gave him the piece of white gold.

And when he came to the magician's house, the magician opened to him, and brought him in, and said to him, "Do you have the piece of white gold?" And the Star-Child answered, "I don't have it." So the magician fell upon him, and beat him, and set before him an empty trencher, and said, "Eat," and an empty cup, and said, "Drink," and flung him again into the dungeon.

And on the morrow, the magician came to him, and said, "If today you don't bring me the piece of yellow gold, I will surely keep you as my slave, and give you three hundred stripes."

So the Star-Child went to the wood, and all day long he searched for the piece of yellow gold, but nowhere could he find it. And at sunset he sat him down and began to weep, and as he was weeping there came to him the little hare that he had rescued from the trap.

And the hare said to him, "Why are you weeping? And what do you seek in the wood?"

And the Star-Child answered, "I am seeking for a piece of yellow gold that is hidden here, and if I do not find it my master will beat me, and keep me as a slave."

"Follow me," cried the hare, and it ran through the wood till it came to a pool of water. And at the bottom of the pool the piece of yellow gold was lying.

"How shall I thank you?" said the Star-Child, "for lo! This is the second time that you have succoured me."

"No, but you had pity on me first," said the hare, and it ran away swiftly.

And the Star-Child took the piece of yellow gold, and put it in his wallet, and hurried to the city. But the leper saw him coming, and ran to meet him, and knelt down and cried, "Give me a piece of money or I shall die of hunger."

And the Star-Child said to him, "I have in my wallet but one piece of yellow gold, and if I don't bring it to my master he will beat me and keep me as his slave."

But the leper entreated him sore, so that the Star-Child had pity on him, and gave him the piece of yellow gold.

And when he came to the magician's house, the magician opened to him, and brought him in, and said to him, "Do you have the piece of yellow gold?" And the Star-Child said to him, "I don't have it." So the magician fell upon him, and beat him, and loaded him with chains, and cast him again into the dungeon.

And on the morrow, the magician came to him, and said, "If today you bring me the piece of red gold I will set you free, but if not I will surely slay you."

So the Star-Child went to the wood, and all day long he searched for the piece of red gold, but nowhere could he find it. And at evening he sat him down and wept, and as he was weeping there came to him the little hare.

And the hare said to him, "The piece of red gold that you seekest is in the cavern that is behind you. Therefore weep no more but be glad."

"How shall I reward you?" cried the Star-Child, "for lo! This is the third time you have succoured me."

"No, but you hadst pity on me first," said the hare, and it ran away swiftly.

And the Star-Child entered the cavern, and in its farthest corner he found the piece of red gold. So he put it in his wallet, and hurried to the city. And the leper seeing him coming, stood in the centre of the road, and cried out, and said to him, "Give me the piece of red money, or I must die," and the Star-Child had pity on him again, and gave him the piece of red gold, saying, "Your need is greater than mine." Yet was his heart heavy, for he knew what evil fate awaited him.

But lo! As he passed through the gate of the city, the guards bowed down and made obeisance to him, saying, "How beautiful is our lord!" and a crowd of citizens followed him, and cried out, "Surely there is none so beautiful in the whole world!" so that the Star-Child wept, and said to himself, "They are mocking me, and making light of my misery." And so large was the concourse of the people that he lost the threads of his way, and found himself at last in a great square, in which there was a palace of a king.

And the gate of the palace opened, and the priests and the high officers of the city ran forth to meet him, and they abased themselves before him, and said, "You are our lord for whom we have been waiting, and the son of our king."

And the Star-Child answered them and said, "I am not the king's son, but the child of a poor beggar woman. And how do you say that I am beautiful, for I know that I am evil to look at?"

Then he, whose armour was inlaid with gilt flowers, and on whose helmet crouched a lion that had wings, held up a shield, and cried, "How says my lord that he is not beautiful?"

And the Star-Child looked, and lo! His face was even as it had been, and his comeliness had come back to him, and he saw that in his eyes which he had not seen there before.

And the priests and the high officers knelt down and said to him, "It was prophesied of old that on this day should come he who was to rule over us.

Therefore, let our lord take this crown and this sceptre, and be in his justice and mercy our King over us."

But he said to them, "I am not worthy, for I have denied the mother who bore me, nor may I rest till I have found her, and known her forgiveness. Therefore, let me go, for I must wander again over the world, and may not tarry here, though ye bring me the crown and the sceptre." And as he spoke he turned his face from them towards the street that led to the gate of the city, and lo! Amongst the crowd that pressed round the soldiers, he saw the beggar woman who was his mother, and at her side stood the leper, who had sat by the road.

And a cry of joy broke from his lips, and he ran over, and kneeling down he kissed the wounds on his mother's feet, and wet them with his tears. He bowed his head in the dust, and sobbing, as one whose heart might break, he said to her, "Mother, I denied you in the hour of my pride. Accept me in the hour of my humility. Mother, I gave you hatred. Do you give me love? Mother, I rejected you. Receive your child now." But the beggar woman answered him not a word.

And he reached out his hands, and clasped the white feet of the leper, and said to him, "Thrice did I give you of my mercy. Bid my mother speak to me once." But the leper answered him not a word.

And he sobbed again and said, "Mother, my suffering is greater than I can bear. Give me your forgiveness, and let me go back to the forest." And the beggar woman put her hand on his head, and said to him, "Rise," and the leper put his hand on his head, and said to him, "Rise," also.

And he rose up from his feet, and looked at them, and lo! They were a king and a queen.

And the queen said to him, "This is your father whom you have succoured."

And the king said, "This is your mother whose feet you have washed with your tears." And they fell on his neck and kissed him, and brought him into the palace and clothed him in fair raiment, and set the crown upon his head, and the sceptre in his hand, and over the city that stood by the river he ruled, and was its lord. Much justice and mercy did he show to all, and the evil magician he banished, and to the woodcutter and his wife he sent many rich gifts, and to their children he gave high honour. Nor would he suffer any to be cruel to bird or beast, but taught love and loving kindness and charity, and to the poor he gave bread, and to the naked he gave raiment, and there was peace and plenty in the land.

Yet ruled he not long, so great had been his suffering, and so bitter the fire of his testing, for after the space of three years he died. And he who came after him ruled evilly.